ARNOLD DAGHANI'S MEMORIE
THE ILLUSTRATED DIARY OF A SLAV

Photograph of Arnold Daghani at his desk with the album 1942 1943 *And Thereafter* (*Sporadic records till 1977*) (1942–77)

Arnold Daghani's Memories of Mikhailowka:
The Illustrated Diary of a Slave Labour Camp Survivor

Edited by Deborah Schultz and Edward Timms
with a contribution by Petru Weber

VALLENTINE MITCHELL
LONDON • PORTLAND, OR

First published in 2009 by Vallentine Mitchell

Suite 314, Premier House,
112–114 Station Road,
Edgware, Middlesex HA8 7BJ

920 NE 58th Avenue, Suite 300
Portland, Oregon,
97213-3786

www.vmbooks.com

British Library Cataloguing in Publication Data:
Daghani, Arnold, 1909-1985
Arnold Daghani's memories of Mikhailowka : the illustrated
diary of a slave labour camp survivor
1. Daghani, Arnold, 1909-1985 - Diaries 2. Daghani, Arnold,
1909-1985 - Criticism and interpretation 3. Daghani,
Arnold, 1909-1985 4. Mikhailowka (Concentration camp)
5. Concentration camp inmates - Ukraine - Diaries
6. Concentration camp inmates as artists - Ukraine
7. Forced labor - Ukraine - History - 20th century
8. Concentration camps - Ukraine
I. Title II. Schultz, Deborah, III. Timms, Edward
IV. Weber, Petru V. Memories of Mikhailowka
940.5'3174779'092

ISBN 978 0 85303 638 8 (cloth)
ISBN 978 0 85303 639 5 (paper)

Library of Congress Cataloging-in-Publication Data:

Printed by the MPG Books Group in the UK

Contents

Illustrations

Titles are given in italics for those works titled by Daghani.

Frontispiece: photograph of Arnold Daghani at his desk with the album 1942 1943 *And Thereafter (Sporadic records till 1977)* (1942–77)

Map: Durchgangstrasse IV in 1942–43 (drawn by Petru Weber)

Between pp.132 and 133

1. *Nanino at the window (in Czernowitz) awaiting full of apprehension my coming home. Too much of a risk in the streets...* (1942), in 1942 1943 *And Thereafter (Sporadic records till 1977)* (1942–77), ink and watercolour on paper (G2.053r) (Arnold Daghani Collection, University of Sussex © Arnold Daghani Trust).
2. *Ivan, third sentry* (1943), watercolour on paper (Collection of the Yad Vashem Art Museum, Jerusalem © Arnold Daghani Trust).
3. *Pieta* (The death of Selma Meerbaum-Eisinger) (1942), pencil on paper (Collection of the Yad Vashem Art Museum, Jerusalem © Arnold Daghani Trust).
4. *New Year flowers for Nanino* (1943) in 1942 1943 *And Thereafter (Sporadic records till 1977)* (1942–77), ink and watercolour on paper (G2.060r) (Arnold Daghani Collection, University of Sussex © Arnold Daghani Trust).
5. *Camp interior* (1943) in 1942 1943 *And Thereafter (Sporadic records till 1977)* (1942–77), watercolour on paper (G2.063r) (Arnold Daghani Collection, University of Sussex © Arnold Daghani Trust).
6. *Camp interior* (1943) in 1942 1943 *And Thereafter (Sporadic records till 1977)* (1942–77), watercolour on paper with tracing paper overlay (G2.063r) (Arnold Daghani Collection, University of Sussex © Arnold Daghani Trust).
7. *The stables at Mikhailowka* (1942), ink on paper (Collection of the Yad Vashem Art Museum, Jerusalem © Arnold Daghani Trust).

8. Portrait of Pita Mihailowski (1942), watercolour on paper (Collection of the Yad Vashem Art Museum, Jerusalem © Arnold Daghani Trust).

9. *Work on the highroad* (1942), watercolour on paper (Collection of the Yad Vashem Art Museum, Jerusalem © Arnold Daghani Trust).

10. *Eintritt Verboten* (1942), gouache on paper (Collection of the Yad Vashem Art Museum, Jerusalem © Arnold Daghani Trust).

11. *Evening Prayer* (1943), pencil on paper (Collection of the Yad Vashem Art Museum, Jerusalem © Arnold Daghani Trust).

12. *The life-giving soup* (1943), ink on paper (Collection of the Yad Vashem Art Museum, Jerusalem © Arnold Daghani Trust).

13. *Against the wind* (1943), pencil on paper (Collection of the Yad Vashem Art Museum, Jerusalem © Arnold Daghani Trust).

14. 'Intestinal T.B.'(*Mussia Korn, 18 years old*) (1943), watercolour on paper (Collection of the Yad Vashem Art Museum, Jerusalem © Arnold Daghani Trust).

15. Kaiser's room (1943), watercolour on paper (Collection of the Yad Vashem Art Museum, Jerusalem © Arnold Daghani Trust).

16. *One of the five tailors* (1943), watercolour on paper (Collection of the Yad Vashem Art Museum, Jerusalem © Arnold Daghani Trust).

17. *The sight of Bershad* (1943) in 1942 1943 *And Thereafter* (*Sporadic* records till 1977) (1942–77), watercolour on paper (G2.101r) (Arnold Daghani Collection, University of Sussex © Arnold Daghani Trust).

18. *Ghetto market, Bershad* (1943), watercolour on paper (Collection of the Yad Vashem Art Museum, Jerusalem © Arnold Daghani Trust).

19. *Mass graves, Bershad ghetto* (1943), watercolour on paper (Collection of the Yad Vashem Art Museum, Jerusalem © Arnold Daghani Trust).

20. *What a Nice World* (1943–77), spiral-bound sketchbook with mixed media (G1) (Arnold Daghani Collection, University of Sussex © Arnold Daghani Trust).

21. *Mikhailowka Camp* (1943) pencil on paper (Collection of the Yad Vashem Art Museum, Jerusalem © Arnold Daghani Trust).

Between pp.180 and 181

22. A page from *Let Me Live* (1980s), typewritten manuscript (H5, p. 49) (Arnold Daghani Collection, University of Sussex © Arnold Daghani Trust).

23. A page from *What a Nice World* (1943–77) including *Romanian gendarme* (1963), ink on paper (G1.035r) (Arnold Daghani Collection, University of Sussex © Arnold Daghani Trust).

Acknowledgements

We would like to record our indebtedness to the late Norbert Lynton, to Carola Grindea and to the late Mollie Brandl-Bowen for generously sharing their memories of Arnold and Anişoara Daghani and donating works of great artistic and historical importance to the University of Sussex, where they now form the Arnold Daghani Collection, part of Special Collections in the University Library (hereafter ADC). It is largely through their efforts that the collection has been preserved and made available for systematic research.

Our research has been supported at various stages by grants from The Leverhulme Trust, the Ian Karten Foundation, the Conference on Material Claims against Germany, The Rothschild Foundation Europe and the University of Sussex Centre for German-Jewish Studies. We would also like to acknowledge the assistance we have received from the principal institutions holding works by Arnold Daghani: Special Collections, University of Sussex Library; the Art Collection of Yad Vashem, Jerusalem; and the Museum of Art, Constanţa.

Finally, we would like to thank Stewart Cass and the staff of Vallentine Mitchell for the skill with which they have prepared our book for publication.

PART I

INTRODUCTION

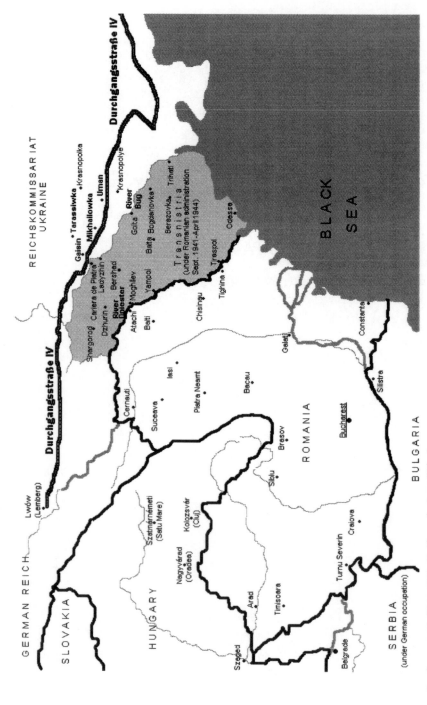

Durchgangstrasse IV in 1942–43 (drawn by Petru Weber)

1

Arnold Daghani's Original Diary

EDWARD TIMMS

The artist Arnold Daghani (1909–85) came from a German-speaking Jewish family in Suczawa, a small town in the Bukovina on the eastern frontier of the Austro-Hungarian Empire (now Suceava in Romania). Although he visited Vienna, Munich and Paris as a young man, he scarcely seems to have received any formal artistic training. Indeed, his career began under the most adverse circumstances – in the Mikhailowka labour camp in Ukraine. He and his wife Anişoara (nicknamed Nanino), whom he married in 1940, were Romanian citizens living in Czernowitz at the time of the German invasion. In June 1942 they were deported across the river Bug to Mikhailowka (see map), together with 400 other Jews who were forced to work as slave labourers. Among the few personal possessions which Daghani took with him when they were deported was a set of watercolours and a sketchbook (a Romanian guard had persuaded him to keep them in his knapsack). He was thus able to complete a remarkable series of paintings and drawings recording the appalling conditions in the camp, a selection of which are featured in this volume. He and his wife had to endure a total of twelve months' forced labour under extremely arduous conditions, working for the August Dohrmann company on the construction of a strategic military road, known by the abbreviation DG IV (Durchgangsstrasse IV).

During this period Daghani and his wife witnessed the arbitrary execution of many of their fellow prisoners by German officers or Lithuanian armed guards. There was also an outbreak of typhoid at the end of 1942 which resulted in many deaths. In the summer of 1943, however, Daghani's artistic gifts earned them the opportunity to spend some nights outside the barbed wire in the neighbouring town of Gaisin, when he was commissioned to design a mosaic of an eagle (or a vulture, as Daghani refers to it) for the headquarters of the Dohrmann company. They were treated with some sympathy by members of the Dohrmann staff, including the engineer Werner Bergmann and the foreman Josef Elsässer. It was this that made it possible for Daghani and his wife to escape in July 1943, aided by a Jewish cobbler named Abrasha, who was a member of the resistance. They were able to smuggle out of the camp about fifty of his artistic works, concealed in a metal tube. While hiding in the ghetto of the small town of Bershad, they learnt that the prisoners from Mikhailowka had been transferred to Tarassiwka, after the camp was attacked by partisans. In January 1944, as they were preparing to return to Bucharest, they received the terrible news that the camp in Tarassiwka had been liquidated and all the remaining prisoners exterminated.[1]

These events left an indelible impression on Daghani's personality, especially as the victims included close friends. In March 1944, after he and his wife had reached the relative safety of Bucharest, he compiled a narrative of events at Mikhailowka in the form of a diary. This was written in English, based on entries he had secretly made in shorthand notebooks at the slave labour camp and the Bershad ghetto. This diary was published after the war, first in a Romanian (1947) and then in a German translation (1960). The English text, entitled *The Grave is in the Cherry Orchard*, appeared in 1961 in a special edition of *Adam: International Review*, a literary magazine edited by Miron Grindea.[2] It is this original text that forms the basis of the present edition, followed by a selection of Daghani's illustrations, some of them completed under circumstances of extreme danger.

The experiences of the labour camp formed the core of a remarkable series of commemorative works which Daghani undertook later in life, combining documentary materials with collage, artistic representation with the meticulous re-transcriptions of his personal memories of the Holocaust. For this purpose he created several large-format albums, juxtaposing visual images against forms of illuminated calligraphy in a style reminiscent of medieval chronicles. The most ambitious of these pictorial and calligraphic manuscripts, which bears the ironic title *What A Nice World*, was completed during the 1970s, but has remained unpublished. A second substantial album, *1942 1943 And Thereafter* (*Sporadic records till 1977*), contains a number of original paintings from Mikhailowka, in addition to an extended series of textual and pictorial reflections on events at the camp. The earliest of these works, dated April 1942, captures the mood before their deportation: *Nanino at the window (in Czernowitz) awaiting full of apprehension my coming home. Too much of a risk in the streets* (Plate 1). This evocative image, his earliest surviving work, shows that by the early 1940s he had already acquired a confident artistic technique, together with the ability to empathize with the emotions of others.

During the post-war period Daghani had an extremely varied and productive career. Although he had no sympathy with the communist regime, he remained in Romania until 1958, developing a personal style which made no concessions to Socialist Realism. He and his wife then emigrated to Israel, but even here he felt that his gifts were not fully appreciated. Between 1961 and 1977 they lived in France and Switzerland, and Daghani's creativity remained undiminished despite the lack of public recognition. He continued to use his artistic and narrative gifts to reflect on the terrible events of the Second World War and its aftermath. In 1977 he and his wife moved to England, where they spent their final years in Hove. Here they lived in an apartment directly above that of Anişoara's sister Carola and Carola's husband, the author and editor Miron Grindea, who had both come to Britain from Romania in 1939. The final years of the Daghanis' lives were relatively peaceful, although they were plagued by illness, partly attributable to the privations they had endured in the camp. Anişoara died in August 1984 and Daghani, who had developed Parkinson's disease, died in a Hove nursing home on 6 April 1985.

THE ARNOLD DAGHANI COLLECTION

In 1987, two years after Daghani's death, the University of Sussex received a collection of approximately 6,000 artistic and commemorative works from the artist's estate. This is the most significant British collection of work by a Holocaust survivor, and it may seem surprising that it should be located at a university. Carola and Miron Grindea, acting as trustees for Daghani's estate, did consider other locations, both at home and abroad. The Imperial War Museum in London was unwilling to accept works that were not 'original' in the sense that they were produced during the Second World War.[3] The municipal museums in Brighton and Hove were also approached, but without success.[4] Public collections in Israel were also considered. In 1960 Daghani had presented a selection of the works completed at Mikhailowka to the Yad Vashem Museum in Jerusalem in return for a token payment, but he later became embroiled in a dispute with Yad Vashem, feeling that they had shown too little respect for his work and ignored the significance of the Nazi slave labour camps in Ukraine. Nevertheless, the home for Daghani's estate might still have been a Jewish museum.

In February 1987, Miron Grindea offered the collection to the Israel Museum. The following month his offer was politely declined by the Mayor of Jerusalem:

> Dear Miron Grindea,
>
> Thank you for your letter of February 2nd. Please forgive my somewhat belated reply.
>
> Permit me to begin by thanking you for your very generous offer concerning the collection of Arnold Daghani. Unfortunately, it is an offer we shall regrettably have to decline. Neither our Museum galleries or storerooms would be adequate for anything of this nature. The space we have available is very limited and the scope of our collections is such – covering antiquity, modern art, Judaica, ethnography, Old Masters, Impressionist art, ethnic arts, Israeli art, etc. – that it would be impossible to make such an addition.
>
> Our curators did speak with the museum at Yad Vashem which would be happy to receive the calligraphy manuscript. Our curators would also be interested in having two or three works of Mr Daghani for our prints and drawing collection.
>
> It is not easy to turn down the major part of a generous offer but such is our reality.
>
> Yours,
>
> Teddy Kollek[5]

The most striking feature of this letter is not the familiar complaint about inadequate storage space, but the emphasis on the structure of the Jerusalem collection. It appears that various departments of the museum were consulted, but that Daghani's work did not conform to the categories used by the curators: 'modern art', 'Judaica', 'Impressionist art' or 'Israeli art'. Even for Yad Vashem, with its extensive archive, the Daghani collection proved unacceptable, since it did not conform to prevailing conceptions of Holocaust commemoration. Yad Vashem was willing to accept the commemorative volume *What A Nice World*, since it was clearly a work of both historical and artistic significance. But how could they be expected to make space for the scores of sketchbooks and hundreds of sheets of drawings and paintings devoted to other subjects: life drawings, nudes, clowns, landscapes, religious motifs, satirical sketches and illustrated literary works?

In their own terms the curators in Jerusalem were right, since Daghani's work does defy conventional categories. It is not 'pure' enough to count as great art, and it is too personal to count as 'authentic' historical documentation. It is an extraordinary bundle of diverse artistic and writerly impulses, reflecting the career of one of the most idiosyncratic artists of the twentieth century. However, Miron and Carola Grindea remained convinced that the collection had an underlying unity and should not be broken up and dispersed. The University of Sussex was fortunate in having a professor of the History of Art, Norbert Lynton, who shared their sense of the collection's importance. 'As a refugee who has lost many relatives and some childhood friends in the Holocaust', Lynton later recalled, 'I could not but be sympathetic.'[6] He was supported by Sir Hugh Casson, past president of the Royal Academy of Arts, who submitted to the university a five-point memorandum. While acknowledging that the collection was 'so vast that it would be difficult for a single institution to agree to accept responsibility for all of it', Casson argued that the university should accept a generous selection of Daghani's works, since this 'would be of more interest to scholars and students – and incidentally much more valuable as a group – than a few isolated pictures'.[7] When the trustees offered the collection to the university, Norbert Lynton piloted the proposal through the channels of academic bureaucracy and ensured that the collection found a haven on the campus.

'MAJOR ART COLLECTION COMES TO SUSSEX', proclaimed the university bulletin on 12 May 1987. But at Sussex, despite its interdisciplinary ethos, the collection again fell between different schools. Professor Lynton decided to take early retirement, and his colleagues in History of Art had other priorities. The gift, which was to form part of the University Art Collection, was not their 'departmental' responsibility.[8] And they apparently felt that the collection was not of sufficient artistic quality to merit their attention. For political historians, on the other hand, it was too subjective to be regarded as a reliable source, while it was too pictorial to be acceptable as part of the Manuscript Collection in the library. For ten years the collection languished in storage, neglected and virtually forgotten. It is only now, since the founding of the Centre for German–Jewish Studies, that the essential tasks of cataloguing and analysis have been tackled.

A grant from the Ian Karten Trust made it possible to employ a gifted young art historian, Dr Deborah Schultz, to compile a computerized inventory of the collection and develop a strategy for its conservation and display. Further generous grants from The Leverhulme Trust made it possible to place Daghani's oeuvre in the broader context of a research project entitled 'Pictorial Narrative in the Nazi Period'.[9] This research also took account of the expanded version of Daghani's diary, which he compiled with the assistance of Mollie Brandl-Bowen during the final decades of his life. This includes a wealth of additional materials, reviewed in Part 3 and Part 4 of the present volume under the headings 'Memory and Creativity' and 'Testimony, Justice and Reconciliation'.

THE MIKHAILOWKA DIARY

Nothing could show more clearly how Daghani's work defies conventional categories than his diary of events at Mikhailowka, *The Grave is in the Cherry Orchard*. The account it gives of experiences in a slave labour camp raises disturbing questions about the role of ordinary Germans in the Holocaust. However, the status of this text is not easy to define. It appears to have the authenticity of a diary, with each event recorded as it occurs. But the book as a whole was not composed until after Daghani and his wife had escaped from the camp and returned to Bucharest. When the English edition of *The Grave is in the Cherry Orchard* was published in *Adam* in 1961, the editor's introduction recorded that Daghani originally wrote the narrative in English. This may seem surprising, since his English cannot have been very fluent at that time, even though he had worked as a commercial translator during the 1930s. Indeed, his written English remained rather idiosyncratic even in later life, with fractured syntax and persistent traces of German idiom. Since these qualities accentuate the disconcerting style of his narrative, they have been left unaltered in the present edition of the diary.[10]

An explanation for his use of English can be found in a deposition which

Daghani made in Lübeck in June 1965, when he was interviewed by the German Public Prosecutor investigating war crimes in Ukraine. At Mikhailowka, in addition to his paintbox, he had with him two practice books for English shorthand, small enough to slip into his pocket, and he was able to make brief notes about dates, events and persons in these books and on other tiny scraps of paper. He succeeded in keeping these notes concealed on his person and was able to save them when they escaped. The diary in its more polished form was 'composed later, as a factual report, on the basis of these notes which I had saved' ('später auf Grund der Aufzeichnungen, die ich gerettet habe, als Tatsachenbericht niedergelegt'). Daghani also recalls that when he and his wife emigrated from Romania in December 1958, he was obliged to leave those original notes behind.[11]

Using English shorthand was a sensible safety precaution, since anyone discovered keeping a record of events in the camp would certainly have been shot. Daghani continued to use English on his return to Bucharest in March 1944, when he began to transcribe his notes into a more coherent form. One might have expected him, like his fellow countryman, the poet Paul Celan, to choose German as the medium for reflection on the atrocities of the Nazi period. Celan had survived in a Romanian labour camp, while his parents were deported to Ukraine and shot. When reproached for writing in the language of his parents' murderers, Celan replied: 'Only in one's mother tongue can one express one's own truth, in a foreign language the poet lies.'[12]

By contrast, Daghani's aim was to record events, not to express a personal, poetic truth. He was a lifelong Anglophile, frequently choosing to write in English even when he was living in France and Switzerland. In 1944 he evidently took a conscious decision not to write in German, unless circumstances made this necessary. Perhaps he felt revulsion at the way the Nazis had abused his mother tongue, or perhaps it was once again a safety precaution. In the spring of 1944 Bucharest was still controlled by Marshal Antonescu's pro-German regime, and it would have been dangerous for a Jew to be caught in possession of an anti-fascist manuscript in German or indeed in Romanian. However, the situation was transformed on 23 August 1944, when Antonescu's government was overthrown, and a week later the first units of the Red Army reached the city.

During the following months Daghani revised the text of his diary for publication in Romanian. The Introduction to the original edition is dated

Bucharest, July 1944, and a short excerpt – dealing with events in September 1942 – appeared on 1 December 1944 in the magazine *Răspântea*. Daghani later recalled that the complete diary was originally scheduled for publication in January 1945 in the Romanian magazine *Forum*. But the text was received with scepticism, not only by the editor of *Forum* but also by other publishers to whom it was offered, both in Romania and in England.

The original English manuscript was brought to London by a friend in 1946, but rejected as unsuitable for publication. As Miron Grindea recalled in the preface to the *Adam* edition, people felt that it was 'good' but contained 'too few atrocities'! So the first edition of a diary written in English was actually published in Romanian in 1947 under the title *Groapa este în livada de vişini* (The Grave is in the Cherry Orchard). This version runs to 164 pages and includes reproductions of sixteen of Daghani's watercolours and drawings from Mikhailowka. Apart from a brief introduction and an afterword, each section of the diary bears a specific date, starting with 18 August 1942, and this dating system was retained, with minor variations, in subsequent editions in other languages. Occasionally, details which occur in the Romanian and German editions are omitted in the English version, possibly as a result of careless copy-editing. Among those who died during the typhoid outbreak of the winter of 1942–43 was Selma Meerbaum-Eisinger, a gifted young poet. The entry for 16 December 1942, which records her death, is omitted from the *Adam* edition.

The compelling power of such a diary does not depend on entries being composed on the date of the recorded events or in the linguistic medium in which they were originally experienced. The most significant models for Daghani's use of this narrative form may be found among those memoirs of the First World War which convey an impression of immediacy but are actually re-transcriptions, composed in the aftermath of the terrible events they record. Ernst Jünger's *In Stahlgewittern* (Storm of Steel), first published in 1922, is the most influential example of a war 'diary' which owes its impact to the skilful rewriting of notes originally made by the author as a front-line officer. But by contrast with Jünger, Daghani's aim was to record events as accurately as possible, not to use them to propagate a dubious ideology.[13]

It was this overriding concern for accuracy that led him to revise his narrative later in life, when new information came to light. The 'diary' ultimately evolved into a more elaborate form of memoir, but this does not diminish its value. For Daghani, as for other survivors, memory became an 'insomniac faculty'.[14] According to those who knew him best, Daghani had an exceptionally retentive memory for events, names, dates and places.[15] And since his wife Anişoara had shared every hour of their ordeal, he was able to draw on her recollections for further confirmation.

The original text of *The Grave is in the Cherry Orchard* owes its effect to the cryptic economy of Daghani's style, accompanied by passages of anguished reflection. His distinctive achievement, both in the text and in the accompanying illustrations, is to give a human face to the sufferings which the Nazi system inflicted on slave labourers. The description of events at Mikhailowka provides a microcosm of the system of mass murder, with the precise dates and details of mindless atrocities. In place of the impersonal machinery of 'the Holocaust', we are presented with the names and ranks of individual perpetrators, the individual characters of their victims, and the identities of the bystanders – officials of the construction company who colluded with a system of institutionalized barbarism. 'Anişoara was mercilessly beaten by Ivan the guard', Daghani reports on 18 January 1943, 'because she dared to nibble some stale bread while she was shovelling.' The watercolour of Ivan that he had to paint the following month captures the gleeful face of petty tyranny (Plate 2). Ivan 'was pleased at first', Daghani explains, 'but in the end did not particularly like it, so I have kept it' (2 February 1943).

One of the principal themes of the diary is the discrepancy between the routines of forced labour and unpredictable eruptions of violence. Certain scenes depicting the family life of prisoners in their cramped sleeping quarters have a reassuring domesticity, and on one occasion Daghani recalls that it is not the first time that a child has been born in a stable. As an artist familiar with Christian iconography, he is reminded of both 'NATIVITY and PIETA' (30 December 1942). It is as a modern version of the Descent from the Cross that he represents the death of Selma Meerbaum-Eisinger in a striking pencil drawing entitled *Pieta* (Plate 3). Such religious allusions enrich Daghani's verbal and visual narrative, reflecting both his Jewish upbringing and his debt to Christian iconography.[16] However, there is a continuous awareness that violent death lurks in the background, and it is behind the stable buildings that executions frequently take place.

The entry for 21 September 1942 records that the German camp commandant, Arthur Kiesel, came to inspect the road construction work as usual.

Then a Lithuanian guard named Wisotzkas ordered two elderly women workers to drop their shovels and follow him into the fields. 'Two shots. A shriek!' There was no obvious explanation for the killings, although it was rumoured that the guards had taken a dislike to the two women-slaves and used to sneer at one of them for wearing snow boots during the summer. It was all so 'nightmarish' that the prisoners seemed to be merely 'players in a gruesome, highly imaginative comedy of errors, or should it be a comedy of horrors – but who can say what part one really has in the cast'. The unpredictability of this reign of terror intensified the demoralizing effects of exhaustion, malnutrition and illness. The entry for 6 October 1942 records that one prisoner became so depressed that he attempted suicide by swallowing tablets. He survived the attempt, but was shot dead by a guard the following day on the orders of Walter Mintel, deputy commandant of the camp.[17] There were further shootings in the spring of 1943, after SS-Oberscharführer Bernhard Maass had taken over command of the camp.

It is against this grim background that the remarkable story of the Daghanis' escape unfolds. Despite the dehumanizing pressures, the Jews in the camp tried to keep alive the spirit of family life. On New Year's Day 1943, Daghani presented to his wife a beautiful painting of tulips in a bowl (Plate 4). The painting bears the poignant inscription (in Romanian): 'To Nanino: Happy New Year! May God help us that in 1943 we should be home, united with the family.' Daghani also painted views of the prisoners' sleeping quarters which convey a strangely homely atmosphere. His aim, as he explained, was to show that the prisoners retained a certain dignity while enduring hunger, lice, brutality, disease and arbitrary execution. His artistic skills enabled him, uniquely, to bridge the gap between the two worlds, testifying to the residue of shared humanity which survived within a system of organized atrocity.

On 19 June 1943, Josef Elsässer arranged for the Daghanis to travel to Gaisin and stay there, sleeping in a garage, so that they could continue work on the mosaic of the German eagle which they had begun earlier that year. The pages describing their experiences in Gaisin are among the most compelling in the whole diary. Although still under the threat of death, they now experienced certain gestures of humanity. It was in Gaisin that the Daghanis came to know two young German women employed as secretaries – the sisters Martha and Atti (nées Grae). On 22 June 1943 Werner Bergmann gave Daghani some drawing paper and asked him to do a watercolour of the room occupied by the Grae sisters. It was to be a present to Atti Grae, with whom Bergmann was on affectionate terms. Atti treated the prisoners with contempt, even though she herself relied on a woman from the camp named Rosa Tabak to work for her as a dressmaker (28 June 1943). Her sister Martha, however, showed greater sympathy, even lending them books on their wedding anniversary.

There is a dramatic change of key as the narrative describes the Daghanis' escape. The disjointed series of short diary entries gives way to a gripping adventure story. By 15 July they had completed work on the mosaic. They were terrified that they would once again be imprisoned at Mikhailowka, but they were allowed to stay in Gaisin for a further night, when Bergmann gave Daghani another more personal commission. He asked him to paint some flowers on parchment, to make a lampshade as a present for Atti. Prompted by Anişoara, Daghani used the pattern on some Rosenthal porcelain in the Grae sisters' room as his inspiration. It was this task which gained them time to make their escape, aided by a Ukrainian Jewish shoemaker named Abrasha. They hid overnight in a deserted building in Gaisin, narrowly escaping detection when the building was searched by German soldiers.

After a series of further alarms and adventures, they were taken by a guide to a shallow place on the river Bug and were able to wade across to the relative safety of the Romanian shore, carrying their possessions (including the precious pictures) above their heads. One of the finest paintings in the Daghani archive, an untitled interior of the prisoners' living quarters inscribed 'Done early 1943 ...', still bears signs of damage from the waters of the river Bug (Plate 5). After the section describing the Daghanis' stay in the Bershad ghetto, the diary entry for 10 January 1944 records that all the remaining prisoners from Mikhailowka have been liquidated, including some of their closest friends. The final detail, based on the testimony of peasants who witnessed the atrocity, is that the shootings lasted for six hours and the graves 'are in the orchard'. A poignant postscript records that Abrasha, the Jewish shoemaker to whom they owed their lives, was also shot by the Nazis.

NOTES

1. For a more detailed account of Daghani's experiences, see M. Bohm-Duchen, *Arnold Daghani* (London: Diptych, 1987), pp.11–45.
2. A. Daghani, *The Grave is in the Cherry Orchard*, with twenty-four reproductions of watercolours and drawings by the author, in M. Grindea (ed.), *Adam: International Review* (London) 29, 291–3 (1961), pp.4–118.
3. Information provided by Carola Grindea in an interview with Edward Timms, 17 December 1996. The Imperial War Museum would have been willing to accept only works which were actually painted in the labour camp.
4. 'Hove turns down genius' was the headline on the front page of the *Brighton and Hove Leader*, 11 May 1985. The Hove Town Council rejected the offer of 100 works by Daghani for the Hove Art Gallery because there was 'no room'.
5. Typewritten letter of 28 March 1987 from Teddy Kollek to Miron Grindea (signed 'Teddy'), ADC.
6. Letter of 2 February 2000 from Norbert Lynton to Edward Timms, ADC.
7. Letter of 2 July 1986 from Sir Hugh Casson to Carola Grindea, enclosing a draft memorandum for the attention of Professor Norbert Lynton, ADC.
8. Letter of 2 February 2000 from Norbert Lynton to Edward Timms.
9. D. Schultz and E. Timms, *Pictorial Narrative in the Nazi Period: Felix Nussbaum, Charlotte Salomon and Arnold Daghani*, special issue of *Word & Image*, 24, 3 (July–September 2008), pp.207–335.
10. Small typographical errors, such as 'wark' for 'work' (10 December 1942), have been silently corrected. Otherwise, the only significant emendations made in the text of this new edition of *The Grave is in the Cherry Orchard* are as follows: the spelling of Roumania has been modernized to Romania; the misheard name 'Minte' has been corrected to 'Mintel'; the missing entry for 16 December 1942 has been restored; and a small number of copy-editing changes have been made to correct minor inconsistencies.
11. 'Zeugenschaftliche Vernehmung', Staatsanwaltschaft Lübeck bei dem Landesgericht, 2 P Js 1629/64, 9 June 1965: vorgeladen Arnold Daghani. A carbon copy of the twenty-four-page transcript of this testimony is now in the Arnold Daghani Collection, University of Sussex. References to this document are identified by the abbreviation ZV followed by the page number.
12. Paul Celan in conversation with Ruth Lackner, quoted in I. Chalfen, *Paul Celan: A Biography of his Youth*, translated by M. Bleyleben (New York: Persea, 1991), p.184.
13. The tendentiousness of Jünger's use of the 'diary' form is analysed in M. Travers, *German Novels of the First World War and their Ideological Implications, 1918–1933* (Stuttgart: Heinz, 1982), pp.32–42. For a more detailed account of the differences between Jünger's original notes and his published texts, see U. Böhne, *Fassungen bei Ernst Jünger* (Meisenheim: Hain, 1972).
14. L.L. Langer, *Holocaust Testimonies: The Ruins of Memory* (New Haven, CT and London: Yale University Press, 1991), p.xv.
15. According to his sister-in-law Carola Grindea, Daghani never forgot anything and 'had the memory of an elephant' (conversation with Edward Timms, 24 January 2000).
16. The Christian undertones in Daghani's depiction of Jewish suffering are analysed in D. Schultz, 'Religion and Identity in the Work of Arnold Daghani' in F. Ames-Lewis, P. Martyn and P. Paszkiewicz (eds), *Art-Ritual-Religion* (Warsaw: Instytut Sztuki PAN, 2004), pp.109–19 and in Bohm-Duchen, Arnold Daghani, pp.59–70. As a young man he was apparently baptized as a Protestant, since in his court deposition he describes himself as 'protestantischer Jude' (ZV 2).
17. The original Romanian edition gives the victim's name as Dr Arnold Goldenberg. In the early editions of the diary the name of the German commandant is given as 'Minte'. It was only during the legal investigations of the 1960s that his actual name was identified.

PART II

THE DIARY

2

The Grave is in the Cherry Orchard

ARNOLD DAGHANI

INTRODUCTION

Eight road contractors, August Dohrmann, Eras, Kasper, Emmerich, Horst, Kaiser, Stöhr, Teeras and Ufer – all belonging to the Todt Organisation [T.O.] – were in charge of repairing the main road from Gaisin to Uman in the South-Western Ukraine with labour drawn from both sides of the river Bug: three thousand and five hundred Ukrainian Jews, raided from various ghettos of the region and three thousand and eight hundred 'exiles' recently deported from the northern part of Romania.

Since the labour had been 'purchased' from the SS the contracting companies did not consider it necessary to pay any wages to the workers themselves. The price had been duly fixed between the SS and their contractors at sixteen Reichspfennigs per head – paid daily! A wise precaution on the part of the companies – to have daily accounts! If something unforeseen happened to a worker, (if, for instance, he or she would ... 'cease to exist') the contractors would have been in an awkward situation had they made payment in advance for his or her labour.

Officially we were under the command of Engineer Werner Bergmann from Hagen, who was assisted by a large number of camp-führers and overseers who, in their turn, were constantly watched by the SS, the Reich's police (the Fifth Schutz Company) and scattered contingents of Lithuanians and deserters from the Russian army.

The fact that there was nothing but death waiting, a single step away, for anyone who, for some reason, could no longer work led to many odd results: boys between the age of thirteen and fourteen who, according to the regulations, were too young to do their full share of work and so enjoy the right to live, tried at the beginning to hide from the searching eyes of the sentries, but after a while they would stand on tiptoes so as to look taller and older. Likewise, older people were doing all they could to look younger than they were. Those who had formerly indulged in a beard or moustache solved the problem by becoming clean-shaven. The sick simulated the healthy.

'Let me go to work, *please, please!*' was the imprecation of all those who have been decreed as unfit for work, in other words selected for immediate execution. Our motto was: *work sweetens life*, and even when one's husband or wife, children or parents were taken to the grave, one would still go on working and afterwards queue for his pea-soup. There was no time for bereavement.

The road-building companies left this daily plea for survival to the inmates and their destroying elements – guards and sentries. With them, the one essential thing was that work should go on smoothly: not only were the contractors profit-making concerns, but the work on the main road provided their own staff with an excuse for staying behind the front line.

This desire that everything should go forward as efficiently as possible became evident in a conversation I had one day with a T.O. camp-führer, Karl Ulrich. He asked me if I had not been wondering over the fact that for a long time past executions had ceased to take place on the actual working-plot. In fact, I had not given it a thought; the decrees of those who owned our lives were too unfathomable for any of us to question them, even in our minds. The T.O. man, however, insisted in offering his own explanation. The company, August Dohrmann Arbeitsgemeinschaft, had protested against any execution taking place on the working-plot on the grounds that it would have an unfavourable effect on the fellow-workers of those shot dead. The manager, therefore, expressed his opinion that any 'purge' carried out well away from the highway would have a far less depressing effect on our zest for work.

But, who among us was still so susceptible to outside impressions?

True enough, at the very beginning of all these events, a twenty-year-old lad, Barasch Jr, had been on the point of fainting as he cleaned up the blood-stained bicycle and truncheon, which the Lithuanian N.C.O. Zelinskas had handed over to him after returning from a 'pruning' that took place in the background of the working-plot. But that was a long time ago now!

And yet, in spite of everything, youth will be youth. Thus, on Sundays, enjoying their day of rest, the people, cleanly dressed, would sit just inside the barbed-wire fence, pursuing with their glances the boys and girls, also neatly dressed, who were on their way to the church opposite. The priest, a neighbour of the T.O. overseer, Kaiser, never missed an opportunity to slip some food to any of us who were lucky enough to be detailed that day for menial jobs around the camp or who were on odd errands for Kaiser. In a furtive way he or his wife would pass the food into the worker's hands as they passed. One day, seeing me do a painting for Kaiser, the priest gave me some writing-paper to use for water-colours. Precious paper! — everyone wanted it. Buder, the police-sergeant, temporary commandant of the camp, retuned one day in a furious temper from the near-by town. He had gone into the only shop in the town to ask for a writing-pad only to be told that the shop was reserved for officers. Buder was a sergeant. It is easy, it seems, to become a master over the lives and deaths of men: for that, the rank of a sergeant is sufficient — but it is not enough to enable one to buy writing-paper! Buder told us this himself! In fact it was nothing out of the ordinary to be told such things by the camp staff. The T.O. men were sometimes willing to air their grievances: they could be quite sure that any such confidences would be taken to the grave — all too literally.

The prisoners, on the other hand, being talkative human beings themselves, and ignoring altogether where they were, took their role as partners in the conversation quite seriously. Strange as it may seem, they never lost the habit of considering themselves as equals ...

Then, too, in their thinking, they were planning ahead for a different life after liberation, because liberation would never fail to come — or would it?

Hearing a girl sing the song 'Wir sind die Moorsoldaten' which, she told us, had been born in a Concentration camp in Germany, many women in our camp asked her to sing it more often. They clung to the vision of liberation in that song. And their conversation voiced this certainty also. Thus, one woman, Mrs. Jurmann, said to a neighbour: 'If Heaven saves us and we go back home again, I'd like my Martha to be led to the altar to the nuptial march, "Zu fünf, zu fünf"' '(In fives, in fives), which was the N.C.O.s' daily working order: 'Get on parade in five ranks.'

'Won't that be glorious, Madame?'

Both of them were laughing heartily.

There was something irrational in this use of 'Sir' and 'Madame' by the inmates of the camp.

19

'You ought to hold the shovel in another way, Madame', was an expression that was heard quite often in the beginning, when a man or woman, who had learned the trick, wanted to teach the other. Nor was the sentence: 'I'm afraid, Sir, I can't let you have the potatoes now because I haven't been able to barter my underwear', something at all out of the ordinary in our lives: it described a true situation, but it sounded grotesque, as if corpses already lying on the bier were exchanging politenesses.

But there were others who were utterly sceptical regarding the watercolours and drawings I was making. What if there *was* a chance of such things being looked at afterwards, after the general purge of the camp? What use would that be?

Unfortunately, it is they, the sceptical ones, who have been proved right. On the 18th July 1943, my wife and I made our getaway, but between the 10th and 18th December, the same year, all the camps across the Bug along the highway between Gaisin and Uman were dissolved – by the wholesale extermination of the inmates.

The graves have no sign; nor are they otherwise conspicuous. Mass-graves and single ones in orchards; in some ditch; in front of stables; at the back of them; in corn-fields, close to a well; everywhere ...

MIKHAILOWKA

18th *August* 1942

Some of us were still asleep in the derelict garage at the outskirts of Ladijin, on the river Bug. The night before, Anişoara – my wife – had, through the mediation of a dentist, Klein, managed to get two armfuls of hay from a peasant woman. This is how we, too, had a good night's rest for the first time for weeks.

All of a sudden, came the bawling of a strange voice: 'Get out!'

A thickset man in SS uniform was standing on the threshold. 'Get going with all your trash!' he added impatiently, fidgeting with his menacing baton.

His unexpected appearance made us jump to our feet. In a great hurry we succeeded in getting outside, dragging our things behind us.

In the area, rounded off, we saw people running to and fro, terrified. The arrival of some lorries, chalkmarked T.O., added the final touches to the confusion.

An old woman stooped to pick up the scattered potatoes she had let fall in her bewilderment. An SS officer stopped her: 'Don't you bother, you'll get plenty to cram down over there.'

In lorry-loads to the river Bug, where an improvised ferry took over. For an hour or so, the ferry crossed back and forth disgorging a mass of misery across the Bug. Every age between six-months and ninety-one years was represented. A conglomeration of humanity: a few still good-looking people, others frail or blind or hunchbacks; children and sucklings; finally workers, shanghaied for the Todt Organisation. We were loaded up again. Before the lorries started up, T.O. men and regular soldiers came up to each group for any money we might still have hidden or which had not been handed over as ordered. 'Where you're going, you won't need any money', they said.

We passed through villages, the inhabitants of which looked at us furtively from behind their windows. Some of them kept grinning.

We passed a sign-post: GAISIN, and not long after we came to a halt in front of a building. Soldiers, in uniforms, which were unfamiliar to us, were loitering about, outside. One of them changed a few words with one of our sentries, in a language likewise unfamiliar to us. On leaving Gaisin, we came upon signposts directing to Teplik and Uman, and then we were on a road that fringed a wood. PoWs with big letters S.U. on the backs of their bluish-green jackets were working there. Finally, three lorries of our convoy drew up at the end of the village.

MIKHAILOWKA

In front of two stables. A villager-sentinel was standing by the barbed wire. We seemed to have arrived at the terminus.

One by one we passed through the gate, to be counted. The shock produced by the succession of events was such that we trotted in only half-conscious of what was going on.

A sergeant-major of the Police delivered a short address of 'welcome':

'It's forbidden to get in touch with the peasants or to barter with them: anyone who contravenes this order will be executed on the spot. Anyone who tries to make a getaway will be shot dead or hanged.' He then pointed to the gibbet over the gate. According to him, a fugitive had been caught and hanged a few days before. 'We make no distinction between the educated and simple folk. All of you have to work. A Jew is a Jew. Is that clear?'

When he went off, Anişoara called my attention to some heads that had appeared at the low windows of the stable. Now a sentry opened the gate leading into it. An appalling sight: shapes of what had formerly been human beings, dressed in tatters, were to be seen on the threshold. Our fellow-workers. From Teplik and Uman respectively, they had been transferred from the Ghetto in May, to work in the near-by gravel-pits. Some of those we were talking to had become ill, the others were 'commandeered' – a newly-coined word, I had to learn – to work as craftsmen or kitchen-hands. In the cook-shack, a woman was just lifting the lid of a huge boiler; there was a strong smell of sourish pea-soup. We were advised not to tell our true age when asked by the police. Those under fourteen and the ones over forty-five were listed on a special roll, together with anyone who was foolish enough to report himself ill.

The Police in charge of us are: Arthur Kiesel, a Berliner, (the man who greeted us on our arrival). He is the commandant. His A.D.C.s are SS Scharführer Walter Mintel and a Lithuanian N.C.O. So, the unfamiliar uniforms of the soldiers loitering in front of the barracks are Lithuanians. As to food, there is the salt-less pea-soup with fusty millet in it, and every eighth or ninth day three quarters of a hard, green-veined loaf of bread. Of course, those who have something to sell or barter (the Umaner Naiman, for instance, shifted his glance pointedly to our bundles) would be able to change it for potatoes, onions or bread from the passers-by. Forbidden? He poo-poohed our interruption. The police and the Lithuanians, including the village-guards, are only too glad to receive a bribe.

A young woman, holding her baby tightly in her arms, joined our group. Her baby was born a fortnight ago, she told us. 'Some day', she remarked, looking sadly, 'they are going to take it away from me … '

A cloud of dust was approaching, while an ever growing noise was bursting upon our ears.

The convoy.

Several hundred men and women, in separate groups, escorted by local guards and Lithuanian soldiers, stopped outside in front of the gate. After having been counted by the N.C.O., they were ordered to enter. What followed was a bedlam! Men, women and youngsters were hurrying in, shrieking, shouting, pushing, and swearing at one another. We watched them lining up before the window of the cook-shack. Worn-out faces; destitutes. Greedily they kept stretching out their hands, to take the earthen dish. Some we saw standing aside, pursuing with their envious looks those who had managed to get to the window earlier.

I exchanged a look with Anişoara and shuddered.

Would this be our life, too?

... Dusk came.

Since there was no room left in the stable for all of us, the newcomers had to pass the night in the open.

19th *August*

We were awakened as the day was breaking. After each of us stowed away our things, we were ordered to form files by five; men and women separately. Mintel did the counting: four hundred and eighty newcomers. Seven mothers of sucklings have been commandeered as cooks and kitchen-hands. Segall, our self-styled spokesman, will be distributor of food. Pepi has been 'appointed' both cook and interpreter with the T.O. man in command of the Ukrainian peasant-women camp in the village.

After the working-convoys were taken to the gravel-pits, some of us, myself included, had to clean the second stable of the dung. Since only part of the horses in this stable has been dislodged, we shall share the abode with the remaining horses.

Two more lorries from 'beyond'. A baby and her grand-mother are amongst the recent arrivals. The baby's parents were in a lorry bound for another direction.

At noontime, a lorry with supplies arrived, driven by a T.O. man. I managed to peep over his shoulder as he was making out the allowance: two and a half ounces of millet and three and a half ounces of pea per capita each day. We are 'owned' by the August Dohrmann Arbeitsgemeinschaft of Remscheid in Rhenania. The same lorry is also taking supplies to the camp of Tarassiwka and Braslav. How funny: Braslav is situated on the other side of the Bug from which we have been brought, and as far as I know, it was only on this side that there was German jurisdiction!

... Sunset.

The convoys are approaching. Trudging along afoot, some people with tiny sacks in their hands or on their backs, still containing a little food from the other side, they are all coming closer and closer. No face stands out from the mass. All of them are covered with dust.

Tired and hungry, they can hardly wait to be given the 'life-giving' pea-soup.

After the meal we are moved into the stable.

Divided only by a latticed partition, people are penned together with the horses; others find accommodation in the loft. Everywhere it is so over-crowded that we have to cram down next to one another.

20th *August*

At the gravel-quarry.

Men are working with picks; women and children are shovelling gravel, gathering it into heaps.

The mechanical calls of 'get working' come from the local guards. Ever so often workers are knocked to the ground by an 'encouraging' blow from a baton. T.O. man Kuehne is the overseer. According to those who have been working under him for the past three months, he is decent and will never abuse or beat anyone.

Nearing the stable, on our way back 'home', we saw a covered ladder being carried out of the gate. It is a seventy-year-old woman who has died of heart-failure while we were out working. We also learn of two more dead, shot by Mintel and Zelinskas, within the enclosure of the barbed wire. What has happened to their bodies? I don't know.

23rd *August*

Sunday ...

Mintel had a talk with Segall in the afternoon. We are told he is claiming one thousand Reichsmarks to accede to the babies remaining with their mothers – in plain language a bribe in order not to shoot them.

The sum is quickly raised by collection.

24th *August*

One convoy has left for the gravel-pit, another for the highway. Anişoara and myself are amongst those to start work on the road.

The way to the main road led through a wood. It was a sight to remember. Some of us were trying to escape, even for a moment, putting out of our minds any thought of barbed-wire or the villagers who guarded us. But even this was impossible for the guards kept on bringing us back to reality with their rifle butts and their curses.

T.O. men Kaiser, Ulrich and Schneider are the overseers.

It is a very warm day, which makes us thirsty to a man. Fortunately, we have been given a barrel of water to ourselves. The T.O. men are having coffee. On account of typhus and typhoid fever prevailing in the district, they are not allowed to indulge in water-drinking, as we do.

Back home, we are told that Zelinskas, a Lithuanian, has sent word that anyone who prefers work at the gravel-pit to work on the road, should pay into his hands a subscription either in money or in valuables. As a favour, Zelinskas will see to it that barter with the passers-by should be set on a truly great scale. The number of the people to work at the gravel-pit has been fixed by him at a hundred.

25th August

Homeward along the highroad.

Serskus, the Lithuanian, knows but one German word, 'schneller', and he means it. 'Get moving!', he tells us, 'get moving!' As we reached the outskirts of the village we were in the last stage of exhaustion. Just then we had the bad luck of running into Mintel, who was riding a bicycle. Some of us took our hats off to him, while others, simply not noticing him, kept their hats or caps on. That put him into a rage. He got down.

'Don't you know', he snapped, 'that you have got to take off your hats on seeing a German soldier? I'll make you atone for that, so you won't do it again!' Mintel waited for us all to march past and then rode off.

Some while later we found ourselves waiting for the pea-soup. Hardly a week has passed, and now we, too, would hurry in at the gate to be amongst the first to line up before the window of the cook-shack. There was a time, now dim in our memory, when people used to be decent and give way to women and elderly people. It is strange to recall that such a time ever existed.

There!

Something was stirring up.

Mintel!

Mintel was at the gate, people were whispering to one another. What was he up to, some of us were anxious to know.

I couldn't guess what passed through his mind then – for the moment he only gave us a quick glance and rode on.

26th August

The Lithuanians and other guards have extorted money to buy brandy with. As the majority of those working on the main road are provided with too little or with no means at all, the extortion is felt as a heavy burden by all of us. On the other hand, Zelinskas and a few guards seemed to have had a good time at the gravel-pit by placing empty bottles of brandy as targets into the excavated walls over the heads of the workers. By order, no inmate is ever allowed to leave the spot where he is working: and when an elderly woman got wounded by a detached stone of some size, Zelinskas looking at the bleeding wound remarked casually: 'A good job you are a woman. If it were a serious wound, I'd have to polish you off right away.'

29th August

This morning some of the Lithuanians stayed behind in the guard-house. Serskus said casually to one of us 'that lot over there have a holiday today'.

In the afternoon, however, they came to the road riding a cart. Whistling and radiating and smelling of brandy the Lithuanians shook hands with the T.O. men and the guardian.

... Sixteen inmates have been shot dead!

Amongst them the mother with her three-week-old baby who spoke to us when we arrived, also the cook's daughter whom we noticed at the cook-shack. Segall watched the whole thing from a small window in the loft.

This is how it happened. All craftsmen and kitchen-hands as well as Segall were locked in the stable. After the two convoys to the gravel-pit and main road were marched off, those to be executed were goaded to a grave behind the stable. A man of ninety-one led a seventy-year-old blind man by the hand. Segall overheard them say their prayers in a fairly loud voice. All were then told to remove their clothes, piece by piece, their backs turned upon the Lithuanian firing squad. Naked they sank into the grave.

Passing by some youngsters, I overheard them whisper the word 'purge' – another word newly-coined by the new Order.

There was a blank in my mind as I looked at Anişoara. The thought that ...

30th August

Sunday ...

Life went on.

Throughout the morning the women were engaged in setting up 'house-keeping': two clods, an earthen pot over it, and then it was just a matter of luck or skill whether one had a pumpkin, potatoes or just warm water in it. Men and children kept kindling the fire, entreating one another every now and then for at least two or three spoonfuls of water.

The Guards did not feel inclined to take our water-carriers to the village-well more often than they considered necessary. Anişoara and I have been given a share of a pumpkin, some people are dusting their clothes and cracking lice, while the two hairdressers are busily engaged in hair-cutting and shaving. Indoors, people are standing around, discussing the latest 'piece of news' heatedly. Professor Henner is deep in his grammar-book. He is known to have brought English and Italian grammar-books in his bag. Twelve-year-old Nori is reading the Luther Bible. A few steps further, Rosa, surrounded by young and old, is telling them their fortune in the cards. Nothing about love-affairs, or windfalls of money. No! Instead of this Rosa pretends to read in their cards the forthcoming liberation.

Liberation? After yesterday? Deliverance will not fail to come, she keeps on saying, even though there are others who voice their disbelief. On the whole, people would get good cards. Only Mia's were different. After she left the group, Rosa told us that something was wrong with Mia's cards.

While I was slowly going down the loft to get some potatoes from the Landmanns, I heard a shriek and at the same time a lot of dust fell from above. Looking up, we saw a woman's leg sticking out through the ceiling. A rotten plank had given way. Luckily, nothing serious had happened.

2nd September

The bustle in the stable resembles some main street in a forlorn market-town, the shake-downs and horse-cribs, turned into infant-beds, playing their parts as houses on both sides of the 'street'. Two improvised lamps – tiny bottles of Eau-de-Cologne – give off a dim light. Not too far away from the centre there is a young man surrounded by a group of men and women: he has potatoes. Another group of men are swaying to and fro in the rhythm of their prayer. The voices from time to time defeated by the neighing horses beyond the latticed partition.

Silence has fallen all of a sudden.

People are signalling one another cautiously.

Zelinskas!

He wants our tinker and the watchmaker to come out at once.

The murmuring voices are being heard again, while Gutman has resumed selling his potatoes. Unobtrusively, the tinker and the watchmaker come back from outside, limping and bleeding heavily. Zelinskas, furious at their having bought some cheese and tomatoes from a stable-hand, without giving him a bribe first, had them flogged.

3rd September

Zelinskas, talking in a friendly manner to one of us, has dropped this remark: 'If I shoot you or another Jew, I only serve my country. The Jew is our enemy!'

4th September

We were awakened long before the reveille by Susi, the five-year-old daughter of Dr. Siperstein.

'Mummy, I'm hungryyyy!'

Poor child! She could not be soothed so easily.

Some of the women, working in the gravel-quarry, availing themselves of the short space of time till the unvarying call 'Aufwachen und fertig machen' put on several dresses; they might get the chance of bartering them for some food.

The call.

In the files, people were discussing their dreams with one another. Most of them had seen dishes of food set before their delighted eyes. Lilli's eyes were still sparking as she told Mizzi about a fish she had been eating in her dream.

Esoteric Hammerling remarked suddenly:

'I'm positive that by the eighteenth of September we'll be back home again!'

5th September

People have returned from the gravel-quarry in a bad state of nerves. Mizzi offered me the explanation: they were working for two hours or so when Zelinskas was seen talking excitedly to Mintel. Then they watched Zelinskas leaving the quarry. Mintel remained behind, keeping a close watch on all of them. Each one of them went on working hard, straining every nerve. Something was in the air … Zelinskas returned, this time in a cart, accompanied by guards. The car stopped at the entrance to the quarry. Stealing a glance, Mizzi saw the guards drag a girl of about eighteen from the cart. Her clothes were torn, the hair dishevelled. Though her countenance was terror-stricken, it still bore the traces of charm. Probably, Mizzi thought, she had run away from another camp, and went astray, thus falling into the hands of her captors. In the meantime, the girl was told to take up a pick and to start working, isolated some distance from the others. Zelinskas and a woman-companion seated themselves in the very neighbourhood of the girl, enjoying a hearty breakfast. The girl was working in a strain, and dared not look up. Without any other warning, Zelinskas interrupted his breakfast and, jumping to his feet, dashed upon her. He started to kick and beat her with his truncheon. She tried to fend off his blows: 'Oh! – Oh! – Don't! I do work!' yet all was in vain. Finally, getting tired of hitting her, Zelinskas returned to resume his breakfast. Still masticating, he ordered the digging of a grave.

The girl was told to step down. She refused to. Encouraged by the blows of a stick she made a step, halted, and was thrown into the grave after a short struggle. Another order, to lie face down at the bottom.

A shot …

6th September

Sunday …

Looking straight at me, Hammerling volunteered the remark: 'Your bad luck will be over by the time you have finished your thirty-seventh year of age. You'll cross waters and your name will become very widely know.'

Four and a half years ahead, if we do not take Mintel or Zelinskas or the like into consideration.

7th September

We have seen our owners for the first time. August Dohrmann's brother came on a lorry to pay wages to the overseers. He was accompanied by Werner

Bergmann and Josef Elsässer, manager and foreman respectively. The three of them were in the uniform of the Todt Organisation. Bergmann and Dohrmann wore the distinction of *Sturmführers*, Elsässer that of a *Truppführer*. While they were inspecting the works, the driver, another T.O. man, availed himself furtively of the opportunity to sell some boxes of matches to those close by.

10th September

Twilight.

Some of us were just discussing the purchase of two pails of potatoes, to cover the needs of our four families, when a voice announced from below:
'SS!'

Very soon, indeed, a voice was heard storming:
'Dalli! Dalli! Out with you and your trash!'

Heinz seemed completely changed. We had heard those words before, hadn't we? 'You'll see', he whispered to us radiantly while we were stepping down from the loft, 'they have come to send us back across … Annie, dear, cheer up: we'll celebrate your birthday across the Bug.'

Outside we recognised one of the SS-men – the thick-set man who had taken us from across the river.

Silence fell.

I saw an officer beckon Dolfi, our monitor. Soon Dolfi's voice made itself heard over the area:

'We have to deliver at once upon pain of death: furs, fur-lined coats, fur-hats, leather and soles, wash-basins, cooking-lamps and money.'

About twenty minutes later the collection was stopped. It was getting too dark.

Off they drove.

No potatoes to be bought. Heinz, who yesterday was successful in selling a suit of his against cash, has delivered the money to the SS …

11th September

On our return home, we saw a civilian, a stranger, lolling against the lintel of the stable.

A man from the Ghetto of Uman, we learned later, who having his wife and sister in the camp, had got permission from the GESTAPO to take them back to Uman.

Mintel and Zelinskas had a long talk with him and checked his papers. Then he was told to pass the night in our stable. Why on earth was he not asked to stay in the stable over there, where his wife and sister were?

12th September

In the morning, before the call, on my way to the cook-shack for a cup of hot water, I was stopped near the second stable by the stranger's sister.

'Has anything wrong happened to my brother?' she asked anxiously. Not that I know of, was my reply. 'What should have happened to him?' I added.

I was to learn all about it, as soon as we formed in files. Last night, some of those that were lying next to the entrance were awakened by the loud drunken voices of Mintel and Zelinskas. They were out looking for the stranger. Finding him, they summoned him to follow. A few minutes later, a shot was heard from near-by ...

No trace of the stranger in the morning.

13th September

Sunday ...

The thickset SS-man and other members of the SS turned up again in the morning. This time, we were indoors and they had all of us open our bundles ...

Sheer joy in the stable upstairs in the loft and down below. Kaiser is said to have given his opinion that by the first of October work on both the high-road and gravel-quarry will have come to an end.

Speculations as to our future are running high. The odds are that the groups of peasant-women who also work on the main road (they sometimes pass by our convoy, riding in packed carts, singing) will be disbanded. But what about us? Some voice their grave doubts. These are the ones who, by nature, are unable to believe in any change for the better. Others simply radiate hope. Our release is forthcoming! The Dohrmann Company is sure to send us back! However, the first group shudder when hearing this; they cannot help thinking of the mass misery across the Bug; of the typhus; the grinding poverty; the down-fallen houses in which the sick and the healthy are penned in together; of the cart that used to go round from house to house everyday, to collect the dead; of the call of the cartman, knocking at the doors: 'Have you any dead?' Receiving sometimes the reply: 'Not YET!' – the London of 1665 at the time of the plague transplanted to Eastern Europe

1941/42. Still, compared to Mikhailowka ...

Late in the evening, the fibre-bags taken from a couple this morning, have been returned by the SS. In the end they decided they were not to their liking. Happy owners!

14th September

The call.

Kiesel and Mintel have made their appearance. Although the Lithuanian N.C.O. has counted us, Mintel seems to delay the signal to march off. Suddenly, our looks are taken by the N.C.O., who, pacing up the first close files, motions to a woman to step out. The latter looks aghast ... An impatient gesture with the truncheon, and she totters from the files, to be led by a guard to the end of the stable. Again the N.C.O. paces slowly, focusing his eyes on each of us. I look over the heads of the men towards Anişoara in the women's convoy, meeting her startled eyes. Whose turn will it be next?

One by one, twenty-five or so are summoned to join the group by the end of the stable. The Lithuanian seems to have accomplished his task, for I watch him now go up to Kiesel and Mintel.

The signal to march off has not been given!

A woman from the group by the stable calls her boy out of our files, and removing her worn jacket, gives it to him. No tears. Neither does the boy weep. A short embrace, then she is forced to let him loose – the convoy has started to move.

My legs felt wobbly as I stumbled out of the gate. No one has any eyes for the other. Everybody seems to be hastening their steps, one dreads looking behind. Yet hardly were we outside the gate when I saw Wisotzkas drag a woman from the foremost files. Desperately she tried to defend herself against him, wailing: 'I want to go to work! Do let me go to work!' Unmoved, the guard dragged her along, back to the stables. Her screams were dying down.

'Get going!' yapped the guards, shepherding us with batons and rifle butts, to make up for the lost time.

On our return, I looked absent-mindedly at the big gate that leads to the area of the two stables. An outwashed sign over the gate: 'SCAB' written both in German and Ukrainian. Well, that's that. Have we not been making home with horses, sharing also the cribs for the infants? August Dohrmann Co.

seems to own the horses as well, but we have the odds against us, for it is unlikely that they will kill the horses. Horses are expensive. Jews? 'One shovel is worth more than ten Jews', a T.O. man is said to have decreed in a fury, as he saw a shovel lying about in the middle of the road this morning.

We have been told by the craftsmen commandeered to remain in the camp that they were ordered to fill the mass-grave after the execution. Approaching it (it is in a glade about four hundred yards off the stables) they heard a whispering voice coming from within the grave. However, the voice was also heard by the N.C.O. Silently, he took his gun and discharged it. The grave was filled ...

In the evening, some Lithuanians came into the stable. They were drunk. One of them said they had been given money and valuables by those to be shot, so that the bullet should have immediate effect. Bragging?

15th *September*

An SS Untersturmführer by the name of Friese was on a tour of inspection in the camp during our absence. It is reported he has also looked into the case of the shot stranger from Uman. I am at a loss, I don't understand any more ...

16th *September*

It transpired this morning that, as a consequence of Friese's visit, a list of one hundred and fifty had been drawn up, to be removed to the camp of Naraewka.

On our return to the stables, after having read the list to us, Mintel was implored by Mrs. Kron and her daughter, not to send them away. He made condescending gesture. Happily, the mother bowed and kissed his hand. I am told the Kron-women used to be civil servants. It is strange: hardly half an hour ago, wading along in the dust on our march back from the road, a man kept arguing with the man in the rear file, why they of all people had to work on the road, while others were allowed to lead a life 'of leisure' at the gravel-pit, and now, he too, is to go together with his family to the camp of Naraewka. He may even feel happy ...

17th *September*

We were trying to dry our drenched clothes – we had just come back from the highroad without having started work, since Kuehne found the rainfall too heavy – when a lorry appeared before the gate. The thickset SS-man again! Only male-workers to line up in file. Quick! Anxious looks of mothers, wives, sisters, children …

Thirty craftsmen are to be removed to Gaisin. Amongst them Esoteric Hammerling, who is by the way an architect, and the builder Anschel. Poor Hammerling! He seemed so positive of the fact that by the 18th September he would be back HOME again.

20th September

Sunday …

People close to us were cracking their crawlers. Some of the women had their hair cut off. The usual scene of 'housekeeping'.

Professor Gottlieb was quoting to his audience from Jeremiah.

There!

Some Hooting!

Approaching cars!

SS!

People like rabbits disappeared into the inside of the stable.

The place lay deserted.

Again that voice 'Dalli! Dalli!' The voice – as I have learned since – of SS Oberscharführer Maass. Incidentally, his brother-in-law, the T.O. man Hennes, is overseer in a camp near-by, where he has been staying with his wife. Their son, Ernst Josef, is one of the lorry-drivers for Dohrmann.

We were ordered to draw up in a circle in front of the stables and to empty our sacks. SS officers came up to each heap, taking every thing that attracted them: Ladies' shoes, male shoes, towels, soap, knives, forks and so on. An officer, observing Mizzi's contemptuous look as he slipped her half-full bottle of Eau-de-Cologne into his pockets, made a gesture as if he was about to hit her, but on second thoughts passed on. Meanwhile another officer, attended by Kiesel, collected wedding-rings and jewellery. We had to throw them into a leather-bag, as if *we* were the liberal donors. After that we were told to hand over any personal documents some of us might still possess.

Landmann is almost out of his wits; the jewellery he hid in the search under his shake-down has vanished. He strongly suspects his former neighbour, who was sent to the camp of Naraewka on Thursday.

Hammerling and Anschel have arrived from Gaisin, to fetch their wives and things. They are rather reticent as to life there.

21st September

Zelinskas has made his appearance on the main road. It is most unusual for him to do so. As a rule, it is only Kiesel and Mintel that come on inspection. Mintel will ride past on his bicycle, while Kiesel will sit in a cart, as though he was in a Sedan-Chair, pretending not to see us; a Lithuanian will come up to his cart and give him the report.

Soon after Zelinskas, Kiesel also came. They shook hands and had a long talk. Wisotzkas joined them after a while.

After Kiesel left the working-plot, Zelinskas started riding on his bicycle up and down among our groups. Wisotzkas, too, paced up and down. Up and down! It was unbearable to feel his eyes on us.

While we kept working under the strain, Leova, our interpreter with the Lithuanians and guards, came up to one of us, his face livid and distorted.

'For heaven's sake', he whispered, 'don't look about you, and mind your work. All of you. A grave's been dug in the maize-field.'

A grave?

Anişoara and I looked at each other ...

Wisotzkas had stopped pacing up and down. Watching him out of the corner of my eyes, I saw him asking the two elderly ex-nurses to follow him. Sally, the daughter of one of the nurses, looked frightened; the women, however, dropped their shovels almost mechanically, and kissing Sally good-bye, went slowly after Wisotzkas, to disappear into the field across ...

Two shots.

A shriek!

Sally fainted, but immediately was struck by a hard blow, dealt by the abusive Sukerka.

On the way home, people discussed the event in a whisper. Some asserted they had been expecting it, as Zelinskas had taken a dislike to the two women, and would often sneer at the snowboots Sally's aunt was wearing. I still cannot understand why people should have expected it, but there are so many things I do not understand ...

In the camp, Sally has been left to herself. We have not condoled with her, nor are we able to. It is of no use; cattle selected to be slain, do not condole with one another, or do they? It's all nightmarish. Players in a gruesome highly imaginative comedy of errors, or should it be a comedy of horrors – but who can say what part one really has in the cast? It just depends on the inventive and ingenious mind of the director.

22nd September

A desperate shriek of a child: 'Mummy!' followed by screams of other people from below awakened us all of a sudden. Somebody felt his way to the stairs to get to the bottom of the hubbub. The screams were dying away ...

Nothing serious. Nine-year-old Hannerl had had a nightmare. She had dreamt Mintel was telling her to lay down in the grave together with her brother Poldi, as they were going to be shot dead. She shrieked and awoke. On hearing her shriek, some people unaware of the cause had just given free rein to their stretched nerves, so that it all degenerated into a general tumult.

23rd September

Quite by chance I have learned that a young man has for some time been suffering from camp-fever. God know what that may mean, I never heard of this complaint before. It seems as if a horse-crib has been removed for him into the den inhabited by Segall and his family. Apparently Zelinskas has called on the patient and, more-over, has had some food sent round ...

25th September

Ernst Joseph Hennes, the driver, remarked casually this morning to one of us:

'You're like cattle purchased by the butcher. One of you will be slain today, the others tomorrow. The turn will come to all of you.'

That remark passed off for sympathy. Was it?

26th September

Reaching the plot on the main road, we saw a party of Soviet PoWs, guarded by civilians with Swastika armlets, work a telephone-line along the field. One of us recognised in a guard an old friend of his, and called out: 'Lennert!' The latter, surprised, looked in our direction, and then came round to shake hands. I saw him draw out some cigarettes, holding them out. The name conjured before my eyes another Lennert. Its bearer was a young man who had done military service with me more than a decade ago. One day, learning that I had lived some time in Germany, he wanted to know whether the peasants in Germany speak Romanian (as they naturally do in Romania). My negative reply seemed to disconcert him. God knows what might have lingered on in his mind then.

28th September

Wisotzkas arrived late on the plot. He alighted from a cart and then looked down at a piece of paper in his hand. Then he went up to a woman, the former civil-clerk. Curtly, he summoned her to mount the cart.

'No, no!' she cried out. 'For goodness sake, let me live! I do work well! I am sure you won't find fault with my work!'

Alas, try as she did, he remained unmoved.

'Come on!' He swore at her.

Mother and daughter started to cry, trying their best to persuade Wisotzkas. Impatiently, Serskus joined his fellow-Lithuanian, and giving the woman a violent push in the direction of the cart, encouraged her daughter with the rifle-butt, to resume work.

Sitting on the cart, the woman kept crying, stretching out her arms:

'My child, do help me!'

The cart was moving slowly, and stopped in front of another group. Here an elderly woman was also summoned to join. Lest his grandmother be beaten, her grandson lifted her by himself, placing her gently upon the cart.

The cart set off under looks of stone, and it soon disappeared into the field.

... Two shots.

29th September

On the highroad, Sukerka gave me two apples for a pencil sketch I did of him.

People say that Wisotzkas has committed an error in mistaking the former civil-servant for another woman, to be shot. How do they know such things, on what 'authority' do they base their deductions, I wonder?

In the evening, the Lithuanians gave an accordion to one of us, to play in their guard-house. His wife was restless and couldn't find any sleep. Her husband had promised to bring her some food from the Lithuanians.

30th September

The Lithuanian newcomer, Romko, was pacing to and fro, and looking fixedly at each of us, concentrated most of his attention upon our neighbour. Finally, he stopped before him, and told him to follow. The wife gasped and was on the verge of swooning away, yet she quickly regained her composure and watched them both disappear into the field.

Silence ...

Time passed slowly, then two were seen coming, our neighbour taking up his work.

Romko had set his heart on the neighbour's boots, and tried them on in the field. They did not fit.

At the gravel-quarry, Landmann has been warned by Fedya to hand him over his suit, unless he prefers to be shot dead. Segall is said to have persuaded Landmann to comply with the guard's wish.

2nd October

This morning Heinz was complaining that somebody had stolen his scarf and both his and Annie's bread-ration. People suspect a former industrialist ... Annie has fallen ill a few days ago. They say it is typhus or typhoid-fever. Cases have grown in number.

Mintel had a long discussion with Segall. He has asked for a large sum of hush-money, to leave the sick alone for the moment. He has not been told that most of the cases are typhoid. As for the sick, they have been left in the care our two doctors. To what avail? There are no proper medical supplies.

3rd October

Heinz's scarf has been found, but not the bread.

4th October

Mia has died. The first case of 'natural' death. So Rosa saw right in the cards! But what about the forthcoming deliverance?

The T.O. man Kustin, the commandant of the Ukranian peasant-women camp, has come on a roving visit. Segall introduced me to him as an artist who has studied in Munich. Kustin shook hands with me saying:

'Never say die! Let's hope for the best!'

It is the first time I have heard a T.O. man talk like that.

5th October

After Kiesel was given the report, Lilly had a nervous breakdown. He had been staring at her, she said sobbing, before he went off in his cart. As she is looking at her worst – she is but twenty-two – he was sure to have given an order to have her executed. We could not soothe her.

Shortly after the break, another elderly woman, who had been working with her husband and three daughters, was summoned by Serskus to mount the *hearse*. So was a second woman.

Were the two shots heard properly?

It all seems so natural that on the surface it affects the workers no longer.

Whose turn will it be next?

6th October

A man has committed suicide by swallowing tablets. He preferred suicide to an unavoidable end – to be shot dead any time.

It has only been an attempt of suicide, I learn, and our two physicians have been taking charge of him.

7th October

The man has started bleeding. On Mintel's order he was shot dead by a guard. Poor doctor! He had tried his very best to avoid such a form of death, but the producer of the play has once again proved to have an eye for macabre acting. Why not kill a self-murderer for a change?

I learn that yesterday, a neighbour of the shot man, saw him eat bread and butter and apples! His last meal …

9th October

I was just returning with Anişoara from the cook-shack when some head-lights flashed the area. In no time a lorry stopped near us.

'Hi Jidane!'

The call gave me, or rather both of us, a shock of surprise: we had been addressed in Romanian, here of all places! And it was a Romanian, I saw now, who had stuck out his neck. My brain reeled.

Impatiently, the man repeated:

'Hi, Jidane!'

Well, he wanted to know the whereabouts of some family. On orders of the Romanian Provincial Government and by special Gestapo permission he had been looking for the family in different camps on this side of the River Bug. I called for Segall ...

The case is the great event of the day, and is being discussed accordingly. Perhaps ... ?

10th October

I watched Mintel and Segall deep in conversation at the back of the stable.

11th October

Mintel has again asked for hush-money, to leave the sick alone. The ransom amounts to fifty marks per head. He is not aware that typhus or typhoid fever are raging in the camp, otherwise ...

12th October

I have been working today in the guardhouse at a sign-board: 'It is strictly forbidden to enter the camp for Jews without permission.'

Taking advantage of the Lithuanians who were entertaining a fellow-countryman, a Chaplain, in the adjoining room, I did a rapid brush in grey water-colour of the stables across the way [Plate 7]. My first. Let's hope, I shall be able to do some more. Vera, the cook for the Lithuanians, a Ukrainian peasant-woman, gives me some hot soup for Anişoara, who has remained in the stable with some pains.

From the returning convoy I learn that Misha, an Ukrainian Jew, was executed by Wisotzkas right on the plot. Misha, a strong young man, was said to have been ordered by Wisotzkas to follow, but he succeeded in snatching the gun away from the latter, and to fire at once. The Lithuanian was slightly wounded. Meanwhile another guard took aim at Misha who fell on to the ground relaxing the grasp that was holding the gun. Wisotzkas seized the gun eagerly and pulled the trigger ...

Mintel has left today for Berlin and will be back again by the end of the month, when I have to make his portrait. Segall has proposed to Kiesel that he should sit for me for a portrait. What black looks Kiesel had for it. No!

13th October

Another Romanian constable has been outside the stables, I learn. He has expressed the opinion that we are going to be sent back across the river. Asking for some shirts, he was gladly presented with them as a reward for his being a harbinger.

16th October

It is getting very cold ...

Not a ghost of a chance of being sent back, say the pessimists amongst us. A suggestion is made by Heinz, who is himself a road-engineer, to find some means for Segall to enable him to go to Gaisin and have a talk there with Bergmann and Elsässer. They are likely to listen to a sound officer and – who knows? – send us back as soon as the campaign is over.

17th October

Evening ...

Following a call from Segall, we have all come to the loft.

Were it not for the shouts of the guards outside, one would have taken these scenes as being very romantic: dim shapes cautiously moving up to the spot, lit by two tiny bottles of Eau-de-Cologne (cotton-wool-wick and some kerosene).

Segall was giving an account of his interview in the morning at the HQ of the T.O. in Gaisin. First, he had succeeded in persuading the N.C.O., who was on his way to Gaisin, to take him there. At the Dohrmann Co., he had obtained an interview with the big two. His point-blank offer of jewellery and dollars for their contacting surveyor Stracke of the 'ABSCHNITTSBAU-LEITUNG II', was accepted. It would be a matter of days to settle it.

'I'm convinced', Segall concluded, 'that all's going to turn out well!'

The assembly dispersed in high spirits.

'What an extraordinary thing', a man was saying musingly as he limped to the stair-case, 'that we should pay for our being sent back across the river. Here we die of a bullet we pay for, there, of misery, likewise paid for.'

18th October

Sunday ...

A girl [Selma Meerbaum-Eisinger] promised to lend me 'Das Heim und die Welt', the only book she has brought with her. Now it is with somebody else. Rabindranath Tagore's book has come into a strange environment, but even here it may bring about some peace of mind.

21st October

Disquieting news. The T.O. man Kustin is reported to have said we are going to be kept here during the winter; our work will consist of clearing the snow off the highroad.

Leova has suggested I had better go on Monday to the gravel-quarry instead of to the main road; in fact, he will see to it that I get on the list, for Wisotzkas seemed to have looked at me very long, just as the convoy had arrived back at the stables. Is it on account of the fact that I have not shaved today? At any rate, he was very displeased that I had pulled the shawl over my hat. And, of course, I look my worst. Well ...

23rd October

No work at the gravel-quarry. Work has been stopped. All of us are to work on the road. A ditch, to serve as snow-collector, is going to be dug along the road.

Sukerka encouraged me with some heavy blows over my back and held out the prospect of some more beating if I should remain, as I was, behind the target of the day. Two women and a man helped me to achieve it.

Wisotzkas was not in sight.

24th October

A heavy downpour.

By order of Kiesel, we have stayed behind in the stables.

After the call, Zelinskas ordered all males to go the gravel-quarry for spades and picks. No man, no craftsman to remain behind; no one to be commandeered to any other work. All have to go. From the quarry we should be taken *somewhere*. His vile smile and mysterious hints brought forth a feeling of apprehension.

On the way to the quarry I kept thinking of Anişoara and the others ...

Escorted from the quarry to the village-centre, we were told to stop at the school-building, now deserted, for the peasant-women had been sent home. The T.O. men, residents of the village, were approaching.

After some minutes, Zelinskas made his appearance, too. We were still standing in front of the school when we saw the women-files come along under escort. They disappeared into a small, detached house, next to the church. At the same moment we, too, were signalled to leave our picks and spades behind and to enter the school-building. Indoors, we were ordered to lie down in the three rooms – one next to another, so as to leave no space at all ...

After we had been lying for a while, they told us to stand up, and leave the building.

They had simply wanted to ascertain whether the school-building could accommodate all of us, as new quarters.

Now our task was to dig holes for the barbed wire fence.

Meanwhile the women were sent back to the stables.

Anişoara told me afterwards that in her file one woman, frightened of what might happen, had been consuming almost the whole of the loaf of bread she was able to barter yesterday for a dress ... At least, she knew how to still her hunger ...

25th October

This morning Pita Mihailowski wanted me to paint his portrait in water-colours, and allowed me to exchange the pick for the brush [Plate 8]. Of course, not when the commandant or the Lithuanians were in sight. After a long while my fingers got numb with the cold, and I had to interrupt. Mihailowski gave Anişoara a few picked apples.

27th October

It has transpired that the Company – I really do not know whether it is the Dohrmann Company, the police or the SS – are still not decided whether to quarter us in the school, for there is not sufficient room for all of us. The T.O. man Kustin is to continue to use two rooms and the kitchen as his residential quarter, and they are part of the school-building.

A violent wind kept blowing on the road and made work very strenuous. Kiesel, seeing an ex-woman teacher at some distance from our group, asked her to get nearer; nothing would happen, he shouted if people saw her do her needs.

28th October

Some fifty men and women have arrived from across the river.

29th October

The newcomers have been fired at with questions about the frontlines and all that. They do not know much either, only that the Germans have taken Stalingrad.

In the evening, I was involuntary witness of some, to my mind, interesting conversation in the dark:

'And what, if they have taken Stalingrad?' a weary woman's voice asked. 'To tell you the truth, I'm fed up. It's no purpose, to cherish any hope. Suppose, the Soviets do hold the line and drive them back. So what of it? Do you really think they'll be in time to liberate us of all people? I very much doubt it.'

'You're wrong here, madame', a male voice interrupted eagerly. 'Quite wrong. It's not our lives that count, it's the deliverance of mankind. But, if we were delivered, suppose we survived, wouldn't I have the joy of my life, taking vengeance on Mintel, Kiesel, Zelinskas, and on those of the Dohrmann Company? I certainly would.'

'Here you are, Poldi', Dr. Seidner said derisively. 'Alright, you lifted up your own grandmother and placed her on the cart! That was really decent of you! But why didn't you kill the Lithuanian? And now I notice you have left Wisotzkas's name out, he who murdered your grandmother. This lapse might mean a lot to psychologists, you know? Well, don't interrupt me, please. Look at me. Wasn't I thankful the other day when Serskus, the murderer of my father, held out a cigarette to me? What is dignity, young man? You're talking of vengeance. Nonsense! I don't see any of us taking revenge; besides, I don't believe in it. Perhaps in justice. But, what is the use of talking? Mind you, we're in for it.'

1st November

Sunday ...

Anişoara and I have become rich, having succeeded in bartering my last shirt. A guard has provided me with some food – beans and tomatoes – but at the same time cheated me of the rest of the food bargained. Never mind. For hours both of us kept blowing into the fire, our eyes getting red, but the fire went out constantly, and the beans would not soften. Finally, we appealed to a neighbour, who had a splendid fire.

As usual conversation slipped from food on to the situation in general. Mrs. Vogelhut said, heaving a sigh: 'I'm afraid it will be difficult for those at home to believe all we shall tell them. It is almost beyond belief to ourselves.

But it will be the more striking because of its truth. It's simply beyond endurance what we have been through. It can't be worse; I think it's the limit.' She started to cry.

2nd November

We were digging at the extreme end of the ditch. Mihailowski had placed us here, so that I could give his portrait the last brush, without being noticed by either Kiesel, the guards or the Lithuanians. So I worked alternately with pick and brush, for the target had to be achieved, too, and Anişoara could not do the work herself.

After the break we were startled by two shots!

I had been so much absorbed by the portrait that I nearly forgot where we were, or our status as free game.

After some frightful minutes, word came that Fredi has been shot. But no! At that very moment we saw him, together with other youngsters coming down from the opposite direction! ... Lilli's face was a blank; her brother, Gerry, was working down there ...

After knocking off work, and already in the files, neatly arranged to be counted, we came to know who it was: the seventeen year-old son of Mrs. Vogelhut – LOTHAR!

He and his mother had been somewhere, about ten yards off the ditch, close to a heap of beetroots. Wisotzkas is reported to have aimed at the boy, hitting his kidneys.

'Mummy, I've got pains!' those digging the earth heard Lothar cry out as soon as the shots had been fired. They even saw him fall down. After a short time he was dead. Mrs. Vogelhut started screaming and threw herself over the bleeding body. Wisotzkas and another Lithuanian, a newcomer, were swearing at her to resume work. Beaten on her head she got hurled to the ditch.

A grave was then ordered to be dug, and Lothar was laid in naked. Wisotzkas took possession of his clothes.

In the evening, Zelinskas came round to express his sympathy to Lothar's mother, offering her a loaf of white bread ...

Anişoara, witnessing the scene, turned to me with a bitter smile: 'Poor woman', she whispered. 'Flaubert depicts in SALAMBO how Hamilcar Barca is forced to sacrifice his son Hannibal, but in the end he substitutes the son of a slave for him. After the slave's son is taken out the room, Hamilcar orders a hearty meal for the slave. And the slave swallows the dishes greedily while tears keep dropping down his cheeks.'

Wisotzkas told Zelinskas that he killed Lothar while catching him stealing beetroots.

3rd November

People know, however, that Lothar has been killed for quite a different reason. Some time ago, Wisotzkas asked a man to hand him over his winter clothes; the latter assumingly refused to. Lothar's death should therefore be a warning to all those who might be tempted to do the same. Locker tells me that he, too, expected to be a victim. Why he? Is he taking pride in it, to be a would-be victim? And why was Lothar killed and not that man who refused to hand over his suit? Was that man immune? My mind simply refuses to understand what is going on around me, besides the wanton shooting of my camp-mates.

6th November

Mintel has come back from Berlin. He looks his worst. How lucky of him now to have Wisotzkas or Serskus sitting on his back; they or others could well take his hollow cheeks as a very sound reason to have him 'purged'.

8th November

Sunday ...

When the day was breaking we found our improvised beds snow-topped. Shaking with cold, we took refuge in the mouldy warmth below ...

After the call, which took place inside the stable, each of us was struggling hard to get a tiny space for a shake-down. The loft has become wholly uninhabitable.

Anişoara and myself are 'organising' our own bunks next to the feet of another family; thus, the big toe of the man can't help touching Anişoara's cheek, while I myself can't change places since my wife would get the worst out of it. In our neighbourhood, an elderly woman, laid up in a horse-crib, is being at her last gasp.

In the dead of night someone was crouching over us smelling heavily of brandy. We shuddered. It was Zelinskas. He came to offer Trude some drink so that she might get warm. Still full of sleep, she refused at first. Zelinskas was drinking by great gulps, as I could not help hearing it.

9th November

Anişoara has manufactured herself a pair of snowboots from ropes of onions. The people in the village-hall have protested against the horses being kept outside in the snowstorms; they are claiming the whole stable for them.

10th November

Mintel orders our removal into the school-building, actually only part of us; the others have to stay on in the stables till some more accommodation can be found.

When our group reached the school – on the way there Anişoara's snow-boots have become ropes of onions again – we were met by an infernal noise. Everyone was claiming the right to sit, or to lie down precisely where someone else had already set his eyes before. There were shoutings, people swearing and pushing one another, with squalling children as a background. No light. All moving in darkness. Nothing but utter confusion.

11th November

Three school-rooms, a bigger and two smaller ones have been turned into a hen-roost. Two 'floors' – posts and mobile crab-sticks between them meant to serve as bed and ceiling. Each cage, with no partition-wall between, sixty-three inches wide and two feet and five inches high, will house four people ...

... A hundred of those left behind in the stables have been sent to another camp.

Towards evening, Zelinskas dropped in. He was anxious to see whether another one hundred and thirty-seven could find accommodation in the rooms. After an all-round inspection, he reached the conclusion that about forty could still be penned, that is, doing one's utmost.

12th November

Mintel has given orders that all those looking wretched shall be *shot dead*.

One hundred and seven people!

The T.O. man Kustin is said to maintain his two rooms and the kitchen in the school-building ...

15th November

We have still been working at the ditch. The ground is frozen, but we have to dig it. The Lithuanians have a fire for themselves.

A man staggered; he was feeling sick. Wisotzkas, keeping a close eye on him, ordered some of a close-by group to dig a grave at the mouth of the ditch ... He then went up to the man, summoning him to follow ...

Afterwards, a young man was told to pull out the gold-crowns from the man's mouth, as he was lying in the grave.

Back in the camp, the man's family, mother and son, seriously ill were only told that he had died of heart-failure.

17th November

In the evening, Zelinskas came round to bid us farewell. He and the other Lithuanians will be off to their regiments tomorrow. He shook hands with some of the inmates.

20th November

It could not be said that, from a sanitary point of view, life in the stables was exactly ideal, but here in the school-building it is Hell.

Three hundred and thirty people in the rooms. Two mobile ladders serve for moving up and down. The unvarying call during the day 'The ladder, please' stops after the Eau-de-Cologne bottle lamp has been extinguished. Then one has to climb down from cage to cage in complete darkness.

The sick have indiscriminately been lying down next to their still healthy neighbours.

Just after a corpse was taken out into the corridor, a woman profiting by the fact that she was staying on the second floor was doing her needs, to the accompaniment of a pell-mell of voices and shoutings.

'Shut the windows! Our sick have got fever!'

'Open the windows! We're getting suffocated!'

And now a woman speaks: 'It's a mass-grave we're penned up in. Nobody will escape!'

One hundred and twenty human beings in a classroom of about eleven square-feet.

23rd November

Kiesel and Mintel have been transferred ... Kustin is to take charge of the camp.

24th November

It has been getting stormy.

On our way to the road, we were overtaken by Kaiser, who had come by sledge after us. He gave us orders to turn round. Work at the ditch had been interrupted. What a joy!

30th November

At the morning-call we saw a sergeant-major of the Police. Looking sharply at me, he asked me whether I had not been at DACHAU. I replied in the negative.

He's to take charge of the camp. Kustin will be the second-in-command keeping his old rooms.

1st December

I have started on a portrait in water-colours of Kustin. The name of the first commandant, as I got to learn at the sitting, is Willi Buder.

5th December

Our number in the rooms is growing less and less, most having died of typhoid fever, others of inanition.

Taking a tape-measure from the tailor, I now have the size of the water-colour I have made of the stables. It is eighteen by eight centimetres, done in a greyish colour [Plate 7]. Let's hope I shall be able to make another one of the interior of the school, although I don't see how I can manage in these surroundings. The portrait of Pita Mihailowski, in brighter colours, is twenty by fourteen and a half centimetres [Plate 8]. I have kept it, renouncing the bread. Pita wanted me to darken his hair, I said I couldn't, and so he left it with me. A loaf of bread would have meant something to us, though. So far I have the following: 'Work at the gravel-quarry', twenty by sixteen centimetres, in one colour, and 'Work on the highroad', likewise in one colour, it is seventeen by eight centimetres [Plate 9].

8th December

It has transpired that Buder wants to get rid of the mothers and their babies, as well of the families with children under fourteen. Nine year-old Hannerl wearing a long skirt; her parents hope she will look much older, as if the lists set up by the police would not speak for themselves.

9th December

In the evening, a woman is having labour-pains. Cowering in her cage on the ground, her thirteen-month-old daughter is playing by her side, while her husband looks helplessly at his wife. In the other cages, life is going on as usual. Quarrelling about several inches of room in the cage; Rosa is telling Mizzi what kind of cake she used to prepare at home; fifteen year-old Hardy can be heard from below whistling a few broken themes from a Brahms Sonata. In the welter of happenings, the event of the woman bringing forth the baby has passed unnoticed. As our doctor is coming in at the door, everything is all right. We have *increased* in number ...

I can't help thinking of an analogous case which happened two thousand years ago. Then it was a publican's wretched deed, now it is a plurality's affair.

10th December

Stefan Bregula, a private in the Wehrmacht, has come to the camp, to ask Buder for a batch of people to do some work for him. He has taken up residence in the village and could do with a cook and men to perform the menial work.

Arriving back at his rooms, Bregula was followed by a party: Frieda, as cook, two lawyers and an elderly man as wood-cutters, and myself as a sign-painter. One of the signs is to bear the inscription: *W.C. for Germans only.* Bregula belongs to a transmission unit.

12th December

Aisic, Frieda's fiancé, has been shot dead by T.O. man Karl Ulrich after having been subjected to tortures. Why tortures, I wonder?

13th December

It is curious that at the bottom of Aisic's execution for once there should seem to have been a very unusual motive: a complaint from the inmates. They had made a complaint to Kaiser and Ulrich of his alleged inhuman behaviour towards them, asking for his transfer. But it is a strange transfer anyway.

14th December

Whilst working at Bregula's I had a glimpse of the transferred people passing in sledges. Should we ever see one another again?

16th December

Towards evening Selma Eisinger passed away.

17th December

Professor Gottlieb and Selma have been buried together. When alive, both were at loggerheads ...

I once wanted to paint Prof. Gottlieb's portrait, but the others were against his sitting for me in the room; his coat swarmed with crawlers. As if one single person among us was without them. Anişoara is wont to pray: 'Lord, make our lice healthy ones!'

18th December

Selma's mother has told me that her daughter was on the verge of making a getaway with a guard's help before she was taken ill. She has it from a farewell-letter addressed to her, found in Selma's coat. To my surprise I also learn that Selma used to write poetry that was highly thought of.

Christmas-presents to be prepared for Buder, Kaiser and Kustin: a pair of gloves, a muffler, a pullover, a silver-comb and a hand-mirror. Of course, they will have to be cleaned first.

Christmas Eve

Kustin and his fellow-countrymen are celebrating. A hunchbacked spinster from our room has been invited to oblige them with carol-singing.

30th December

I have made a pencil-drawing, fifteen by fifteen centimetres, having Selma being taken down on two ladders, a subject-matter which I witnessed about a fortnight ago [Plate 3]. It reminds me strongly of 'Deposition of the Cross.' Here we are, then, when NATIVITY and PIETA are presented again to our eyes. But do we really see? I have also made a water-colour on note-paper, seventeen by fourteen: it shows the guard standing by the gate to the camp [Plate 10]. All in all, till now, I have six works, including the guard, Fedya's portrait, which he refused to acknowledge as his own. Its size is twenty by fourteen and a half centimetres.

31st December

Buder has given me red chalk to write A HAPPY NEW YEAR on a live pig, owned by Kustin. I wonder whether it is a custom to do so.

At midnight, Mizzi, Anişoara and myself were awakened by whispering voices coming from our neighbours.

Rosa was reading the fortune in the cards of Pepi and Paula by candle-light. 'Joyful things: They would reach their homes again: uniformed men would come and open the gates!'

1st January 1943

I learn that while last night three of us were fast asleep, Buder is said to have entered the room. After having wished all the inmates A HAPPY NEW YEAR, he added he'd feel glad to know that by the end of the year all of us would have reached home safely.

I have painted some tulips for Anişoara [Plate 4]. Bregula gave me a sheet of foolscap-paper. Sitting next to me in the cage, Anişoara was murmuring a song: 'L'étang', the old French tune. Tears stood in her eyes. Some reminiscence of the time when she did secretarial work for the actress Alice Cocéa in Paris, she explained to me afterwards.

2nd January

A guard who had spent his Christmas as Krasnapolka told some of us that the camps at Krasnapolka, Kublicz and Nemirow had suffered a severe 'pruning' during the holidays.

I have started on a water-colour depicting the room. It is 'genre'-like and the personages are meant to be portraits. The size is twenty by nineteen centimetres. Anişoara is to be seen in the upper cage [Plate 5].

3rd January

At Kublicz, some of the inmates that were shot were Romanian Gypsies.

4th January

I have started on portrait of Buder's at his village-room. He's from Erfurt, he told me. Before joining the police with which he has been for ten years, he was in the bookbinding trade.

He confirms that there has been a 'purge' in other camps. After some time

I remarked casually: I wondered whether Anişoara and I would ever be back in Bucharest again.

'Bucharest? I think not!'

Then musingly: 'I'd rather be elsewhere and not here as commandant when the general purge takes place.'

Well, it's point-blank!

In the evening, an ex-high post-official and his two sons were entertaining us by imitating a village orchestra on the fair-grounds, and the speech of a bell-man. Great fun, with the discussion of this morning with Buder still in my mind!

5th January

Acting on the permission of Buder and Kustin, to get in touch with the villagers and to barter clothing of the inmates for food, Heinz and Naiman have returned with potatoes and other victuals.

In the evening, having at first given the share to the owners of the clothes, the remaining food supplies were distributed amongst the needy and the sick. In addition to potatoes, I have been given a quarter of a cup of honey! After the distribution, Dr. Rudich climbed the ladder to our cage. As from tomorrow morning we'll have potato-soup before being marched off to the highroad. Fifty Pfennings daily is the cost of the soup. By collecting this money one will get the means for the purchase of the potatoes. The needy are going to be given the soup without pay. Anişoara and I insisted Dr. Rudich should not be ashamed to get the soup for nothing.

6th January

Dr. Kiermayer has been accused of having stolen the bread which belongs to his neighbour. Having seen the bread lying about, he explained to Segall, he could not resist breaking off a little bit, greedily. Little by little, he was breaking off larger bits, and then three quarters of the bread, the week's ration, were eaten up. His female-neighbour flushed and looked very embarrassed as she heard the indictment and the explanation given. She is on very good terms with the doctor and his wife.

8th January

I have made a pencil drawing: 'Prayer in the evening' [Plate 11]. Its size is twenty-two by sixteen. Looking down from our cage into the dimly lit room, it's rather a weird scene. Yesterday I made a grey-brush of people queuing to get the soup [Plate 12]. It is eighteen by sixteen.

14th January

The epidemic is subsiding: the toll of death is decreasing.

18th January

Shovelling on the road has become very strenuous. Anişoara was mercilessly beaten by Ivan, the guard, because she dared to nibble some stale bread while she was shovelling.

21st January

As the highroad was clean, the groups were ordered to clear the snow from the fields. Kustin was roaring with laughter watching the groups working in the field from his sledge; he's mocking at Dohrmann Co.

22nd January

Even the neighbouring village had to be cleared, so that twenty miles had to be made on foot, in the icy steppe-wind [Plate 13]. Kuehne, Ulrich and Schneider – I learn that Kaiser has gone on leave to Germany, where he took many presents for his wife and daughter, taken from and presented by us – were of good cheer as they were making themselves comfortable in the village-houses, leaving the groups in charge of some guards.

23rd January

Peasants distributed some potatoes, bread and onions among the groups that were cleaning the snow in the village of Adamowka. The guards allowed it for some time, but in the end many of the people got beaten.

In the evening, I 'called' on Ludo at his cage. He'd been laid up with a complicated typhoid. After having shown him the water-colours and drawings – I have enlarged the portfolio by a portrait of Naiman with the school building as background, a water-colour fifteen by fourteen centimetres, and by a pencil-drawing twenty six by nineteen, 'On the Way to the Road' – he said to me in a feeble piping voice:

'I know some villager whom we could entrust with your album. As soon as I recover I will talk to him. Our chances of getting liberated are next to nothing, they will not even find our grave. A thousand pities that the world should not have a glimpse of our tortures through your work.' All of a sudden his voice went down to an eager whisper: 'Do you see the lorry outside? They've come for my brother. They're going to take him away.' He started crying. Ludo's brother was deported to Siberia in 1940, as far as I could learn from Lilly, Ludo's wife.

At night, we were awakened by loud and insistent voices. I understood from the arguments that while he was asleep, a man suddenly felt some warm liquid flowing down his cheeks. Urine! After some minutes of embarrassment, the young woman from above apologised. It was true. The mishap took place as she was dreaming she had come home again and, full of joy, opened the taps in the bathroom. Harmony was restored in the room.

24th January

The guard and overseer Yasha asked me to paint his portrait. Not content with a simple sketch, he wanted a highly-conceived portrait. As a rule the room was overcrowded, people moving about, while I myself pushed and jostled was trying hard to keep my balance on the stump. Finally, exhausted, I begged him to postpone the sitting. 'Go on!' he said curtly.

2nd February

Elsässer has come to tell Segall that their quartermasters have almost run clean out of peas for the camp, while the bread-ration is likewise to be cut down.

Standing in the courtyard, I had to make a portrait of Ivan. He was pleased at first, but in the end did not particularly like it, so I have kept it [Plate 2]. I have made another pencil-drawing of the interior; it is twenty-one by fifteen. Thirteen works till now. People have been making fun of me. What's the use of depicting 'life' in the camp they keep asking. Can I promise them liberation instead? they sneer. Others will exclaim sentimentally 'If only the Americans would once see them, they would learn how much we have suffered!' I am nonplussed by both attitudes.

3rd February

Working at his portrait, I am told by my sitter, Buder, that he has received a letter from his wife. She asked him to get some dress material from us.

Having got in touch with Segall he has been given it, and showing me the fabric, he asked:

'D'you like it?'

'Yes, of course, I do.'

It was some fine silk fabric, no doubt. Whose had it been? Was it the man's who wears his expensive fur-hat with his ample fur-lining outwards, so as to stifle any wish?

After a pause, our conversation fell upon Architect Superintendent Schweser of some Headquarters, who had been to the camp this morning for about half an hour. He was accompanied by Dr. Shaiovici, the spokesman for those in the camp in Teplik. Schweeser introduced Shaiovici, and here Buder flew into a passion:

'Imagine, Shaiovici dared to meet me with his hand outstretched. I ignored it, and was on the point of smacking his face.'

Sledge-bells prevented me from making a comment, but would I have made any to him? Certainly not.

Buder rose quickly to his feet.

'If it is someone from the SS, you must hide at once in the kitchen. Two of the SS died of typhus last week, so we have been strictly forbidden to come in close touch with you. Besides, should you be found here, you will be shot dead at once.'

The sledges went past the house.

6th February

Pepi has it from Kustin that the Wehrmacht has sustained a defeat, I am told. If the news is true, I think it comes from Schneider, who is against the regime.

8th February

One of us has been assigned to fetch bread from Teplik. It is bitterly cold, and not one of the Todt Organisation felt inclined to go for their bread and provisions.

Livia, Segall's second daughter, has been looking fondly after the sledges. Of late, an affection has sprung up between her and the young man, Edy Weiss.

10th February

Disquieting news brought back from Teplik.

A T.O. man there is said to have given it as his opinion that by springtime another ten thousand Jews will be brought over from across the river, so that work on the highroad may be continued. Among us there will be a purge, to get rid of the weaklings.

Edy scoffed at all this alarming news. Springtime? Rubbish. Hasn't the Wehrmacht been reported to be in retreat? Haven't we seen loaded lorries moving over westwards? That man was only boasting surely. I still have to think of what Buder told me more than a month ago. The 'general purge' taking place some day ...

11th February

Our black-smiths that work in the village-smithy for men of the T.O. have come back with a piece of sensational news: the villagers know that the Soviets are nearing Kiev.

12th February

Many cars bearing the index-mark 'Police' have gone past the camp, westwards ...

13th February

Buder is said to be leaving for Nemirow, where a bridge is going to be built over the river Bug. It has leaked out that all the commandants belonging to the Police will be removed.

14th February

Buder has left us.

Paula is dispirited. Only today I have learned that there were strong sentimental ties between her and Buder.

Villagers have told some of the water-carriers that the Soviet ground-forces have reached the region of Dniepropetrowsk. By the end of the month things will be all right, they assured our men.

15th February

Having come back from the village-well together with his fellow-watercarriers,

Max called some of us aside and showed us a tiny note a villager had slipped in his hand. 'It's your deliverance!' the villager had whispered. All were showing impatience to see what it was about. Max started spelling it out closely. The more he was gazing at it the more disappointed he looked. The note ran: 'You must believe and have trust in our Lord. Copy it out nine times, and pass it on.'

17th February

Schulte, commandant of the camp at Krasnapolka, is said to have given orders before he left that the spokesman for the camp be executed.

Kustin has given orders that his pig should be slaughtered.

Are they ready for the last hop?

In the evening, everybody was speaking *sotto voce*. What is going to happen to us? Here we are trapped behind barbed wire, where we can expect things to happen at any moment, if orders come?

18th February

Edy Weiss has again left for Teplik, naturally escorted by guards. Is he going to bring bread? Although we are badly in need of the bread ration, we should prefer to hear from him that Teplik is about to be evacuated, instead of mere rumours.

A villager has told Mizzi on the road that the Red Army is going to launch a formidable offensive on Red Army Day.

19th February

Edy has not only brought the bread rations, but also sacks full of provisions for men of the T.O.

20th February

Kaiser has returned from his leave spent in Germany. To think that when he left about a month ago, we were firm in our belief that there would be no unit for him to return to ...

He has ordered a frame for his portrait of Hitler.

Wherever one looks one sees low-spirited people ...

23rd February

It's Mizzi's birthday. As the villager had told her the Soviets would launch a big offensive on Red Army Day, that is today, she hopes her birthday will be a good omen for her. I presented her with a water-colour depicting the room.

27th February

The hairdresser had a hot argument with Segall and Heinz about a trench-coat. Kustin had voiced his desire to have a pair of breeches made by our tailor, and now they had to look for the material. The hairdresser's trenchcoat would have done, but its owner would not part with it. In the end he had to give in, and he receives twenty Marks for it. They say Kustin is going to pay.

2nd March

Elsässer has told Segall he'll bring some more peas, though he is very doubtful whether they are fit for eating; they are six or seven years old. Segall accepts eagerly.

Coming into our room, Elsässer is asked by the hairdresser's wife what has become of the Doctor who was sent to the camp at Braslav some months ago.

'Ah the dentist? Apparently a priest has put a flea in his ear, which has made him, his wife, and some others run away. I can't understand why. They had nothing to complain of, had they?'

3rd March

Towards noon the door swung silently open. Some of the Wehrmacht had barged in. Passing by the barbed wire and the signboard over the gate 'CAMP FOR JEWS – NO ENTRY' they had expressed their desire to see what it looked like inside. Kustin was leading the way. The sergeants, or whatever rank they had, were looking at us as if they had been visiting Madame Tussauds's Exhibition: just for curiosity's sake. One of them asked Kustin, 'How long are they going to stay behind and not work on the highroad?' Another of them hastened to answer anticipating Kustin: 'Till they get putrified.' Kustin did look embarrassed, as I watched him from my cage. In the room there are a few convalescents and some with frostbitten limbs.

During the night, an eighteen year-old boy gave his last breath. Intestinal T.B. [Plate 14]. His mother died some months ago of inanition; his father was shot dead on the road, I think in November, by Wisotzkas.

5th March

A lorry has brought sacks of peas. A large quantity of it has been put into barrels of water to get softened.

8th March

We have learned that Dr. Shaiovici has been swept away by typhus after a three days' illness. It is a great loss for those in the camp of Teplik.

12th March

The inmates of the camp at Tarassiwka are going to be removed into our camp. Now after the raging epidemic, we have plenty of room ...

13th March

Today about two hundred have arrived from Tarassiwka. Worn out, tattered, gaunt girls – apparently there are no elderly women among them – men and youths; their rags are hanging loose; some of them are bloated.

What do *we* look like in their eyes, I wonder? Much the same as they do in our eyes? I should certainly think so. Especially the female inmates. Everything has made them slacken, lose their womanly appearance, and look untimely old. Even nature itself struck, refusing to give the younger ones the monthly 'allowance', so as to get things going. Nevertheless, or is it just for that, some of our female inmates will use lipstick, for fear that their hollow cheeks and pale lips might incite the destroying angels to prune them. A painful sight!

As for men and women being in the same camp, that is *mixed class*, there is no danger of enticement. The fact that a woman or girl is washing herself thoroughly next to other people has nothing provocative in itself. Sometimes a blanket will screen off the cage, sometimes not even that.

14th March

Anişoara, myself and others have been taken to Tarassiwka to clean the camp for peasants to come. They are said to be replacing the Jewish inmates who have been removed to our camp.

The camp had the same hen-roost arrangement in two tiny wretched filthy rooms. Simply sickening. Cleaning the place seems a task beside which cleaning the Augean stables must have been a trifle.

60

22nd March

Broaching the topic of Selma, who died in mid-December, a neighbour of ours showed me some English verses Selma's mother had found amongst her daughter's papers:

All day I muse, all day I cry,

aye me.

I feel the pain that on me feeds

aye me.

My wound I stop not, though it bleeds

aye me.

Was I sharing her opinion that the rhymes expressed Selma's grief about camp-life, or were they copied by Selma from memory?

25th March

We shall be regular workers on the road again. Those who up till now have been assigned to carry the water from the village-well are going to be replaced. Six girls are to fill their places.

Leova has been appointed interpreter in the camp at Cicilowka; his father and sisters have remained with us.

26th March

A long convoy to the road ...

Only those having frozen legs and feet or really the worst cases have remained behind.

The woods we passed through have burst into leaf. A marvellous, gorgeous sight indeed. The guards, full of joy themselves, made us hurry. Owing to the molten snow, and to the obstacles on the narrow path, it was almost impossible to keep pace. Many stumbled. I felt the hard blows of a truncheon on my back:

'Painter, why don't you get hurrying?'

At the same time, Sukerka also encouraged with his truncheon Anişoara, who was hurrying along by my side. She tripped herself up.

... Kaiser, Schneider and Ulrich were seen later arriving in a cart. They sat down on a bench in a clearing of the wood, watching those that had the bad luck to be working in their close neighbourhood. As the T.O. men were still feeling cold, another man and myself were told to move away a couple of the piled-up logs. Kaiser called after us, to take care that we be seen by no wood-reeve ...

28th March

A narrow-gauged railway is to run along the road for the conveyance of earth. Men, women and girls have been carrying the rails.

2nd April

I have to portray Hierl, an inspector of the Todt Organisation who for some time now has been sharing rooms with Kustin.

Having no brush any longer, I first tried a handful of the shaving-brush, but it didn't work; then I tried some of a horse's tail, but it didn't work either; in the end, Fedya's sheepskin did the trick, and so the tinker has fixed it for me.

11th April

The goading to and from the road has become hellish. Toiling on the road is small beer compared to the quick march imposed by the guards throughout the time. Uphill, downhill, we get pushed on by roaring guards. As shepherds and cowherds respectively, they would not dare do such things to the entrusted live stock.

12th April

Anişoara and I have been 'commandeered' to embellish Kaiser's and Ulrich's garden. We have to carry coloured stones from the quarry close-by, and break them with a hammer. The material serves as a lay-out of the German Vulture; an improvised mosaic. Having no adhesive, we use simple sand to lay coloured stones in. Sand ... Everything is built on sand now except the fate of the camp, (Would to God Buder were not right) I was going to say Anişoara, as we were laying the stones.

13th April

As I entered the house in the morning, to get the hammer, I saw Kaiser, Ulrich and Schneider having breakfast together. I could not help stealing a glance over the laid table, though I managed to resist temptation: eggs, potato-pancakes, marmalade, margarine, lard, coffee, and brown bread. I felt so sick that, murmuring an apology, I turned off without taking the hammer.

15th April

Kustin has left for Teplik. The camp will be in charge of the two sergeants, or sergeant-majors. His two rooms with the kitchen have graciously been given to the camp. To think that in December one hundred and seven people were killed simply for lack of accommodation in the school-building.

16th April

Pepi has retained her 'appointment' as cook and interpreter with the new commandants. Both have taken up residence in the village, sharing rooms.

17th April

This morning, a third sergeant turned up. Having brought with himself a *body-guard* of twenty-odd villagers, the camp is left now in charge of three Commandants and thirty-odd guards. The new one seems to be hot-tempered; finding fault with our forming in files he takes violent measures, especially aiming at our heads.

I have learned the names of the commandants: the first two are Hartmann and Louis Glasbrenner; the third is called Luneville.

18th April

Hardly was the convoy outside the barbed wire than we were ordered to stop.

A car had drawn up in front of the camp.

SS Oberscharführer Maass! (I really don't know how he spells his name, Mass or Maass), but I think I was not really interested in either spelling, but in the little man himself. He gives me the creeps.

After a few minutes talk with Hartmann, they told us to stand in files on the other side. Maass was pacing up the lines inquiring now and then of Hartmann about the age of those whom he kept watching closely. The procedure lasted but a few minutes, and then he took himself off into the inside of the camp.

Hartmann looked uneasy.

Both the commandeered and the sick were running out of the building. A man who, on account of his furuncles, was unable to put his foot to the ground, was encouraged with a blow over his head.

The SS man had all the outcomers set up near the gate, and looked at each face fixedly.

Turning abruptly, Maass went up to his car.

We were given orders to step out quickly, so as to make up for lost time.

For some months past the SS has left it to the epidemic to bring about a natural pruning. It looks as if they are going to handle it again by themselves.

23rd April

I was called to Hartmann's to paint Easter-eggs. He also did some. The task finished Hartmann told Pepi to give me half a loaf.

Easter-Sunday

Maass's car was seen on its way to the house where Hartmann and Glasbrenner have taken up residence. On an Easter Sunday? He couldn't be invited, or could he? People are feeling the strain ...

After an hour or so, orders were given that we should wear a badge, any badge, to distinguish us from the villagers, or rather to distinguish ourselves as Jews.

Close on midday there came another order: All of us have to register, stating age and profession.

I overheard Lilli entreat Segall and Heinz, who were about to make up the list, to misstate the age of her parents.

26th April

After reveille we were prevented from leaving the building; instead we were told to wait in the corridor.

The front-door leading into the enclosure was locked!

Segall and Heinz seemed extraordinarily nervous, looking livid.

Time passed ...

Thoughts were playing havoc with me ...

Finally, the door was unlocked from the outside.

Hartmann's voice was heard; he wanted us to come out for the call.

As a rule, the call is taken at the same time for ex-inmates of the camp of Tarassiwka. We learned, however, that the call had already been made for them.

Kaiser was seen, too, though of late, he used to come straight to the road. Someone whispered in my ear that Hartmann and Kaiser had been checking those from Tarassiwka, before we were allowed to come out.

A young man was just seen leaving the detached little house of the Tarassiwka-group, his cheek wrapped up. Yesterday he was complaining to me of tooth-ache.

Addressing himself to Kaiser, he said beseechingly:

'Do let me go to work!'

Kaiser shook his head negatively.

The boy kept imploring. Kaiser reddened and threw his baton at him. Hartmann witnessing the scene, motioned to a guard to take the boy back into the little house.

'Get going', he said.

Hershl, on my left, said in an undertone:

'I'm feeling miserable. My mother has been told to stay behind today, to mend for the T.O. men, or for the commandants. She's not at all clever at sewing. I wonder why they have commandeered her. I'm afraid for her.'

I was trying to calm him.

'You see', he continued, 'last night, when you were probably asleep, the list of the commandeered contained more people than usual to work in the camp today. If only I could manage to take my mother to the road. I'm miserable, I am really.'

'Itzku', an anxious voice was heard suddenly over the heads of the files.

'Join the line; you are not working in the camp today.'

'Of course, I am', the voice of the husband came over from the group of the commandeered. 'It has been my job for a long time.'

... The call.

I kept thinking of Herschmann: 'Itzku.' With what pride he showed me the other day a photograph of his, representing him as a civil servant. A senior post-official. Now commandeered to clean the latrine, he has refused to come with us to the road, out of his sense of duty. The latrine ... Half of its thatch has been used up by the people. One of the many reasons for the raging furunculosis.

... Judging by the burning sun, it was getting on toward ten when Maass's car stopped on the road, near our small group. Jumping out, it was Hartmann who huskily asked for some shovels.

Who was among the victims?

The gloomiest forebodings have come true: fifty-five victims.

The printer Ungar was followed voluntarily by his wife Anna. A man, pushed together with his wife to the lorry, lifted her up gently, and placed her carefully on the lorry, standing next to her:

'Don't despair; with God nothing is impossible.'

Ludo was lifted by the soldiers of the Commando, and thrown upon the lorry. He fell by the side of it. It was not until they threw him once more that he fell into the lorry over the heads of those cowering or standing in it. Hershl's apprehension has proved to be too right. Not only his mother, but also his sister ... With the lorry loaded, one of the soldiers in search for his lost purse – it contained six Marks – came also to the cook-shack where he told the women: Hands up! Thus he perceived the invalid hand of Hershl's sister. She, too, was then ordered to join the others in the lorry. Strangely enough, prompted by her ardent wish to help her mother whom she had seen in the file of those 'specially' commandeered for today, she resolved to stay behind in the camp on her own, insinuating herself into the file of the women-water-carriers, changing places with one of them. Pushed and already in the lorry, Itzku kept shouting: 'Commandant, I have been commandeered!' Segall himself was pushed into the lorry, being ordered to board it. Hartmann, however, intervened for him, as Segall was already standing in the lorry, telling the soldiers that he was our spokesman. Three girls of the Tarassiwka-group had managed to vanish into thin air. The soldiers picked out a water-carrier in their place (so far I have not been able to find out whether they meant Hershl's sister, or a commandeered water-carrier girl). After the lorry left with the people in it, Stefan Bregula turned up in the camp. Learning from Hartmann of the vanished three, Bregula set out to look for them by himself. He found them hidden in the cauldrons of the former kitchen. Turning a deaf ear to their entreaties, he had them immediately dragged out by guards. Together with Hartmann he forced them to enter Maass' car, and took them to the glade: the place of execution.

Mucki, eighteen months old, the only baby left with us by consent of Buder, and afterwards of Hartmann, had a narrow escape. As a rule he would hide himself in the cage as soon as his mother called out: 'Mucki, the commandant!' Today, having acted upon the advice of our doctor and Segall, his mother administered some drug to him and put him to sleep in a rucksack. Sukerka, knowing of the existence of the baby, was looking for it everywhere, and thus came upon the rucksack. Feeling it, he detected Mucki!! Luckily Sukerka was open to a sound bribe offered by Segall. Now, the baby was found playing with his mother ... Amongst those executed there were also some youngsters of the Tarassiwka group that suffered from itch.

29th April

I have finished a water-colour, twenty-one by thirteen, depicting Kaiser's room [Plate 15]. A peasant-woman embellished Hitler's portrait this morning, that is hung up in the corner, icon-like. I have also made a portrait of Segall. Of the inmates, I have besides the genre-like one (in which all the personages seen are portraits), four more portraits, and a scene, depicting our doctor on duty. The number of my works has risen to twenty.

30th April

Anişoara and I have started on an improvised mosaic for Glasbrenner's and Hartmann's garden.

Luneville is on leave.

6th May

Bergmann and Elsässer came to see Kaiser while Anişoara and I were working in his little garden in front of the house, repairing the mosaic.

It has gone on raining for two or three hours. Learning from me that Kaiser was not in, they remained in the car as simple onlookers. Some minutes might have passed when an approaching sound of shouting voices came from the village-lane. We looked up: the convoy of men and women, escorted by guards, was taking the corner close to the barbed wire fence. It must have been nine or ten o'clock. Looking at the convoy, Elsässer called out violently:

'What the deuce does that mean? Where are they coming from?'

He beckoned the guard, Yasha. The latter came up to the car and reported they had been forced to interrupt work because of the heavy rainfall. Yet, the other day, I overheard Kuehne quoting a General as having said that the highroad Gaisin-Uman is of no strategic importance whatsoever. Then whose 'hobby' is it?

Elsässer stormed:

'Get that out of your head! Off with 'em at once, and see to their marching in close files, not as they have been doing, like partisans.'

I exchanged a look with Anişoara. There are about four miles to the road. The convoy had thus already been marching about eight miles on muddy lanes.

8th May

The guards are showing some nervousness, but we cannot get to the bottom of it. No exit for us into the barbed wire enclosure.

There!

Single shots followed by continuous fire of MGs.

... Partisans have attacked the soldiers in the village.

Deafening silence.

The tramp of cantering horses.

Silence ...

9th May

Armoured cars went past the camp in the morning. A battle is reported on the outskirts of the village.

No work on the road; we have been kept behind.

People have been feeling anxious at the presence of soldiers near the camp. What if ... ?

In the afternoon, we learned that Andrei, Bregula's aid, was shot dead by partisans while he was trying to send out an SOS to Gaisin.

10th May

Yesterday's battle has added some horse-meat to our pea-soup.

11th May

By Glasbrenner's order I wrote with charcoal the first line of the LILLI MAR-LENE on their whitewashed wall.

On my way back to the camp, I kept upbraiding myself for my lack of guts; I should have picked up the German newspapers lying about on the floor in their room.

14th May

As Anişoara and I presented ourselves in the commandant's little garden, we found that straw had been scattered on the mosaic. Hartmann told us harshly to clean the mosaic at once; the scattered straw was making him angry.

We set to work, but the wind proved stronger; it meant fighting the storm. I went back to the camp to fetch a 'pincette' from Rosa. Together with the one used by Anişoara, we succeeded in picking up straw by straw, throwing the stalks into a pail filled with water.

With that task accomplished, we had likewise to clean the yard of the straw. Filling in a few sacks, we carried them into the barn. After a while, we were joined by Pepi, and not long after by Hartmann himself. Anna and Pepi filling the sacks, Hartmann and I carrying them into the barn. Soon, however, Anişoara and I were left to finish off the work by ourselves.

17th May

Bergmann has told me to make a sort of mosaic for Dohrmann Co. at their Headquarters in Gaisin.

Together with about fifty men and women, assigned to work at Tarassiwka and at the Gaisin-station respectively. Anişoara and I were taken in a lorry load to Gaisin.

18th May

On the way back from the Gaisin to Mikhailowka, a distance of eight miles, Hennes, out of humour, told us harshly to get off the lorry at once, we continued our way on foot.

Pepi has volunteered an explanation of why Hartmann was working together with us the other day filling sacks. In fact, she said, she herself was the reason. Having seen her help us, it was like a slap in his face, as he expressed himself, and so he, too, came out. No comment.

19th May

Back from Gaisin, we met with agitation. Some twenty villagers had gone past in the morning, carrying shovels on their shoulders. Where to? Why?

20th May

The lorry did not turn up in the morning to take us to Gaisin ... All of us have been ordered to go to the road.

21st May

The lorry did not turn up this morning either.

The smiths commandeered at the village are said to have come back to the camp yesterday with disquieting news. Allegedly a mass-grave has been dug, and SS are about to come tomorrow ...

While working at the slope on the road, I kept meditating upon the wild rumours, resolving in the end to get at the truth of them. At the first opportunity when Glasbrenner came near us, I asked him whether I could start on the water-colour for him tomorrow, Sunday. He replied in the affirmative. Then, I asked casually whether it was true that the SS would come tomorrow to have all of us executed. He was not at all disconcerted at my question, answering just as casually:

'SS is going to come, though it hasn't anything to do with you.'

At noontime, he left the road.

Back in the camp, we were told by Segall that Luneville – I did not know he had returned from his leave – had been showing his anger at the rumours about the mass-grave and the 'general action'. 'If anything is going to happen', Luneville said, 'it's for the police to learn first, but speaking for myself, I haven't got any information.'

22nd May

SS in the village ...

The guards have been given a check up by the SS physician, we were told. Those found suitable for service are to get uniforms.

So Luneville and Glasbrenner were right, after all, and the villagers proved mistaken.

23rd May

At the road Ulrich has asked Lisa to give him the stockings she has been knitting for him. He wants them even if they are not ready, for, if she delays, she may have no time to finish them.

24th May

Lisa, encouraged in her hope to receive a bit of bread for her father, kept working at them last night till the little improvised lamp was extinguished, and this morning Ulrich received his stockings, knitted to the last stitch. Lisa received nothing in exchange ...

Some villagers passing by the road have told us confidentially that a mass-grave *has* been dug!

In the camp, we learn from Segall that according to the commandants the villagers have merely been ordered to fill the second half of the grave on the bottom of which are the victims of the 26th of April.

As to the grave itself, a village-driver on a Dohrmann lorry has related the following:

In contrast to previous methods, those to be 'purged' are taken in lorries to the very brink of the grave. Steps, neatly cut, lead down. Three people at a time had to descend on that day of April and lie face downwards. After the shots were fired from above, another three had to descend, and then another three, and another three ...

Savages on some of the Sandwich Islands were known to use a similar method, to get rid of the men over forty. The man, accompanied by his whole family, would go as far as the grave, dug beforehand, and lower himself to the ground. The family would fill the grave with earth, performing some religious dance over it, afterwards, meant in fact to stamp down the ground.

25th May

Our nerves are being strained. Is there any truth in the rumours? Pepi, Heinz and Segall have been whispering to one another ...

26th May

All was as usual on the road, or, at least it seemed to be so till noon, when a guard turned up on the high road looking for Glasbrenner. I did not give the matter a second thought, and kept reflecting instead why Pepi was so pale as I watched her talking with Heinz and Segall before the signal of 'marching off' was given. Something *was* fishy. She was sure to have learned something. To think that once, in Hartmann's (or was it Glasbrenner's?) room, she promised to tell me of impending danger. In fact, she had plenty of time to do so last night ... And what, if she would have kept her promise? Could it have altered anything?

The German-Pole, Eduard Arnold, a T.O. man, is reported to have told someone amongst us that about thirty-five thousand Jews, provided with arms by German deserters, has risen against the German garrison in Warsaw. Armoured cars and dive bombers were being thrown against the Jews. On account of the uprising, Hitler is said to have ordered all Jewish internees in the East-European region to be exterminated. I wonder whether there is any truth in it. Only last week Arnold remarked to me: 'Painter, why aren't you painting yourself a loaf of bread?' and biting through a morsel of bread he was about to swallow, held it out to me – I ate it.

On returning to the camp, we were received with blows of batons by lolling guards. Very unusual and new.

After having been counted, I remained behind.

Then Anişoara dashed out, tears in her eyes. Speaking with sobs she gave me to understand that it was all lost. Pepi, Mizzi and her husband had made their getaway in the morning ...

The last straw ...

I tried nevertheless to soothe Anişoara.

In the cage, the other Mizzi sitting next to us weeping.

'Imagine', she said sobbingly, 'just when it looks like a collapse of Hitler-Germany, we have to die!'

Another convoy has returned from the road.

Great agitation.

Another three have disappeared!

They are said to have been seen slipping away during the break.

As they worked in a separate group, it was not until the counting that their absence was detected.

Frieda, who used to be Bregula's cook in winter, has made her getaway, too. The guards had been watching her movements as she worked in the camp, knowing of the relations between her and Bregula, and, indeed, Bregula had managed – I'm wholly in the dark how – to spirit her out of the camp.

... Some guards who had kept looking in at the windows dashed suddenly into our room, and started beating several women at hand. Was the end near? We 'hid' ourselves in the cages. The screams of women mixed with the murderous yells of the guards ...

Having cooled down, the guards left the room.

There was a call.

'Get the soup!'

The soup!

Who cared for fugitives, mass-graves, beatings?

The soup!

We rushed into the corridor ...

But try as we might, we could not get it down.

Anişoara started to cry again.

When was it about to happen? During the night? Tomorrow? The day after tomorrow?

Most of us decided not to take off our clothes. Why? I am unable to offer any explanation, not even to myself.

27th May

The call.

Hartmann, Glasbrenner and Luneville are present. The latter is warning us that the escorts have orders to shoot quickly if any of us steps out of the file on the way to the road.

The number of the escorts has been increased.

The convoy sets off, Glasbrenner and Hartmann bringing up the rear. They are prepared to take no chances. A last glimpse of Pepi's husband who, by order of Luneville, is to stay behind. He is standing by the wall, his face livid. Thinking of Pepi herself, this time we should have been spared her aping the different commandants. She would always butt in and repeat their order 'March off.' As if we didn't understand German.

On the way, David, the husband of Sophie, the fugitive, gets brutally beaten by Kolea and Sukerka, but on the main road the guards leave us to ourselves; they do not care whether we are working or not.

Someone is whispering that Segall and Heinz wanted to run away together with their families, but were prevented by Edy Weiss, as they were unable or unwilling to take also his parents. These are, perhaps, rumours.

It is the first time that people have tried to make a getaway. For all practical purposes it looks almost impossible for anyone to succeed. First of all one has to get in touch with a villager, to be guided to the river Bug; then, one needs plenty of money, clothes for disguise as peasants, and last but not least, one has to speak Ukrainian more or less fluently, so as to be taken for a native.

Close upon noontime, Bergmann's car, followed by Elsässer's appeared on the road. As it was breaktime, most of us were lying down on the ground. Elsässer went up to Heinz, who was propped up against a tree, not too far from Anişoara and myself. It seemed to me as if I heard the words: ' ... tried', ' ... impossible ... ' but I was not sure. Heinz looked crestfallen.

I haven't told Anişoara anything; what is the good of it?

Time has passed away. Soon they will signal us to knock off work. Each one of us has been working hard to kill thought. For once we want the day to become endless. It is dreadful to think of going back to the barbed wire-enclosure.

... I hear the confused sound of a motor-car and look up.

SS???

The car is coming nearer. It is Elsässer's judging by its index-mark. Bergmann and Elsässer get out, looking for Heinz ...

The news reaches us in no time:

EXECUTION HAS BEEN POSTPONED.

They are radiant people who are spreading the news, although in whisper: 'POSTPONED! POSTPONED!'

A few minutes have elapsed, and now we hear the order:

'Kaput! Stop working!'

Eagerly we form in files, to be counted.

Homeward I watch Edy and a woman talking to each other excitedly.

In the camp, Pepi's husband is in a state. He was mercilessly beaten by Luneville, and it is Segall who seems to have intervened for his life.

Now I begin to understand why the woman who was talking to Edy Weiss was excited. Her husband, having recently worked as a distiller for the T.O., or the like, has made a getaway from the village-house he used to work in. Apparently his wife received a tiny note on the road – a native passer-by succeeded in slipping it into her hand. It was from her husband, who wanted her and their two teenage girls to follow the peasant through the woods. Unfortunately, the woman was seen walking into the woods. Fedya, the guard, summoned her to resume her place at once, otherwise he would shoot her. Now she is in despair.

Lined up before the window at the cook-shack to get our soup, some of us looked furiously at her. Is her husband's getaway making things complicated again?

Segall and Heinz have been holding a meeting after 'supper' in the room. According to Heinz, Bergmann and Elsässer have intervened for us, and consequently all those who are still in possession of USA dollars and jewellery must yield them up to the two intermediaries.

So as to protect the woman and her two teenage daughters from the consequences of her husband's flight, Segall is believed to have made a report to the commandants declaring that the man, subject to melancholia, is sure to have committed suicide by hanging himself. Will the SS not search for the body?

Mizzi has rendered her last eighty dollars for Bergmann and Elsässer. Something looks to me as being rather odd. I wish I hadn't such suspicions ...

28th May

Before being marched off, Glasbrenner pointed out that five people would be shot dead should any of us plan to run away.

It has leaked out that the GHQ in Kiev has ordered a stay of execution in all camps, including Gaisin. Life seems to have been extended till October.

30th May

Toiling on the road has started all over again. So has the beating and goading on to and from the road.

Moreover, the camp at Nemirow is reported to have been exterminated. The stay of execution came too late. I wonder whether Buder was in command when the execution took place. I hope not.

Hartmann has been transferred.

1st June

Kaiser has ordered me to paint a water-colour of his room. I already have one, made in secret some months ago [Plate 15].

Left by myself in the room, I perceived a plate full of slices of brown bread on the table, and the paper 'DEUTSCH-UKRAINE ZEITUNG' under it. The bread I was devouring with my eyes, but the paper I could not help drawing out from under the plate. No interesting items. Battles. Battles ...

2nd June

Back in the camp, we perceived soldiers of a Transmission Unit restoring wires at the back of the camp.

One of us overheard a soldier asking Bregula:

'Do the Jews still hope to get liberated?'

Bregula apparently kept on smiling.

5th June

During the break, Max was asked by Yasha to translate a few items from the German paper 'DER ANGRIFF' which he had pinched from Ulrich. Nothing to encourage hope. 'What bad luck', Max said to me, 'to come at last upon a newspaper, and to find nothing interesting in it.'

The rain that had started turned into a heavy downpour, making any digging into the slippery clay impossible. The guards went berserk.

6th June

I entered into a conversation with an N.C.O. of the Wehrmacht. He stated his name: Willi Martin, formerly a town-clerk in the City of Cologne. His wife, he told me, could not forget the kindness of the Jewish family in which she had been governess before their marriage, and till the outbreak of war was on writing terms with these people, now in South Africa.

'There are many amongst us', he remarked, 'who are against the treatment you are being subjected to, but what can one do? We were also against the pogrom following the attempt on Herr von Rath's life in Paris.'

We were interrupted by Glasbrenner, who was just passing by and ordered me to attend to work.

In the meantime, a cart had stopped near our working-team. With the N.C.O. off, and Glasbrenner's back turned to us, there alighted a peasant woman, who, breaking some bread into pieces, distributed it amongst our group. She hurried off in the cart without waiting for our thanks. I thanked her in my thoughts.

7th June

Passing in a cart by our group, Glasbrenner called out to me that Frieda had been caught and shot dead. I don't believe it, for something in his voice made me rather think it was sheer bravado on his part. Or is there something else at the back of it? God knows what.

Evening ...

The kerosene-lit tiny Eau-de-Cologne bottle had been extinguished, and those still lying awake started talking, recalling unforgettable dates in the past. Rosa was telling us as she has done so many times before, how she and some neighbours of hers, in nightshirts, had to face the firing squad on the very night her town was occupied. As the soldiers had no longer any bullets for their MG's, she was taken to Police Headquarters, but was released afterwards thanks to an officer.

The air had meanwhile become very close.

Unbearable ...

In the clamour that followed I distinguished Selma's step-father: 'Again those above me, of course! As if they couldn't climb down the ladder and use the latrine! And we cannot open a window! Shame on them!'

Those referred to did not say a word.

'So you use the latrine, don't you?' I hear Poldi's voice remonstrating Selma's step-father. 'Why then, if you happen to be so considerate, did your bottle of urine come down upon my face? Or have you forgotten? Should it happen again – well I just warn you.'

Somewhere, hundreds and hundreds or even about two thousand miles away – a home ...

8th June

Told by Kaiser to do some signboards to hedge up the road for all sorts of vehicles. I was sitting down by the roadside, the pick at hand should a car of the SS come in sight. Soon I entered into conversation with a soldier from the Mettlach-Sarre, where he used to work at a mosaic factory of some sort. Thus we broached the topic on mosaic ceramics and painting. After some hesitation I produced the tin-tube out of my pocket and showed him the water-colours and drawings. He looked with care and interest at each of them, and then said deliberately: 'You MUST destroy them. By some means or other they might get abroad, now or in the aftermath of War, and then they'd become a propaganda against Germany.' How foolish of me to have shown him the works. What, if he would have destroyed them himself?

Quickly I let them slip into the tin-tube – bless the tinker who presented me with it – and pocketed it. 'Of course', he continued, breaking the silence, 'you, too, are a Freemason, even if you are unaware of it. All I know is that the Jews are Freemasons; all of them.' I wonder what was going on in his mind, as I did not see any connections between the camp, my works, and Freemasonry. Or am I unaware of it, and there is such a connection? ... But why did he not destroy them on the spot?

In the camp, my neighbour told me that while she was working together with a group of fourteen other inmates in the woods, a peasant cart-driver offered her his help to make a getaway. Though she regrets that she had to refuse his offer, she is comforting herself she could not possibly have left her family behind, especially Turi, her nineteen year-old boy.

9th June

Two T.O. men are reported to have been stripped of their uniforms by partisans somewhere near Tarassiwka.

Peasants tell tales about a young fair-haired commandant of a partisan-group, sometimes donning the uniform of a German officer, who turns up now here and now there. A few days ago as we were returning to the camp three peasants passed our convoy by. One of them, a young reddish fellow, was looking at us intently. 'It's him isn't it?' the man on my left said. 'Yes, I am sure, he is the partisan leader.'

... Glasbrenner has again called out to me that Frieda has been caught and shot dead; and now they will get also Pepi. Why, in this case, have they not brought Frieda to the camp before shooting her? I do not believe a word. But it still puzzles me – why should he persist in telling me all this? Surely he must realise that I would never be able to run away. Poor health, no money, no knowledge of Ukrainian except for a few words, and no acquaintances to hide me and my wife for a time. As for the others, I do not think they have been planning an escape. Dr. Locker, left behind by his brother and sister-in-law, Mizzi, will probably join the elderly people in reading Psalms, or was I mistaken the other day? Sophie's husband? I don't think he would run away; his sisters, and especially his nephew, Turi, are too close to him. Pepi's husband? He is unattached for all I know.

10th June

Bergmann's car drew up in front of the barbed wire. Dressed in a fashionable light grey flannel-suit (with pressed trousers) he got out of the car and asked for Segall. After a short talk at the entrance of the gate – I have never seen him inside the camp – he drove off to Kaiser's.

It is the first time I have seen Bergmann wear civilian clothes. Up to that moment, his military outfit cheated me into the illusion that we were sort of PoWs. Now his civilian suit made me see the difference: we are nothing but slaves owned by a road-making company, with a death sentence over our heads. As soon as the four months reprieve comes to an end, and the civilians outside need our work no longer, we shall have to descend the neatly cut steps and lie face downwards. I wonder whether he has ever witnessed such a scene. It is just a non-sensical thought. According to Heinz, Kaiser's hair had turned white as snow after he regained consciousness and found himself buried alive in a bomb-crater. I can't help being haunted by the thought of what Kaiser's feelings were, when on that day in April he was checking people meant to step down into their grave. Perhaps, it was as natural to him as the fact that a kind father and husband, going on leave to Germany, should take some presents from the doomed internees of a wretched Extermination-camp. Who cared whether Martha, in her prime of life, had as much pleasure out of life as Eva, the daughter of the T.O. man Hermann Kaiser, for whom she had to embroider a present? Admittedly, Kaiser did intervene on that April day for elderly limping Schaerf not to be taken to the grave; although it is highly unlikely to think that Schaerf, had Kaiser's intervention not failed, would have agreed to remain behind while his frail wife was taken to the grave. It is so terribly difficult to be a judge!

11th June

Two men of ours have returned to the camp only in their pants. As usual they had been working in the woods, together with their group, when guards suddenly accused them both of intending to run away. They made them immediately undress and dig a grave. While one guard went into the depths of the wood, to stow away the clothes of the victims-to-be, Ulrich happened to come along. He asked the other guard what was the matter with the two men in their pants and got the laconical answer: 'JUDA KAPUTT!' Ulrich is reported to have gone into a rage, kicking the guard.

12th June

While Anişoara and I were working again in Kaiser's little garden, we saw Bergmann's car in front of the barbed wire gate, and Mizzi get into it. There's nothing bad in it, surely, but what is at the bottom of it? No use discussing it, both of us resolved; we might learn the cause afterwards when we are back in camp.

Well, Bergmann, in need of a versatile secretary, has taken her for a stretch of three days, on the recommendation of Heinz. Groups, standing about, are discussing Mizzi's luck: she will get proper food.

... Bergmann and Elsässer are said to have ordered the removal of the guard who yesterday wanted to kill the two men.

15th June

On the high road, Ulrich started talking to me about the aftermath of war. He has some more brothers at home, near Remscheid, and thus would like to have a small farmhouse of his own somewhere in the Ukraine. The only hindrance to his dream: his wife. Not for a moment has she thought of settling down here.

16th June

The guard has been re-instated by the SS.

Mizzi is not back 'home' yet; she was due the day before yesterday.

We have meanwhile moved our things into another cage, close to Mrs. Vogelhut's. The bugs coming from the cage below were driving us to despair. People in other cages did not want us as neighbours either because of our own bugs. It is really decent of Mrs. Vogelhut to have insisted on having us close to her. While arranging the things in the cage, I just hear a man saying: 'Bet you, Mizzi Hart is sure not to come back. Elsässer and Bergmann will help her to make a getaway. Well, well, he wins whom luck favours.'

At dusk, Mizzi entered the room.

She had much to do there, she relates, and so they retained her. They were very polite to her, but, on the whole, she is rather glad to be back again. Incidentally, she saw Bergmann looking furiously from his big window at the three quarters' wing of the vulture. He is going to take us to Gaisin one of these days, he said, so that we can finish the work. This would be fine! I do hope he is not going to change his mind, and take it to pieces before we get there. It is rather curious that he should have left it alone until now.

17th June

Agitation in the camp.

Maass's car at the gate. The SS man has asked to see Segall ...

He has only come for a few knives. What if under the sign: 'camp for Jews' we had also the inscription BY APPOINTMENT?

18th June

Three have made their getaway from the highroad! Since they are Teplik-born, they are naturally acquainted with the region. So far nobody knows any details about their escape.

Elsässer popping in late in the afternoon, asks me to get ready for Monday. Anişoara and I will be taken to Gaisin to finish the mosaic. As they have no lorry available to take us daily to and from Gaisin, he will see to it that we are put up there in the garage.

19th June

Sunday ...

While I was working at Kaiser's, a soldier strode past the house, whistling. I took him first for a soldier of the Wehrmacht, but the comb in his tuft of hair set me immediately right: some native who volunteered for the SS Brigade.

Towards noon, as I was on the point of getting out of the camp, back to Kaiser's, the guard did not want to hear of it. Orders of the new commandant! Luneville has been transferred, Glasbrenner is on leave, and now the new one, or rather his deputy, does not know me. 'Now there arose up a new Pharaoh over Egypt, which knew not Joseph.' Will the deputy approve of our going tomorrow to Gaisin?

I am told about a letter that has arrived from Hartmann's wife, after his transfer. I still cannot understand how people manage to find out what is written in that letter. The wife is said to have asked Hartmann to try and come on leave. God knows whether they will otherwise see each other again. Their neighbour has already fallen victim to the heavy enemy air-raids.

20th June

At first Glasbrenner's deputy was unwilling to let us go, since he thought we were going straight to Gaisin, and he could not spare an escort. Segall, however, explained that Bergmann's lorry was waiting for us at Tarassiwka, where at any rate a group of us went daily.

On our arrival, we learned that the lorry had already left for Gaisin. Now we shall have to wait for another lorry.

Hearing the sound of a motor-car, I jump to my feet. Bergmann's car has come to a halt in front of the workshop. Noticing me, he says I shall have to ask the head of the workshop for a permit for the two of us, which enables me to stop any passing lorry for a lift.

Getting the permit, we resume our place at the back of the store-house, stretching out our legs. We feel quite at ease in the sunshine, I must say. A young Ukrainian peasant-woman walking near-by, highly surprised, is making straight for me with outstretched hands. It is Vera, ex-cook for the Lithuanians at Mikhailowka. Now she is cook with the peasants that have been quartered in the camp, to work at the gravel-quarry at Tarassiwka. Vera invites me to escort her to the kitchen, as she wants to offer me some coffee and salt. The pea-soup in the camp is altogether salt-less.

On the way to the kitchen I cast a glance over the open dormitories of the peasants. It is the same building that was cleaned by us in March. Now I see boards serving as beds, which are along the walls. Ours in the camp are uneven crab-sticks. They get their rations twice a day, mostly broth and meat, and twenty Marks a month each of them. She is very sorry, Vera says abruptly, that she has no food for us now, but in case we arrive in time back from Gaisin, she will give us some meat. I take the dish full of coffee, as well as the salt, to Anişoara. She is in conversation with Turi. He, too, has got some coffee out of the dish. Heinz and Turi, his aide, have come to the area just now and are continuing their way. They are engaged in some surveying, I understand. Seeing us, Heinz is astonished to find us still at Tarassiwka. He thinks we had better go back in the afternoon, together with the group, and start for Gaisin tomorrow; today there is going to be no lorry, he points out. I show him the permit and repeat Bergmann's instructions to stop any lorry for a lift. Heinz looks at the note: 'It has not even a stamp', he says contemptuously, handing it back to me. 'You can do nothing with it. Well, it's your business anyway.' Shrugging his shoulders, he leaves us, followed by Turi.

We are standing at the gate. Suppose a lorry will pass all the same. It would be a great pity to miss this opportunity. Suppose, again, flying into a passion, Bergmann destroyed the vulture's wing he has been obsessed with for so long a time?

A cart is approaching. Some of our guards, for the first time in uniform, are on their way to Mikhailowka.

A guard is calling out some words to us, in Ukrainian, which I fail to understand. Jumping off the cart, he runs up to us, and his glance falls upon our little haversack. I understand from his excitable words that he is charging us with the intention of attempting to escape. I am trying hard, in a few Ukrainian words I command, to explain to him the true nature of our being here, but he is impervious to my arguments. Another guard has in the meantime joined him, signalling to Anișoara. God forbid, they could search the sack, and they would come upon the small tin-tube, containing my paintings. Unfortunately, it looks like a hand-made grenade. I show him the note signed by the head of the workshop. He is looking at it, muttering through a German spelling. I am aware he has been making out the word Gaisin. Still, it will not do. So Heinz has been right? The attitude of the guard is becoming more and more threatening. Oh hell, why can't he see sense? Finally, I do not know by what miracle, I make him go with me to the head of the workshop. There everything is explained. Leaving us, the guards warn us, though, that on our return to the camp we shall come in for something ...

Shortly afterwards, a peasant passing close by Anișoara whispers: 'You could easily make a getaway, both of you; why not have a try? You don't look Jewish.'

GAISIN

The arrival of the lorry has brought relief from my nagging thoughts. Showing the lorry driver the note, we are given a lift. Sitting next to the native-driver, we pass by Bergmann and Elsässer on the road; their car has a puncture.

Though it was understood that the driver should drop us at Dohrmann's, he won't hear of it now; his business is to take lumber to the station, he argues. Off we go.

We pass through deserted streets, go past shattered houses. There is no one from whom to enquire about the way. The uniformed sentry at the gate of some barracks presumably takes no notice of us. Let's hope we shall not be asked to produce any documents, in addition to the note given us in the workshop. Why has not Bergmann himself given us a permit? Does he not want to commit himself, or has he no right to do so?

Just relying on our former memory of the district, we find the place all right ...

I agree with Bergmann, the vulture's wing in front of the house looks dismal indeed.

We receive permission from Elsässer to clean the den in the garage, before starting work on the vulture itself.

It is not until we have been working at the den for some hours that we can have a proper look at it: a camp bed with a straw-mattress, a window with broken panes that opens to a garden in blossom, the grunt of the pig coming from the improvised sty just beneath. Having turned over a small box, Anişoara has thus secured a table; another box serves as a bench. No linen, no pillow, no blanket, but a bed. How comfortable it feels. Our first step back to normal life, I remark to my wife.

No light. Who cares? We keep talking of the people in the camp. How far away they seem to us now ...

21st June

We have started to undo the vulture's wing. While looking at it carefully, I detected a fault of construction; the wing is too small compared with the head. If only engineer Bergmann would not have been in love with it, he, too, would have noticed the fault.

'Why hasn't he thrown it away, I wonder?' Anişoara asks me in Romanian in front of Bergmann. Looking on for a while, as we are undoing the stones, he walks away towards the office.

Passers-by look at us without addressing us a word.

In the office high ranking officers of the Luftwaffe, of the Wehrmacht and of the Todt Organisation raise their voices.

Besides the vulture, I am to lay out a little garden, as a sort of 'frame' for the bird of prey. Nazi aesthetics!

During the break we see two girls playing with a black wolf-dog and its thirteen litter. They are Germans, working in the office.

22nd June

Bergmann gave me some drawing-paper. He wants me to do a water-colour interior of the room inhabited by the two German girls. They are sisters: Atti and Martha Grae, who is at the moment standing by his side at the open office-window. I show them the water-colour representing Kaiser's room, and, on the spur of the moment also the room representing the interior in the camp. Both look closely at the latter—they have never been inside the camp – then Bergmann remarks: 'I am not interested in interiors. When back again at Mikhailowka you'll have to paint for me a landscape with the village houses. In winter, should we still be together, you'll have to paint a winter-landscape.'

IN WINTER, SHOULD WE STILL BE TOGETHER.

23rd June

Whilst standing in the anteroom near the kitchen, to receive soup for us, Anişoara heard Atti Grae scold one of the kitchen-hands, because she had let some meat fall into our soup.

The pig, the wolf-dog with its puppies, and Anişoara and I receive separate food, that is, only soup. No, I want to put it right. Even in this case there is discrimination. The wolf-dog also receives meat. What should one expect: Atti Grae is so very fond of it.

24th June

Early in the morning, women with big bottles of milk were passing by on their way to market; others were carrying loaves of bread. I pleaded from time to time with some of them to sell us some milk and bread. We are rich. Just about a week ago, a commandeered smith managed to sell some clothing for us in the village: we have ninety-six Marks. The women went past us, without listening to my words. And then, one woman stopped, saying hurriedly she would send round some milk and bread.

Whilst I kept working in the room of the Graes, a kitchen-hand told Anişoara, who was mangling pebbles with a hammer, that a little girl had brought us a bottle of milk and half a loaf of bread, but had flatly refused to take any money. No doubt the little girl tried to avoid being seen by anyone but the kitchen-hand.

26th June

Bergmann seems to be the very life and soul of the Company here at Gaisin. Having asked him yesterday for some sand, he said: 'My foreman will be handling this.' He was referring to Elsässer.

This afternoon Bergmann asked me rather angrily why I stopped working for two hours. 'We are following the example of the natives', I replied, 'who work in the kitchen-garden.' 'No! That should be none of your business. The workers on the main road have a break for half an hour. This is also meant for you, or at the most, three quarters of an hour.'

27th June

Sunday ...

We have been celebrating our wedding-anniversary with a number of

books borrowed from Martha Grae. It was very decent of her to have selected for us translations from the Norwegian. As she emphasises, she has
refrained from offering us national-socialist literature.

Sitting by the window, I started on a water-colour – 'A peasant woman
carrying a basketful of fruit and goose', with a sunny landscape as background. Anişoara's eyes glittered. Was it cruel of me to evoke such an
utopian image? Full of remorse I presented the kitchen maid with the
painting.

My eyes have become so weak that no matter how hard I try I cannot go
beyond the first page, and even this with the utmost difficulty. Anişoara is
revelling in some Norwegian landscapes.

28th June

Working ahead at the vulture, we see the car of the District-Commissioner
passing us slowly by. Rising to our feet, we kow-tow and watch the car stop
in front of the recruiting station, not far away. Today all young Ukrainians are
forced to register, so as to be sent as volunteers to Germany.

Women looking at us, heave a sigh; soon their loved ones will have to
leave the country, and work for Germans. At least, this is what I think makes
them sigh; they may have other reasons, of course.

After a quarter of an hour or so, the car turns round, stopping near us.
The driver in the brown uniform of a German soldier puts out his neck, and
looking fixedly at me says to me. 'You are from Bucharest! Aren't you?'

I am going livid, that's what I feel. Who is he? I am trying hard to detect
some familiar traces in his face. Something is familiar about him, but ...

'Joseph!'

I step nearer; so does Anişoara, perplexed at my sudden paleness.
Explaining to her in a whisper that it is Joseph who, for many years, was
chauffer to Manfred, my eldest brother, we both go up to him.

His glance had fallen on me while we were bowing to District-
Commissioner, and wanting to make sure it was really me he had seen, he
has come back this way. He is very astonished to see me here of all places,
but also worried, as he is perfectly well aware what is going on in the camps
on this side of the river Bug.

He is about to leave for Ploieşti and Bucharest, and as a matter of course
will get in touch with my family. Casting a glance over us, he notices that our

feet are naked. I am wearing a blouse full of holes, instead of a shirt, so Joseph consoles me by promising to bring us some clothes from home ...

At any rate, he promises to be back again in the afternoon.

... Joseph has brought us some note-paper to prepare a letter, as well as a packet of tobacco and matches. He will be back here between the fifteenth and twentieth of July, and then he is going to do something for us. Perhaps, he will be able to drive us in the Commissioner's car as far as Braslav, the village across the river. Money will, however, be of the utmost consequence with the German border soldiers. He will talk it over with my family.

Towards dusk we have yet another surprise: Rosa! Bergmann and Atti Grae were in the camp, to fetch her. Rosa being a skilful dressmaker, Atti Grae wants her to work for her.

In the camp, everything is as quiet as quiet can be, setting aside the fact that men were ordered to fill up the grave, as the dogs had uprooted its thin bed, and the SS were afraid of an epidemic. Rosa claims that the grave was not disturbed by dogs alone. Because a coat showed up conspicuously above the earth, this was pulled up by one of the local people, then other villagers began to search for hidden gold and dollars in the clothes of those killed in April.

Rosa is not going to share our den. She is to be put up in the main building, in a room next to that of the Graes.

29th June

We have handed Joseph the letter. It is written in pencil as we have no fountain-pen. In spite of his insistence that I write as freely as I wanted to, I just could not. I am afraid the letter will seem rather a rigmarole to those at home. I only hope Joseph will explain everything to them. I could not possibly tell them about the grim look of the camp and the month of October as the deadline of the work and probably of our lives. Anişoara has been stressing the need of the small tooth-comb and of some 'Tox' against crawlers, as we can't stand them any longer.

Due to Rosa's staying all day in the Graes' room, I was forced to interrupt the water-colour I have been making for her, and have started instead on a water-colour for Elsässer; he shares the room with Bergmann.

While dressing, Elsässer started a conversation on the outlook for peace. 'The English with their rotten system', he says, 'are doomed to lose. They're behaving as though they're the real masters.' Then full of wrath:

'These gentlemen of England have their hearty dinner and then set off to raid Germany, spreading death and destruction. Imagine', he added, 'a town of ten thousand inhabitants has recently been completely demolished by the R.A.F.'

I am not aware whether he expects me to say something. In fact, what could I say? Should I mention Coventry, for instance, or had I better ask why it is necessary that people should dig their own graves and then walk down the neatly-cut steps in threes to their death? And yet, the shattered town and our descent of the steps to the grave are but links in the single chain of pointless annihilation.

5th July

We keep talking of Joseph. Has he already left for Romania? Will he be back in time, while we are still here? Bergmann very much resents our slow work at the vulture, and wants us to hurry. He fears the SS will take exception to his having us brought over here. Who can say for certain? But, suppose Joseph was not back again by the fifteenth – according to my calculations work will be finished by then – what then? Our stay at Gaisin cannot be extended; on the contrary, Bergmann will be only too glad to get rid of us the day we have finished, and an escape from the camp itself is impossible; at least it has been proved so till now.

6th July

Joining Anişoara, who is in the company of an N.C.O. of the Military Police, near the vulture, I am asked by him whether we are volunteers. 'No', I say, 'We've been shanghaied, if you know what I mean.' The N.C.O. gives me a blank look. Anişoara is sure that he does not believe we are Jews.

According to Rosa, the parents of the Graes have a farm somewhere near Recklinghausen in Westphalia; their brother is believed to have been killed in action at Stalingrad.

7th July

Bergmann, unable to make himself understood in French, tells us to talk to two soldiers of the Todt Organisation. They are French-Algerians, who enlisted in the T.O. in Paris. For once, the Germans have scored a triumph: getting Frenchmen to enlist in a German Legion. Bergmann wants us to persuade them to renounce their position at Teeras Co. and to start work instead for the Dohrmann Co. He is in need of skilled foremen.

The Algerians complain to us of having been cut off from their families, since Algiers has been occupied. We look astonished. Occupied? Algiers? But they, in their turn, too, were surprised by our amazement. 'You don't mean to say, you haven't heard of the occupation of Algiers by American troops?' they ask. We are anxious to learn as much as we can about it, but, unfortunately Paul Leroy, of all people, turns up. I understand he is a German from Mulhouse, a member of the Security Troop of the Todt Organisation.

All three of them enter the house, and then we hear the Algerians talk Ukrainian to the kitchen-hands.

The Americans in Algiers?

8th July

Looking at the vulture, Hennes says to me contemptuously: 'What's the use of working at this? As soon as the Russians come, this, too, is going to disappear.'

The cook Ernst, coming round from the kitchen-garden stops near the driver. They start discussing the ravages made by the R.A.F.

'Is there any God, to allow aged, sick and innocent children to be butchered by the British?' Hennes asks vehemently.

Again I wonder whether Hennes and Ernst are aware that their righteous indignation could be shared by the inmates of the camps on this side of the river Bug?

Ernst says: 'There will be no peace on earth until this damned island is wholly razed off the map.'

Hatred here! Hatred in the camp! Hatred everywhere!

9th July

I have been given permission to take Anişoara's shoes to a cobbler. Perhaps a skilful cobbler will be able to make something of them. Defying the other kitchen-hands, who refuse to show me the way, Stasia offers to do so. She will take me to a good one round the corner.

In the shoemaker's courtyard Stasia points to tiny girl of about six. Do I recognise her? 'No!' I do not know who she is, I answer by a gesture as I cannot find any appropriate word in Ukrainian.

I understand, however, she is the little girl that brought the milk and bread. Her daddy is not in, but her mother is. It is the kind-hearted woman

I talked to about the milk and bread. I explain to her that in a few days time we may be sent back to the camp, and Anişoara is badly in need of the shoes. As I command only a few words, our conversation suffers from many gaps. After a pause the woman says: 'Do try and come again tomorrow at noon. My husband will be in at that time.'

I will, I answer, wondering however whether Stasia will not be detained during lunchtime in the kitchen. According to the cook Ernst's warning I must never go out by myself, as I am liable to be shot dead.

At any rate, I leave the shoes with the woman.

10th July

It is close on noon, and I am on my way to the shoemaker's by myself. Stasia has no time. I do not feel at ease, but I simply had to take the risk. Funny to think that even a female escort could protect me from being shot in the street.

The shoemaker is at the table.

On seeing me, his wife invites me to stay for lunch. Try as I may I just can't help myself to any of the dishes. He motions to his wife, and now the little girl and the baby are taken into the adjoining room.

'Why aren't you joining the comrades?' he fired this question at me.

Hesitating for a moment, I start explaining about Joseph. My host listens carefully to my very broken Ukrainian, mixed, of course, with German words. The shoemaker is very doubtful whether Joseph will come in time to save us, even supposing that he has this intention. No, we should not wait for him. Provided Anişoara agrees, he, the shoemaker will try to get us out of town on Monday night – that is in three days time. We shall have to stay for some days in the woods; from there we are going to be taken to Sobelewka. In the forest we shall be given identity cards valid for the Romanian-occupied territory across the river Bug. At Sobelewka, a market-town, five Jewish survivors are living at present and will help us further.

His wife hands me some packages containing chicken-meat and a bottle of broth, to take to my wife.

What is Anişoara going to say to all this?

11th July

Sunday ...

A chilly rain has made us sit on the bed, looking at the ever-widening pool underneath the window; we have nothing with which to replace the missing panes.

In comes Rosa with two steaming cups of tea, some bits of cake and a blanket on her arm. She has got round Martha Grae to cheer us up with these things.

We tell Rosa about the plan – we have not seen her since Friday – and ask her to join us. No, she can't! Much as she would like to, she cannot possibly leave her family behind, especially Turi, her beloved nephew. We are extremely sorry, but it is only natural that she should feel this way.

Rosa has it from Martha Grae that Bergmann is greatly in love with her sister, Atti. They met years ago in the neighbourhood of the Graes' farm. He is married and has a five-year-old boy, whose photograph is on the desk in his office.

12th July

We have not finished our work yet, and I don't want to leave it unfinished. Tomorrow, then. No, tomorrow is the thirteenth. Well, the day after tomorrow, that is on Wednesday.

I slip round to the shoemaker's to settle our escape for that day. Entering the workshop I come upon a second master, who is working away at some shoes. Perceiving me, my shoemaker says casually: 'So you have come for the pictures? Step into the room will you?'

His wife is in the company of two children. The shoemaker comes in close on my heels. I explain matters. Can we start on Wednesday? Of course, he does not mind at all. The younger of the boys will join us. Where have the children come from? Who are they? Idle questions, for I cannot answer them myself. I do not put any questions nor am I offered any information.

… Bergmann has left in a great hurry for Proskurow. Partisans are said to have blown up a freighter carrying materials for the Dohrmann Company.

After giving Elsässer his water-colour, he wants to know what its value is in Marks. I cannot tell him now, I answer, nor about its value in any other currency. He cherishes it as a treasure.

In the afternoon, surprisingly, Elsässer came out to our hut; he stayed at the door, asking whether we were satisfied with the food. Anişoara kept pulling at my sleeve. In spite of her warning I didn't feel like holding my words back, and so I answered: 'My wife has just been pulling my sleeve, telling me not to complain, but why shouldn't I? The food is as bad as in the camp, so there is no need for us to work here.' Elsässer seemed a little put out, but said: 'I'm going to bring you some food; don't say anything to my fellow-countrymen.'

After a while he brought us a thick slice of lamb and half a loaf.

13th July

The shoemaker, in the company of the younger boy, has just gone by us. Both of them were riding in a cart, with their legs dangling. So they have already started? Will the shoemaker be back tomorrow? Suppose he does not come? It would have been a thousand times better to have started last night. Damn superstition!

A man from the camp has arrived on the lorry, together with the T.O. man, Becker, the quartermaster of Dohrmann Co. We proudly show him our den. We should like to tell him of our escape plan, but we must do our best to keep our mouths shut. His wife is at Mikhailowka, and he is certain not to want to leave her behind. So, instead, I ask him if, as he is coming tomorrow, he could not bring our fur-line waistcoats from the camp. I am thinking of the woods where we shall have to hide ourselves for days, and of my lungs. He tells us about Kustin, who has dropped in at the camp. He bursts out laughing when he's told of the escape made by Pepi and the others, then quite seriously, he asks why there had not been other attempts at escape. While offering the man smoking-paper to roll himself a cigarette, and digging deeply into Joseph's tobacco, I feel I am betraying the man. He has been so decent to me throughout the stay in the camp. We must tell him tomorrow.

Heinz turns up at noon, escorted by a guard, looking for Bergmann or Elsässer. Neither of them is here. Heinz turns down our hearty invitation to see our little room.

14th July

We have finished the flower-beds. Here and there they need a last brush. Luckily, Bergmann has not come back yet.

What about the shoemaker? When I slipped round, his little girl only had a negative shake of her head ... And Joseph will be back between the fifteenth and the twentieth ...

15th July

Bergmann is back again. Bad-tempered as he is – Atti Grae has left for Jitomir in the meantime to see her fiancé – he flies into a passion because he finds us still here.

Two hours or so afterwards, Rosa comes out of the building to tell me to paint some flowers or what-nots on a parchment, meant as a lamp-shade for Atti Grae; Bergmann wants it as a surprise for her. 'You will have to hurry!' Rosa adds, 'since the lorry is about to arrive from Tarassiwka in half an hour's time, *to take us to the camp!*' She speaks casually, but I feel I am going mad. In *half an hour's* time? Where is the shoemaker? But, even if he were here, how could Anişoara and I sneak away in broad daylight? Suppose, I asked Bergmann to let us stay another day? Rosa is against it; I ought to leave the whole thing alone; Bergmann is ill-humoured on account of indigestion.

Well, I shall just have to face his bad temper. Paying no attention to Rosa's warning, I enter his office, quite in a terrible state of nerves and start: 'Since we have to leave, I should like ... '

He cuts in impatiently: 'Get to work immediately. The lampshade must be ready by tonight, and see to it that you make a beautiful thing out of the parchment.'

Now, things look a bit different altogether. Tonight is by no means in half an hour's time!

With a sigh of relief I go out to break this good news to Anişoara.

... Rosa has given me the parchment out of the things belonging to the Graes – she says it has been her suggestion that I get this commission; now let me see, what would I have gained if I had followed her advice *not* to see Bergmann? If I were going to be taken off in half an hour's time to the camp, what difference would it make, whether I was commissioned to paint a lamp-shade or not, since it would not mean, according to Rosa, any extension of our stay here. Anişoara has in the meantime been ordered by Bergmann to level the road in front of the building. A stretch of about thirty yards. Try as I may, inspiration for the lamp-shade does not come. In the end I decide on copying the pattern of some Rosenthal porcelain laying on the table in the room of the Graes.

Anişoara's head has appeared at the window. She is all in a fluster. She whispers that quartermaster Becker has arrived ten minutes ago to take us on his lorry to Tarassiwka. She told him, however, that we had been retained for another day, so he has left without us. Thank goodness!

... Four o'clock. I have accomplished the task.

No longer any lorry to take us away today. Tomorrow? The shoemaker is back again. He went past Anişoara as she was crushing the stones, stealing a nod at her.

I think the nod means *tonight*!

... We are stirred by the sudden arrival of a cart. Paula and Livia, escorted by a guard are sitting in it. What are they doing here? Suppose Bergmann is availing himself of this wonderful opportunity to send us back to Mikhailowka? But Bergmann is not in the office. He has gone to the 'Abschnittsbauleitung-Office', but is expected back any minute. I say 'hullo' to the girls, and dash into the house, to beg Rosa to do something about their leaving at once for the residence of the Polish physician they have come for. She understands me straight away.

The cart has set off.

The girls will be thinking me rude because I confined myself to saying 'How d'you do?', but I really can't help it. Perhaps later they will understand and forgive my brusque manner. This is the first time I've heard that inmates of the camp can be looked after by a Polish physician in Gaisin. Why did they not send the physician with medicines, when the epidemic was raging and patients were dying for want of drugs? Or are only those two girls out-patients? There are so many things I have not been told about in the camp.

Anişoara is doing the room and washing the dishes, arranging them neat-ly on the 'table', together with the blanket and the books borrowed from Martha Grae. Meanwhile I am writing a few lines to Elsässer, asking him not to send the SS after us. We could bear the moral and physical pains in the camp no longer; the thought of returning to that horror has encouraged us to face the ordeal of a getaway.

Together with a letter of acknowledgement for the borrowed books, I slip this letter into Hawthorne's *The Scarlet Letter* – and hand it to Martha Grae. The borrowed books I place on the blanket.

Unable to stand the shack any longer, we go out.

Rosa is still with Martha Grae, who is trying on some dresses. How can one go off without saying goodbye to Rosa? It's awful.

Leaning against a tree, I am rolling myself one cigarette after another. Soon, my thoughts are diverted by the ants bustling about the trees. It all looks like a stream of traffic, seen from a bird's eye-view.

... Dusk is falling.

Bergmann and Elsässer, who were seen deep in conversation in front of the office, are indoors now. It is only we who have remained outside, near the garage. As a matter of fact, it is the first time that we ever came out of the garage after work. I wonder what Bergmann and Elsässer would think if they saw us outside.

The moon is rising.

Lest we should be seen, we have made ourselves comfortable on a stone behind the shrubbery. From here we can watch the lighted window of the office. The people inside are standing by the radio. Ernst's window, which opens into the courtyard, is also lit.

Time is passing.

No shoemaker in sight.

I regret now that I missed asking the shoemaker on Monday, how he was to signal us that he had come for us.

Is there a whisper?

We are looking out through the shrubbery. Nobody to be seen in the street.

There it is again! No mistake! There is some whispering. We can make out the shoemaker's little girl by the tree across the way. Her father will be with us in no time. The girl disappears again from our sight.

We are waiting.

The light in Ernst's room has gone out. Some people are passing close by the shrubbery. We crouch out of sight.

The shoemaker has not come.

Has much time elapsed since we spoke to the little girl? Heaven knows, it seems to us an eternity. Is he going to come? Suppose he does not come? With unmistakeable Central-European clothing, ninety-six Marks, and being lost in the country, any attempt at escape is doomed. There is nothing to be done about it: we shall have to return to the garage, and that is that.

But to do this is plain cowardice. Resolutely we get to our feet.

The overcoats worn like villagers, and walking in socks – the wooden sandals would make us conspicuous – we go past the lighted office window. From there, stealthily along the fence of the kitchen-garden, across the road, past the house in the corner, past the second – here we are.

We look about. The coast is clear. Stepping into the courtyard we open the door to the workshop. The shoemaker is sitting in complete darkness in the anteroom, waiting. He quickly makes it clear to us that he is waiting for the hour when the street will be deserted. We haven't been seen entering the courtyard by anyone, or have we? he asks anxiously. We hope not. He is at a loss to know what to do with us now. His horses are tired, he came back only this morning, and it is very dangerous to take us so late to the peasant whom he had in mind. By God, he isn't going to suggest now that we ought to go back to the garage, leaving it for tomorrow night? His wife breaks the oppressive silence by mentioning a derelict house not far away – again it is guesswork, for I cannot follow all the words – where we could hide ourselves. Her husband – she calls him Abrasha – on reflection, agrees.

Provided with half a loaf of bread and accompanied by her good wishes, we follow Abrasha.

Keeping close to the houses we manage to pass unnoticed by three drunken soldiers, who are bawling a Ukrainian folk-song in the middle of the lane.

Abrasha has stopped before a shrub, which marks the opening of a place. Across it we can see an immense two-storied building bathed in moonlight. He tells us to wait behind the shrub, as he wants to reconnoitre. We see him slip into the extreme end of the building, and then come out again.

He advises us to hide on the second floor, in some corner as far as possible from the staircase. His little girl will be playing outside this place tomorrow, and during this time she will come in and leave us some food on the stairs. In the evening he is going to take us somewhere else, or, perhaps, straight to the woods.

A hearty hand-shake and Abrasha is off ...

Both the staircase and the stairs are moonlit, so we keep close to the wall. On the stairs near the landing on the second floor, we come upon a dented, rusty tin-basin full of mortar.

Many doors open to little empty rooms; another door opens to a corridor. Which room shall we choose? ...

We step into a little one, but don't like the look of it. Of course, it is nonsensical, we have not come to rent a room, and even if this were the case, I couldn't say that I would have any reason not to like it. But there we are. We open the next room close to the corridor. After a brief spell of time in it, we leave this one too, and return to the room on the right, which seems to have formerly been a kitchen; the place for the range can still be seen. Why should we return to it? I do not know either. One room is as good as the other. But did not Abrasha say we should hide in a room as far as possible from the staircase? And this former kitchen is very near to it. I go out to try the handle of the door to the corridor, but on second thoughts go back to the room. Yes, one room is as good as the other.

Crouching down by the open window we cover ourselves with my overcoat.

16th July

Very early in the morning we are roused from a fitful sleep.

We sit up.

I hear voices in front of the building. Passers-by? No! No passers-by. Voices that seem not to withdraw at all. Now we can distinguish German and Ukrainian voices, but can't make out the words themselves.

The house is not tenantless then?

And the tin-basin on the stairs leading to the *second* floor?

All of a sudden a racket is heard coming from below: Hammering and sawing!

Where are they working? Outside – inside the building?

The brakes of vehicle have been applied with a jerk, and the vehicle has screeched to a standstill; it seems to be just underneath our very window.

We have turned pale.

Nervous as she is, and wholly unaware of what she is doing, Anişoara has let the tiny ball of bread she was kneading drop out of the window. The blood is throbbing in my veins. Has it been seen coming out of the window? Where are the people standing precisely?

Some minutes have passed ...

Voices again ...

The voices seem to come up from the ground-floor.

The noise of hammering and sawing continues.

Yes, they are working on the ground-floor!

Snapping German voices ...

Footsteps along the first floor! Footsteps that are dying away somewhere in the corridor ... Doors being opened and slammed ... Footsteps along the stairs, which lead to the *second* floor ...

The door to the corridor has opened. We look at each other. Suppose we hid ourselves there? I close my eyes for a moment, Anişoara is breathing heavily. Footsteps again. A confused noise of voices. We cannot catch the words. The room which we entered and left on our arrival has been opened. So has been the room next to ours. I prop both my hands against the door, while my glance falls on Anişoara. Both of us are paralysed by the same thought: should they come upon us here they will shoot us on the spot as partisans. We hear them leave the little room. Our knees fail us ...

The footsteps are heard going past our room. The door handle has not been tried.

They have entered the room on our left. Some moments pass.

Again snapping voices. The footsteps are on the landing. Now we hear them going down. Thank heaven! The room we are in is, perhaps, of no importance to them.

Anişoara is smiling ...

I leave the door. It is, of course, still too early to think about slipping out of the building. What is it? Let me see ... I have made quickly for the door. Voices again! Footsteps along the first floor ... along the stairs to the second floor ... on the landing ... in the room on our right, yes ... in front of our room – I do not want to meet Anişoara's eyes. The footsteps are back behind our door and enter the room on our left. Very soon they leave also this one and go past our room into the corridor.

I open the door slowly. It is unthinkable to stand it a third time; we simply have to climb up the ladder in front of our room.

The rungs are rattling as we climb, but we can't help it. We might well be seen from below, or by those who, at any moment, are liable to come out of the corridor, but we simply have to go through with it. Voices are still heard from the corridor.

The garret looks as if it consisted only of a stack of bulky chimneys and beams. Soon, however, we get used to the dim light coming in from a small sky-light, and so we slip to the opposite wall. Hoping for the best, we stoop down behind a chimney across the ladder.

Anişoara has fallen asleep ...

I am thinking of rushing to the door and pressing both my hands against it. It could by no means have made them believe – whoever they are – that the door was locked. How damned foolish of me! And then, when I opened the door, why should there not be a man standing on the landing or near the door to the corridor, or anywhere? How irrationally I was acting!

... Has much time gone by since we chose this hide-out? I have an uneasy feeling that something is wrong. It seems as if I heard a slight rattling of the ladder. I strain my ears. Nothing. Can I have been mistaken? I am still uneasy. Getting slowly to my feet I raise my hand to my lips while Anişoara looks inquiringly at me, and I peep out; *a man is standing by the ladder*, some three yards away.

Have they come upon the paper in which the bread was wrapped and the tin-cup? Of course, it is the tin-cup more than anything that could have betrayed our presence ...

I cannot give it a second thought – no time for thinking – and gesture to Anişoara to follow me on tip-toe along the wall.

Now we have put a distance of about sixty yards between the man and ourselves, having reached the extreme end of the wall.

Anişoara is hiding in the narrow space between the chimney and the wall, while I lie down on the ground, to observe the movements of the man. He seems to be talking to someone below; now, another man is turning up to disappear through the sky-light. He, too, is a civilian. What are the two of them up to?

It looks as if everything is alright. They have not come for us. The man next to the ladder has started to overhaul the chimney. The movements of the second man are not heard at all. What is he doing on the roof? Suppose he chose his way back through the sky-light where he could detect us?

Whistling and singing seem now to come from the second floor. The men are working.

The man has vanished through the aperture, but after a short moment is seen again, holding some tools in his hand. Now he is starting on the second chimney. Is he going to check up all of them?

Time is passing while I keep on observing the man. Finally, he collects his tools and gets down the ladder ...

It is as quiet as a churchyard.

They are sure to have lunch now.

We tip-toe to the opening in the roof opposite our hideout and look out of the sky-light. Across the place, half hidden behind the shrubberies, is the red-tiled roof of the shoemaker's house. His name is Jewish, but his wife appears to be gentile. But he doesn't look Jewish either. Having a Christian wife, he, too – if he is a Jew – might be taken for a Christian by the Germans.

No use speculating. Over there, behind the shrubs, on the left, must be the little lane through which we passed last night. Was it only last night? Now we can see the small group of Soviet PoWs in their bluish-green uniforms, the huge letter 'U' on their backs, who pass the Dohrmann building every day at noon. Has Elsässer been given the letter? I should very much like to know what he said, but, of course, we shall never know, unless, he, too, keeps a diary, which is very doubtful. And Bergmann's reaction? What might Rosa's feelings be now? I don't think they will send her back to the camp for that; I don't think that engineer Bergmann has contacted the SS either. It would be awkward for him to confess that we have escaped from Headquarters. He is sure to announce that for some reason or other, we have 'ceased to live.' But are we really out of the woods yet? When Rosa is back in the camp, I hope she will tell Mrs. Vogelhut that we have left her all our things. Things! Only trash, but they might fetch her some loaves of bread, perhaps.

Hammering, sawing, whistling, singing, and banging on doors have started again.

We slip back to our hide-out.

The man has not come up.

How can we get out of this mess?

...Time is passing slowly.

No more hammering or singing. The house is hushed into a profound stillness. Yet, considerable time must pass before we can risk sneaking down to get out of the building.

The garret is getting darker and darker ...

Through the sky-light we look down upon the street; soldiers are coming out or are going in to the building across the way; it is a 'Soldiers' Home' according to a sign.

The silence has been interrupted again by voices coming from down below. Have the workers not left the building yet? I tip-toe to the ladder. A faint reflection of electric light comes from somewhere, and I can now distinguish the voices of two people talking German to each other; then I hear shuffling feet and the pushing of furniture.

Germans have moved in!

Some ten yards from the ladder there is another gap in the ground, as I came to know by a glance during the break at noon. So I tip-toe to that gap.

No ladder! Perhaps there is one more gap? I continue exploring. There is one, and there is a ladder as well, but now the question arises where it may lead to? Bending down, I try to listen. No sound whatever. Has this ladder any connection to the room or rooms occupied by the 'German voices'? I tip-toe back to the first gap. Voices are heard. Quickly I make for the third gap. No voices! In a hurry we get down the iron ladder. It is the rattling of rungs that is troubling me, but what can we do? On the floor we see the door of the corridor ajar. A faint reflection of light is seen on the threshold. Down we go to the ground-floor, making for the outer door.

It is locked!

Losing no time, we open a door that leads to a small corridor with many other doors, and open one by chance. We find a small room whose floor is covered with scattered straw; buckets half-filled with slaked-lime; tools lying about next to the stove. Two large windows open on to the street, just across from the Barracks. A soldier is passing, whistling a gay tune. There is no use staying here, a chance look from outside might give us away. Pushing open another door we come to a backroom opening on to the lane. Now we crouch down by the window, and wait for a large cloud to conceal the moon. People – male and female voices in German – are heard quite nearby, coming from over the garden by the right angle of the building. Could we be seen in case we get through the window?

Taking advantage of the long-awaited cloud, we let ourselves down the window-sill. I take Anişoara by the waist, and behaving just like lovers who have been spending an agreeable time in a derelict house, we withdraw very slowly, and go back by the same lane as we came yesterday.

Abrasha's wife is in the courtyard. Her eyes widen. They were very upset on account of us, she says immediately. Her husband passed by the building in the morning and saw it was undergoing repairs. He was sure we had been caught.

Abrasha comes out the gate. Acting on his advice, we slip to the back of the house, in case we should be seen by passers-by.

He was not only worried, Abrasha says, that we might have been caught, but also by the idea that we might have given him away to our captors. Now he is doubly glad to see us, but we are unlucky again. It is too late to take us to the peasant.

After some deliberation he is of the opinion we should stay the night in the neighbour's garden, under a tree. Tomorrow morning he will see that we take refuge with the peasant, and the day after tomorrow, that is on Sunday, we shall be taken to Sobelewka, the market-town he mentioned in our first meeting.

Abrasha is forcing his way through a gap in the hedge. We do the same. After a few steps he stops close to a shrub, where we are to hide. Early in the morning, he is going to arrange a hide-out for us with a peasant, he repeats. I am quite well aware that it is very dangerous for him to have us about. We, the 'free game'.

It's rather chilly, but we quickly fall asleep.

17th July

Awake at cock-crowing.

From the topographical point of view the garden we are in now seems to be part of the premises inhabited by the District-Commissioner. If that is so, then the Dohrmann building is opposite the cross-road. Two nights and a day we have made our getaway from there. Stasia is probably suspecting something. Not for nothing did she take me the first time to this shoemaker, when on the same street there are two more shoemakers, as she told me then.

People are astir in the street. Some pass close by the garden-fence. It is too dangerous to remain here, as we might be seen either by passers-by or by the Commissioner's maids. At least, I imagine he has some. So I tell Anişoara to get herself ready to leave the garden; keep to myself the ironical fact that we have taken refuge in the Commissioner's garden of all gardens. There is no need to make things worse than they already are. Crawling along on all fours, we creep through the hedge into Abrasha's courtyard. Next to the apple-tree, at the back of the house, there is a tiny potato plot, into which we now creep, making ourselves as snug as we can.

Gradually, life is starting up all around us. Maids are heard calling the poultry in the Commissioner's garden; shots followed by loud laughter. The residents of the house seem to be practising shooting.

Now Abrasha is going slowly up to the hedge. I signal to him discreetly. He is looking for us, unaware of our whereabouts. I get on my knees. Perceiving me at last, he nods approval and signals back that we should stay where we are. Then he throws some apples in our direction and goes back into the house ...

We are dozing away, the sun in our eyes, but we have no means of defence. All we can do is lie motionless. Voices are heard across the hedge of the garden. An elderly woman's voice in German, another voice in Ukrainian. Children's voices at our head, near the apple tree. Sounds of apples falling to the ground, some have fallen nearby.

Some rustling.

A child is kneeling near us, unaware of our presence ...

It startles us. What if – bless her! It is the shoemaker's little girl. We heave a sigh of relief. But now it is the turn of the little girl to make startled eyes seeing us lying there on the ground. At once, she gains command of herself. Anişoara raises her finger to her lips. The girl winks, rises to her feet, withdraws. Now the other children are heard leaving the courtyard.

A hen comes near. Frightened, she flaps her wings and starts to cackle. Other hens join her in the cackling. It gives us a shiver. Could it attract attention? At last, the hens, too, withdraw.

The sun is burning worse and worse. Apples would be thirst-quenching, but none are close enough.

Time is weighing heavily on our hands.

A beetle has crept in. It reminds me how Anişoara and myself would be mindful of those little creatures while we were engaged in digging on the main road; we used to feel compassion for them as by each stroke we were destroying their homes. What is going on at the camp? Is everything all right there? There can be no retaliation-measures against the camp on account of our escape, since we have run away from the HQ itself. How simply that woman's voice called after us on Monday morning as we were passing through the gate on our way to Gaisin: 'Und von dort nach hause!' Dear old Mrs. Rudich! She sensed what we did not. Her soft voice is still ringing in my ears. Perhaps, in the meantime, they have learned something about the fugitives; a peasant might have had a message. It is strange, that we should owe our escape to a poorly constructed vulture's wing. On that particular day, when Anişoara and I, choosing coloured stones at the gravel-quarry for Hartmann's garden, found ourselves without any escort, the thought of making or risking a getaway seemed absurd! But it looked equally crazy that some hours later we should lock the gate ourselves, when we were once again back within the barbed-wire enclosure of the camp. But how could we have set out on such a venture on that day without any acquaintance to help us? The other fugitives had their friendly contacts in the village of Mikhailowka; all except one of them spoke fluent Ukrainian, and perhaps they still had some jewellery about them.

The green leaves over my head deceive me into seeing a variety of paintings, and by some association of ideas lead me to conjure up before my eyes that goat-like bearded priest in his green cassock, who, suddenly appearing from nowhere on the crest of the gravel-quarry, shouted down to Anişoara and me whether we wanted to buy any beans. I should have liked to portray him instead. This symphony in green over my head could make a painting one day, if I could remember it. Things get forgotten easily, I am afraid. I wonder what people at home would say about the works I shall show them. Will they react in the same way, or in about the same way as some of the people in the camp? To Max, the convoy in one of my paintings if shown as going to the right would have been more effective, than going to the left. Likewise, the ex-journalist from Poland took exception to my showing the church opposite. To Selma the works looked tame, as according to her they did not show sufficient cruelty. While all I wanted to do was depict life in the camp. Have I achieved it? Heaven knows. I feel the pictures in my pocket as the tin-tube is pressing hard ...

... It is now getting cooler. The voices that were heard for a long while in our close neighbourhood, have died down.

It is growing dusky. Abrasha comes towards us. He gives each of us a dish full of sour milk and bread.

It is too bad, but we have to stay the night in the potato-field. At last he has arranged with a neighbour of his to take us tomorrow early in the morning to Sobelewka. The fare will be sixty Marks. Naturally, he has told him our plans. At Sobelewka, it will be quite easy for us to get to the Jewish tailors – the five survivors. They live in some alley off the market. In case we don't find our way, we shall have to ask the address of *Stane*, that is the man who makes trousers.

Back in the potato-plot. The place where we lay throughout the day looks trodden. Let us hope that that the plantation itself has not suffered; we should feel very sorry indeed to have harmed Abrasha and his wife.

18th July

We see Abrasha come out of the house. It is three o'clock in the morning, he says. A young man is grooming the shoemaker's horse; he pretends not to see us.

We had rather fitful hours of sleep. The moon's beams could well have betrayed our presence in the potato-plot, as the leaves are sparse, and we were lying on a slight slope. Fortunately, the couple of village lovers who were spending the night on the ground under the apple-tree did not think of gathering apples in the potato-plot.

Abrasha hands me a pair of grey linen trousers, wide-legged leather-boots, and a cap. His wife has sent out a white kerchief for Anişoara, thus we look like natives, or do we really? Before taking us to the neighbour's, Abrasha instructs me once more how to get to the tailors. We are unlikely to attract people's attentions today as, besides the usual market-day, there is also a pig-market being held today, which is a meeting occasion for lots of villagers and townfolk.

Some men are standing about as we arrive at the neighbour's courtyard. Abrasha gives us good, firm hand-shake and leaves the yard. As for us, we have to wait for more local passengers to come, but, in the end, the cart sets off. It is about five o'clock.

Passing by the shoemaker's house, I give him silent thanks. Moving to the right, the cart comes, all of a sudden, to the front of the building in which we were hiding on Thursday and Friday. Anişoara and I steal a glance at the place where we had our narrow escape. My heart is throbbing.

Stopping at another turning, just a few yards away from the Barracks, the coachman takes on a woman passenger, who sits down between his wife and me. As she does so, she looks straight at me. We have already seen each other, at Abrasha's workshop, and while I was working in front of the Dohrmann building. Does she recognise me? It looks as if she does, since I watch her whisper to the coachman's wife. The next glance I get is sympathetic.

The cart passes a building, surrounded by barbed wire; a guard is standing by the gate.

Now, the railway station, a narrow lane, the highroad to the left:
WE HAVE LEFT GAISIN.

Already a string of vehicles wind slowly in the same direction ...

A signpost marks the way to Winnitza. Let us hope that the way does not lead through Tarassiwka or Mikhailowka.

We are passing villages, bouncing over rails and puddles. Our cart is part of a long procession, farm carts in front and behind, packed with market-folk.

The goal does not seem far away now; we pass people on foot carrying baskets.

It looks as though it is going to rain. The landscape and the passing figures are the colour of ashes, broken here and there with a white patch, a headscarf.

We arrive. Our travelling companions descend from the cart and mingle with the market crowd. The cartman asks for our fare. He whispers a warning to us to be careful here – the SS and the local police keep a strict watch at the Sobelewka, especially in the market-place. We too get off the cart close by a small wooden bridge.

Sobelewka – scores of carts on the hill opposite. On our left is the pig market. Farmers on foot and carts are arriving continually.

Right from the start I find the instructions for tracing the five Jewish tailors are inadequate. Where is this alley Abrasha mentioned? True enough the market-place is on a hill, as he described it, but nothing else fits. Although we might pass for natives of the town we hardly dare to ask for the way – my faulty Ukrainian would give us away immediately.

Ignoring the bustle and uproar of the market, we set out straight away in search of some older man we feel we can trust. Elderly people in the Ukraine are more likely to prove trustworthy – at least I think so, though I may be mistaken. In the end I ask for directions from an old shoemaker, whom I find bent over a pair of shoes in his workshop. I thank him for telling us the way, but, unfortunately, I can make out very little of what he said. In fact, we have to go back, to beg him to repeat the directions again. He is kind enough to go over everything a second time very slowly, but to no purpose. Only after I have been through the thing a third time, this time with a hairdresser, are we able to find our way to the tailors [Plate 16].

They live in what was formerly a public house. A wretched place. No sewing-machine or any other tool of their trade. A large table, a board bed and two rickety kitchen stools provide the furniture, spread through the two squalid little rooms.

Their reception is chilly at first. They take it badly that I asked where they lived from a neighbour who was coming out of his house as we arrived. They let us know this might have placed them in danger. However, they grow more sympathetic as I tell them our story. On the whole they are hardboiled people. I hoped that the fact that we were fugitives from an extermination camp would be enough to make them willing to help us. But I had entirely forgotten that Anişoara and I were only two individuals out of a vast multitude of sufferers. What difference would two people make! What really does count is money! My heart almost missed a beat when I heard one of the tailors mention the sum of five hundred Marks for each of us – this is what the guide charges to take someone across the river. I tell them frankly that the sum left on us after we have paid the fare to Sobelewka amounts to precisely thirty-six Marks. The tailor gives us a shrug. They can't keep us in their house – that would be too dangerous. What they are willing to do is to get in touch with a reliable peasant guide for us. I offer my overcoat. It is still in fairly good condition and might fetch a good price. They will see. That is all I can get out of them.

At that point the door opens and two people come in, two former inmates of Tarassiwka camp. Surprise on both sides, but the surprise at seeing the two of us, of all people, here, is the greater. They arrived at Sobelewka an hour ago, coming from Teplik, having run away form the camp at Ivangorod. As they are Jews from the Ukraine it is easier for them to escape without much outside help. At Ivangorod there was an execution on the eighth of June: thirteen people. On the same day in April the babies were killed with their parents, so were all the old people and the sick.

The five tailors are, in fact, four – one is a joiner. They are not allowed out of the house often. As a rule a boy, the son of the joiner is sent out to buy the week's food supply.

The couple from Ivangorod begged the boy to go off to the market and buy them some food. I wondered whether to follow their example. We are certainly hungry! And he might be able to take my overcoat to the market and sell it. After some hesitation he agreed and left with the coat.

Abrasha came here to this house on Wednesday in the company of a young boy. Unfortunately, the boy was spotted by a militiaman. Arresting him on the charge of being a spy, the militiaman locked the boy up in a cellar. The tailors intervened at once, but only a thousand Mark bribe saved the boy from being handed over to the police and bought his release. He is said to be across the river now.

Four ounces of preserved meat, a little bread, a bottle of milk – that's the last I saw of our thirty-six Marks!

The tale of the boy with Abrasha is worrying me – suppose the two of us had been with Abrasha and the boy that day …

After about two hours wait the couple from Ivangorod set off: their guide to the river and over to the other side will be a woman.

According to the tailors there are people in the neighbourhood of Sobelewka who make a business of smuggling people across the river Bug and bringing food from the other side.

Suspense has mounted since the couple left. What are the tailors going to do with us? The son has returned from the market – the overcoat fetched only two hundred Marks.

The tailors have given in in the end. They will provide a guide for this sum and indemnify in one way or another. I am to hand over the sum of two hundred Marks to the guide as soon we reach Bershad on the other side of the river. According to the tailors Bershad contains a fair-sized Ghetto, where life is more-or-less normal. Against this, I understand that this Ghetto has been called upon to provide a contingent of a thousand workers at the disposal of the Todt Organisation within the last month.

But I am given no time to think about this as the guide has arrived, a tall, fair-haired man of about forty-six with a beard and a moustache. His name is Petco and he used to be a sailor.

His instructions are that we are to follow him a hundred yards behind and if the police stop us, we are to pretend we do not know each other.

Petco is first to leave the house. The tailors leave a pause of a minute or two and then open the door for us. They wish us good luck.

We follow Petco through the alley of the town, then down a country lane, and finally onto the highway.

Carts are coming back from the Sobelewka. Market-day is over.

Petco steps out at good pace, we keep the proper distance. We notice he has been stopped by a peasant-woman. They continue their way together. After a while he parts company with the woman and takes a path off to the left over the open fields. We do the same.

By now the sun is scorching us unmercifully. Hours pass ...

We reach a glade of trees. When we come closer we see Petco sitting on the edge of the wood. Dead-tired we let ourselves drop to the ground beside him. Haven't we heard some shots being fired? And now the voices of men? A patrol? My nerves are frayed raw. I do not tell Anişoara anything. But the voices come nearer. Now, she has heard them too. She looks at me ...

A group of five men comes out of the woods. Civilians. Catching sight of Petco they greet him in a friendly manner and sit themselves down beside him, paying no notice whatever to us. Were they the ones who fired the shots? I see no sign of a gun among them. I put my jacket on, while Anişoara settles herself close to me. She is worn out. How far is it now to the river?

From the other side of the Bug it is another fifteen miles to Bershad – that is if we keep to the highway, and I doubt if we will do that.

Petco and his companions get to their feet and start off together. We maintain our distance. He is certain to have said nothing to them and so we must be even more careful.

Losing sight of their party where the wood made a curve, we would have taken the wrong route along the edge if Anişoara had not caught sight of them through a thin patch of trees – Petco and the civilians were some distance away, walking over open fields. They had left the woods some time back.

It was now the hottest part of the day. Four small carrots, each one no thicker than the little finger, found in one of the fields, do very little to quench our thirst.

Petco and the others stop and sit down in a field of stubble. So do we, at the proper distance.

Almost unnoticed by us, the open field has changed into a valley surrounded by low hills. Cows were grazing at the slopes, boys and girls were playing, running here and there. Petco climbs one hillside, while his companions wander off towards a grove. He stops and waits for us to come up. As we come nearer he plucks some apples from a tree and tosses them to us. Then, thinking quickly, he approaches us and whispers as he walks by that we are to go into the grove and wait for him there until it is dark, when he will come back and join us. I ask him in a low voice to be kind enough to bring some milk for us when he comes back.

We enter the grove. As we lie down beneath a tree we hear the gay voices of the boys and girls and the sound of cow-bells comes across to us up the valley. A drop or two of rain falls heavily on our faces, the vanguard of the downpour which has threatened all day. The raindrops increase in number, falling thickly now and hissing against the close-grown foliage of the shrubs and trees, splashing upon our faces and running in rivulets down our necks.

Anişoara is lapping up the raindrops from the leaves to relieve her thirst. I take this opportunity to shave myself. Unfortunately the lower part of the handle is lost while I am trying to clean the razor. A disaster; but it is already dark and in the leaves and the soft soil I cannot feel anything.

We are waiting. It seems very late. Will Petco come? Suppose he changes his mind because of the bad weather? Where are we now anyway? What if he doesn't come? I don't relish the idea of going on alone without a guide – it would be suicidal.

... The rain has stopped. There is still no sign of Petco. The moon is forcing its way through the clouds. Will it be dark enough to cross the river without being seen?

Anişoara tugs my sleeve, steps are heard.

A darker shadow breaks away from the darkness. A form is outlined by the pale moon – Petco?

Yes. He comes into the grove carrying an empty sack over his shoulder. He whispers to us to take off our shoes and to stow them away in the sack together with our little haversack. Before starting off he holds out a small bottle of milk. We drink greedily.

The way leads through the fields and byways. Our naked feet soon become sore on the rough ground.

Petco stops abruptly.

He whispers back not to move. Something has drawn his attention. Is it a man there, standing beside a shrub? Petco steps forward himself ... Nothing of importance. It is only a young tree next to the shrub. Nevertheless, we have to be very careful. On the left, across a field, are some houses occupied by the border-guards. We continue on our way, now in Indian file, now pressed one against the other, to give the appearance of a single person.

At a turning Petco hides the empty milk-bottle inside a shrub to act as a marker on his way back.

We have reached our target ...

The River Bug.

Petco looks at his watch: Midnight.

19th July

We step down the slope very carefully. All the same I slip and reach the bank of the river before either Petco or Anişoara.

Profound stillness. On the other side there is not a sound, no movement either. Yet Petco wants to make sure that we won't be seen. He waits for a cloud to cover the moon.

We follow him along the bank. Finally he stops, and, taking a look round, he sits down and starts to undress. We do the same. He takes one sack and hands me a smaller one in which we put our clothes.

A bank of clouds drifts over, covering the moon.

Petco steps into the water, feeling his way with a stick. We follow on his heels. The water comes up to Anişoara's neck.

The sack which I am carrying on my head has fallen sideways: Anişoara breathing heavily abreast of me whispers: 'Mind the sack! The pictures are getting wet!' Of course, I had forgotten that they were no longer in the tin-tube, which I threw away in the woods. Another two yards or so to reach the other side of the river, but Petco is almost out of his depth; the stick has touched bottom. He stops, looking now to the right, now to the left; he hesitates. Finally he decides upon the right. We wade up-river, and reach the shoal bank at last.

Another step -

Across to the safer (?) side of the river ...

Profound silence.

Anişoara stoops and kisses the soil.

We dress quickly. Now we have to get out of the way of the gendarmes or border soldiers as quickly as possible. Petco warns us, in case we get caught, not to betray the fact that we have come over with him from the other side.

He steps off again.

Hurrying along the footpaths we steal a glance over our shoulders: The sight of the moonlit Bug makes us hasten!

But, slowly, the river drops out of sight. Thirst is tormenting us once more. Fortunately, we pass some four-legged troughs filled with water for the birds ... Petco is pressed for time, and keeps saying: 'Make haste! Make haste!' We come to the outskirts of a forest, but do not enter it. Instead, we follow the road, running beside it. Anişoara keeps close to me. The dense woods frighten her. They seem endless. At last, we see some houses. Somewhere there is a faintly-lit window gleam. It is about two o'clock in the morning. Petco says, inviting us to sit down near a hay-stack for a few minutes rest.

Again, we walk beside trees till Petco stops once more and stretches out under a large tree on the wood's edge. He falls asleep immediately. Anişoara and I sleep only in snatches.

... Day is breaking.

Petco awakes and fumbling in his pocket draws out a pencil and paper.

He wants me to write a few lines to the tailors, assuring them that we have reached Bershad safely. 'Are we already there?' I ask. 'Well', he says, 'there are still some three miles to go ...' but he is going to part with us at the next turning of the hill, in case we should be seen together. I write the words he wants me to, and while handing him two hundred Marks I thank him for his help. Let us hope the tailors will understand the contents of the note, since I have written German words using Russian letters for them, or at least what I think could be considered Russian letters, but I am not so sure even about that.

According to Petco we have walked thirty-eight miles from Sobelewka to this place.

We pass through more woods and a glade and, for all my weariness, I cannot help glancing now and then at the bright-coloured bushes; I am quite under the spell of a variety of hues: If the bush behind which God showed himself to Moses were it not in the Sinai Peninsula, I could quite imagine He could appear from behind a bush right here!

At this point – at the turning of the hill – Petco takes his leave from us. We have to continue our way alone now. There are no more than two and a half miles ahead, he says to reassure us. My left boot is pinching my foot beyond endurance. To take off my boots would rouse suspicion as nobody is barefoot in this part of the country. But now it is Anişoara who, tired though she is, wants us to hurry on.

On a hill in front of us, we see a little hut, an old man standing on its threshold. We see Petco sitting behind him, but as we come near the hut, he rises to his feet and goes off. Getting some water from the old man to relieve our thirst, and to wash, we follow his advice to leave this path quickly. Gendarmes pass here early in the morning and are due to come back the same way. Cattle are being driven to the meadows. Avoiding the village itself, we arrive at the margin of a field, keeping along it. Now and then we pick up a few peas that are lying scattered on the ground. They have a sweet taste. The field comes to an end, and now we are near an area which looks like part of a collective farm. Just at this moment a girl comes out of the gate. A Jewess, as we learn from her immediately. We receive advice to take a round-about way, as we might get caught on the highroad itself by gendarmes. We ask her to fetch us some water. The peas have satisfied our hunger, for the moment, but we did not relieve our thirst. Drinking from the pail in great gulps, we are interrupted by the girl's sudden warning: 'Don't get nervous, a gendarme has just come out at the turning of the road. He's coming up this way; don't run away; walk slowly to the right.'

She lifts up the bucket and goes back to the gate. We turn round and mix with some herd-boys that are just passing. Unseen by the gendarme we break away and slip into a field of turnips ...

The sun is already high in the sky when we wake up. We had some hours of sleep – of blessed oblivion. After raising my head to make sure that the coast is clear, we take our way through the wheat and rye-fields. I discover too late that I forgot my hat in the fields, but I have to put up with this.

The highroad. A young peasant is standing by the well near the roadside. He lets us have some water. This time I only pretended I was thirsty. I wanted to avoid a face to face encounter with eight gendarmes, who were passing in a cart.

We wait for some time until the cart gets farther on, and then continue our way. Where is this Ghetto then?

A peasant-woman directs us ...

BERSHAD

Bershad at last [Plate 17]. Country-cottages on either side of a rather deserted lane, without any other warning I seize Anişoara by the arm and push her into a yard; there we hide down behind some piles of kindling. A dog-cart carrying four gendarmes was coming towards us. Cautiously we creep out of the yard and keep near the fence.

A boy is coming round a turning, the Star of David visible on his lapel. Looking fixedly at our clothes he slows his steps and whispers to me to leave the lane at once. It is too dangerous! We had better try some other way through the courtyards. The Ghetto is straight ahead, about a hundred yards or so.

We get into the first courtyard that we come across. Young peasants, lying in the shade of a tree, are looking at us. We ask an elderly woman, who is seated on a chair, to allow us to pass through. She nods her permission. Then she calls out after us to keep along the side of the brook.

... Joyful voices of children, and a continual splashing of water burst upon our ears from behind the trees. We cannot distinguish anything, so we take a few steps forward. Now we are on a shady, narrow path, fringed by trees and shrubs. A barbed wire stretches out between the trees and brings us up sharply.

I glide behind the tree, to spy out what is going on beyond the barbed wire:

People holding pails are lined up before a well. Some have their pails on the ground. A young man is pouring water into the pails. A gendarme has just taken some water, and, at present, has his back turned on us. Children are bathing and splashing. A few women are in the brook, washing children or rinsing out clothes.

All wear the Star of David.

The man distributing water is relieved by an elderly man, and he comes strolling over to the tree where I am hiding. He caught sight of me while he was pouring out the water, he says to me. The gendarme is likely to leave soon, so we shall be able to slip inside the wire.

After a little while we lift a strand of the barbed wire and creep under it, from the trap of the camp into the trap of the Ghetto ...

31st July

Behaving in much the same way as someone who suddenly comes into a cold room after spending too long outside, exclaiming: 'What splendid warmth!' - we too were tempted to overlook the grim reality of the ghetto, seeing only this 'warmth.' But here, as at Mikhailowka, on the other side of the river, the length of time and the continual cruelty have turned brutality into the normal state of life: here, just as at Mikhailowka too, people have become familiar with it. But it might be Mikhailowka too, when the girls start singing – under their breath of course - as they walk along the main road. Hearing them one day the T.O. man Ulrich said: 'I don't understand where you lot get the strength to sing – I'm writing my daughter in Germany to tell her how you behave.' And didn't the slaves at Mikhailowka come back from their work bringing the first snowdrops to the sick, who had been forced to stay in the camp, with the words: 'How nice it was! What a pity you weren't able to come out and work'? Here in the ghetto, just as at Mikhailowka, it seems that the harsher the rules against living, the stronger is the desire to live. The people here, living in much the same conditions as those on the other side of the Bug, cheat themselves with the same illusion that they are free. For them the barbed wire becomes invisible.

An hour after we arrived, other fugitives from across the river came to see us at the well. The question of where to put us up presented an almost insoluble problem: it was forbidden to give shelter to strangers. In the end, however, they managed to find a relative of Rosa's who agreed to give us lodging for ten Marks a day.

We left the well to be taken, stealthily, to our landlady's house. The houses appeared to lean on one another. People were crowding the doorsteps; in the small, ragged, narrow streets there was a noisy, bewildering vitality, which disconcerted us altogether. It was if we had come from a real world into a wholly unreal one.

In the evening, one of the fugitives (who incidentally, was Mizzi's husband) told us that the three Jewish militia men, in whose precinct we were, had asked for hush money. Two hundred Marks! He would see to it that they came down to one hundred and fifty, and would advance it for us ... And we had thought that those who had not been transported across the river Bug would hold out a helping hand to us. A hand, yes, but for hush money!

The day after our arrival, a physician had to be called in. The boot had played havoc with my foot, and a minor operation had to be performed.

2nd August

Looking out of the room, Anişoara pointed out a man who was just passing. His ascetic figure made him look like Jesus Christ, and I was anxious to meet him. Our landlady said she would invite him to come in: he is a Rabbi.

10th August

I have shown my water-colours and drawings to a pharmacist today. Incidentally, the water-colour representing the interior shows the marks of water splashed when the sack tumbled in the river: I am determined not to show them any more. He has made me furious. Looking at them, he said contemptuously:

'Rot! What you have painted is small beer compared to our experiences. In fact, you don't show anything worth looking at. You ought to have been with us in the woods at Cosautz; there, mind you, things would have haunted you so much you would have had to paint them.'

It's all in vain! We just do not understand each other. How curious it is to vie in outdoing one another in tales of misery and ordeal.

12th August

At noontime, Pepi arrived to see us, breathless. Danger was imminent, she said. It is plain that those from across the river, the fugitives, are in peril. It is said that the gendarmes were searching through the houses tonight. We have no documents at all, nor can we prove that we are inhabitants of this place. In any case, I shall hide my water-colours and drawings.

13th August

The night was quiet.

I cannot help thinking of Abrasha. When I first met him, he said he would take us to the woods, to the partisans, who would provide us with identity-cards for this side of the river. Admittedly we were not in the woods, but he was, either on that Wednesday or Thursday on his way to and from Sobelewka. Why did he not bring cards then?

22nd August

Three more fugitives have arrived in Bershad.

Partisans attacked the camp. Glasbrenner was stabbed to death, a guard hanged, and the other guards stripped naked and disarmed. Taking advantage of the utter confusion that followed, five people ran away. Two remained with the partisans in the woods, while the tinker and the hairdresser-couple were waiting there for an opportunity to cross the river. In the woods they saw Abrasha, who told them about Anişoara and me. It was Abrasha, too, who directed them to the tailors. At the tailors, spending a night in the basement, they saw the boots, trousers and the cap I had sent back from Bershad.

3rd September

We came upon Frieda this morning unexpectedly.

She had been hidden all the time at Mikhailowka, in a house opposite the camp. A peasant-woman had given her shelter. From the window she could see the convoy marching off daily to the road. Then, after the camp was attacked by partisans, she felt safe no longer, and took to the woods. From there she arrived at Bershad.

18th September

Another three fugitives: two women and a young man.

They made their getaway taking advantage of the general break-out, and of the fact that they were working close to a village.

After the attack launched by the partisans, and the escape of the five, the SS and men from the Dohrmann came early in the morning to ascertain the damage. In the afternoon, the inmates were told to pack. All of them were taken to Tarassiwka. There the T.O. believe themselves protected against any partisan attack. The camp is in charge of three commandants, one of them is a Schmidt, who is reported to outdo his predecessors in cruelty. Lithuanian soldiers have been sent to the camp again. It seems that Joseph, the ex-chauffeur of my brother Manfred, was looking for us. One day, as Mizzi Hart was working with other young women at the station, a German driver came close to her, asking discreetly for information about the painter and his wife. Rosa has come back to the camp.

16th November

Segall was on this side of the river. He is said to have been seen together with Elsässer and quartermaster Becker. The latter two continued on their way to Romania, to collect food and things for those in the camp, while Segall was left behind in the Ghetto at Moghilev. Getting back from Romania, they took Segall with them to Tarassiwka. Two loaded lorries were said to have crossed the river Bug heading for the camp.

18th November

Food-prices in the Ghetto have soared up [Plate 18]. A glass of salt is now fifteen Marks; it has risen from about two Marks. Whenever the Soviet Army advances there is a rise in the price for salt. I never thought salt was such a luxury.

3rd December

All the houses of the Ghetto have to be whitewashed.

6th December

Nobody is allowed to leave their house. People learn that a Commission of the International Red Cross is to visit the Ghetto.

16th December

Woollen clothing has arrived for the inhabitants of the Ghetto, sent by the International Red Cross.

The camp at Tarassiwka was entirely exterminated on the 10th of December.

18th December

To her surprise, Anişoara was suddenly embraced by a bearded man in the market. It was one of the tailors – or was he the joiner? All five of them have taken refuge in Bershad. In the afternoon, another of them surprised me by calling on us. He was delighted to see us. He apologised that at Sobelewka they had been so harsh at the beginning towards us. They simply had to. On assuring themselves, however, that we really were without any means of paying the guide, they decided to lend a hand in our rescue.

25th December

We learn to our great surprise that the Red Cross has intervened on our behalf and we are to be sent to Tiraspol. A town on the river Dniester, I think; nearer to Romania, at any rate.

5th January 1944

After leaving Bershad on the 31st December on the way to Tiraspol via Balta, gendarmes took Anişoara and me to the station at two in the morning. We were not the only people: twenty-one partisans, men and women, and two Jewish couples; the latter have to do time at the prison at Tiraspol for having left the Ghetto in Bershad without a permit. They were hand-cuffed two by two. The chains rattled. The convoy was moving slowly, hindered by the chains from going any faster ... After some hours, the slow-train arrived. There was no room left for our convoy. Waiting ... at two in the afternoon, we were driven outside. A freight-train was on the point of leaving. After half an hour we got off the train, exchanging the vans for an open platform – orders. A heavy wind kept blowing. Almost numb we arrived in Birsula, an important junction. Soldiers filled the waiting-room. We were herded on the floor-stones behind a counter. I heard an Austrian soldier being rebuked for his drunkenness by his German comrades: 'Emperor Franz Joseph is sure to come again' I heard him stammering.

Towards morning we boarded a slow-train, and since we are relatively free, that is, not hand-cuffed, or under special arrest, we are seated only the two of us, in a carriage next to German soldiers. One of them, an N.C.O., starts talking to us: 'All that is going on now in the theatre of war is simply strategy', he says. 'There is a world-shattering invention we are going to show the whole world next Autumn.' He laughs heartily.

At Razdelnaia, the junction for Odessa and Tiraspol, we got off and boarded a carriage marked Golta-Bucharest, bound for Tiraspol ...

10th January

A fugitive from the camp at Talalaiwka, who – I don't know by what means – has come to Tiraspol, has confirmed the general action. On Monday, the thirteenth of December, in the camp she heard two T.O. men speaking between themselves; one of them told the other that the camp at Tarassiwka had been exterminated on Friday night. Segall and his elder daughter, Ruth, were amongst the first, Livia and Edy followed. The last seem to have been Heinz with a little child in his arms, presumably Mucki.

18th February

According to statements by peasants, the execution lasted six hours, having started at five in the morning. There are two graves in the orchard, next to the camp, covered with lime ...

Bucharest, 12th August 1945

I have sent a registered letter to Abrasha, thanking him and his wife for their help. Among other things I have mentioned that I am going to publish a book on all the events in the camp, and that I have dedicated it to him, his wife and their little girl.

I have also asked him whether the victims have in the meantime been exhumed, begging him to let me know the details which were available.

Lacking an exact address, and unaware of his family name, I was obliged to write the following on an envelope:

'To the shoemaker Abrasha – in Russian it reads SAPOSHNIK ABRASHA – who has a wife and two little children, and lives in the same street where the German District Commissioner used to have his residence.'

The letter has been translated into Russian for me by my neighbour, Dr. Tarnawski.

23rd May 1946

I have received a letter from Mrs. Jenia Evghenia Efimovna from Gaisin. Translated from the Russian, it reads:

Dear unknown Arnold Daghani, It is most likely that you shall want to know who has written this letter to you. You see, it has been just a matter of chance. Your letter was lying undelivered at the post-office and one day, seeing me, an acquaintance of mine handed me the letter. My name is SAPOSH-NIC, and the letter was addressed to ZAPOSHNIC. Neither of us was aware that the addressee had Saposhnic as profession and not as a second name. Reading the letter at home, I became aware of the grave character of its contents, and resolved to learn the fate of the people you have been showing interest in, and then reply to you. It is with great regret that I have to break the news to you that Abrasha, shoemaker by trade, of Jewish faith, his Christian wife, and their two children have all of them died at the hands of the German barbarians. Abrasha, who stayed behind during the German occupation, enlisted with the partisans, helping them in many respects, and was finally killed, together with his family.

The camps Tarassiwka and Mikhailowka were liberated by partisans at some date, some saved their lives, but most of the people perished. As to the graves you have been asking about, nothing particular has been undertaken.

That is all I can write about.

Excuse the late reply, but it is not my fault; the letter has been lying for a long time at the post-office.

Dear unknown Arnold Daghani, I should like to read your book very much. Do not refuse my request, and let me know the title of the book, which I shall read with interest.

I was born in Gaisin. I have been re-evacuated. My husband whose name was also Abrasha, and his family name was Saposhnic, was killed in action. My name is Jenia Evghenia Efimovna. I, too, have two children.

Address: U.S.S.R. Gaisin
District Winnitza
Tupic, 4-a, Comulnaja
House No. 1
SAPOSHNIC.

THE END

120

Appendix: 'Too Few Atrocities'

MIRON GRINDEA

Editor of *Adam: International Review* (1961)

From the Preface to the *Adam* edition of *The Grave is in the Cherry Orchard*:

There is a danger of a new type of literature being established which literary history might one day classify as 'atrocity writing'. The recent spate of psycho-analytical journalese and statistics on Eichmann, most of them contradicting one another, have appealed to readers for mixed motives, to say the least of it. Even works of poetical restraint and nobility of feeling, such as *The Diary of Anne Frank*, have been mercilessly exploited for commercial or political reasons. Perhaps it is one of the conditions of our half demented society that great human documents cannot be left to speak for themselves. Thus much creative writing, like any other object of modern entertainment, soon becomes subject to publicity fashion.

We do hope that the poems written in the extermination camps, sometimes a few hours only before their authors passed the threshold of the gas chambers, will be rescued from oblivion and translated into as many European languages as possible. [...]

When Daghani's manuscript was submitted in 1946 to a number of London publishers, the author was told – invariably – that nobody would be interested in reading yet one more book about such unpleasant experiences. War memories were too recent and the wounds on the public mind were too raw to be enhanced by further writing in that vein. Perhaps having a right sense of values is to be unpredictable in our approach to life. Indeed, as recently as last year, Daghani's manuscript was submitted to an important literary agent. Her comment was – to quote exactly – 'good, but too few atrocities!' [...]

Since that time *The Grave is in the Cherry Orchard*, which the author wrote direct in English, has appeared in a German translation under the title *Lasst Mich Leben* (Weg und Ziel Verlag, Tel-Aviv, 1960) and is now about to appear in a few other European languages. Arnold Daghani (born in 1909 at Suceava, Bukovina, a fragment of the now legendary Austro-Hungarian Empire, which afterwards became part of Romania) has also become a remarkable painter and ever since he emigrated to Israel, in 1958, his art has grown in deftness and colouristic excitement.

The publication of Daghani's Diary in a full issue of *Adam* is not prompted by the orgy of Eichmanniana to which we alluded already. In 1946 we printed Daghani's first piece of writing in English, *So this is the end*, which showed pronounced literary talent and aroused wide interest in the writer. We feel that *The Grave is in the Cherry Orchard* is not only a haunting document of our time but also a work of literature in its own right. Written with a flaring gift for dense observation it captures a rich mixture of poetry and squalor, of cruelty and goodness which makes these memoirs both wryly diverting and superbly tragic. The striking coinage of words, imperfectly as it may sound from a purist's point of view, brings out the essential contribution made by Daghani to a language which he had taught himself out of sheer indebtedness to English culture.

The story of how one of the inmates succeeded in getting 'preferential treatment' by painting the faces of his torturers and those of their mistresses is as fascinating as the circumstances in which he and his wife (also an artist) had the nerve to take the works away. While crossing the river Bug almost naked they carried the bundle containing the water-colours and drawings on their heads, and whenever the treacherous full moon came out the clouds they risked being shot by the Romanian sentries who were patrolling along the banks. During a second getaway the works were tucked all round Anişoara Daghani's body under an enormous peasant cloak. As to the actual description of the main escape from Gaisin, we consider this to be one of the most accomplished passages in post-war writing. [...]

PART III

MEMORY AND CREATIVITY

3

The Diaries of Arnold Daghani

DEBORAH SCHULTZ

A 2001 book review defines a diary as 'a "perpetual middle". It has no shape or design, no beginning or end. If it reads like a work of art, then the writer is less interested in capturing the moment as it passes than in making an elegant impression on his (or her) assumed audience. The diarist in aesthetic disguise is no diarist at all.'[1] Arnold Daghani's diaries had shape and design, but no beginning or end. They were extensive; indeed, everything Daghani produced can be seen as part of a complex and extensive diary, relating to his experiences and observations as artist, survivor and exile. This impression is particularly due to the way he signed and dated everything, frequently giving the name of the place too. His extensive output of drawings, paintings, folios, objects, books, diaries and manuscripts chart his life; they cover what he saw, felt, thought, his nightmares and his dreams.

These diaries, both verbal and visual, are fragmented and repetitive, with some periods barely covered, while others are examined in minute detail, over and over again; the structural chronology is countered by this sense of unending circularity. Daghani's tireless revisions seem to highlight the impossible space between the event, memory, verbal and visual representations, while the proliferation of different formats give a sense of his frustration at not being able to completely represent in any medium his experience of what happened. For none are mimetic, all involve filters, while even at the time that it takes place the event is transferred through our subjective responses to which memory immediately adds further layers of interpretation.

DIARY?

The term 'diary' may be used for Daghani's written works because he used the diary structure of days. The core of the diary works is the text in English shorthand that he wrote in the slave labour camp at Mikhailowka and the ghetto at Bershad (1942–43). Whether or not on a daily basis, the text was written where and when the events took place. Upon returning to Bucharest in 1944 he wrote up the notes into a manuscript that was published in Romanian in 1947, with translated versions in German, in 1960, and in English, in 1961 as *The Grave is in the Cherry Orchard*.[2] Until his death in 1985, he would keep returning to his experiences of this period, rewriting the text, often painstakingly by hand, and reworking the images. In two monumental handwritten works, the book, *What a Nice World* (1943–77) (Plate 20) and the album, *1942 1943 And Thereafter (Sporadic records till 1977)* (1942–77), he rewrote his diary from Mikhailowka and Bershad, adding further details, drawings, paintings, memories and evidence from the legal investigations in Lübeck. Each of these intensely worked objects comprises around 300 pages, gradually built up and added to during a period of around thirty-five years. These multi-layered works bring together images and writings from different time periods, interweaving memories with current events. During the 1980s in Hove, when illness made handwriting difficult, he worked on typed manuscripts such as *Let Me Live* (1980s). From the 1960s to the 1980s he also compiled a three-volume *Pictorial Autobiography* which combined personal photographs with reproductions of artworks and documentation.[3]

But are these diaries? Apart from the original shorthand version, should any of these texts accurately be described as diaries? More appropriate terms may be 'autobiography' or 'memoir'. However, these terms may also be problematic. 'Autobiography' is primarily constructed for an audience, while with 'memoir' the role of memory is foregrounded; by contrast 'diary' sounds more factual, less manufactured, and less interpretative.

Daghani's bookshelves indicate his interest in writings of this kind. Whilst living in Hove, he compiled a book of text and images titled *Homo Ludens or The Most Personal Catalogue of Books etc.*, in which he listed his books shelved around his apartment.[4] Works he owned included the published diaries of Goebbels, Thomas Mann, Anaïs Nin, Max Beckmann and Witold Gombrowicz, as well as Henry Miller's *My Life and Times*, Nadezhda Mandelstam's autobiography, *The Memoirs of Hector Berlioz*, François Mauriac's

Mémoires Intérieurs, James Joyce's *A Portrait of the Artist as a Young Man* and Isaac Bashevis Singer's *In My Father's Court: A Memoir*.

With regard to his own works, Daghani employed a number of different terms. He used 'diary' for various versions, including the later expanded versions. He also described some as 'Fragments of memoirs' and 'memoirs'. He used the term 'an autobiographical story' to refer to 'Noodles and Buttons in Cakes of Soap', which he wrote in a narrative style of the period in Cernauți preceding deportation, a style more usual for fiction than autobiography. This story is written within *What a Nice World*, the complex structure of which may be seen as a visual analogy for the workings of Daghani's memory. Some events are told repeatedly and in detail, seemingly prominent in his mind, while the various narrative and artistic forms may be seen as reflecting various emotions associated with his experiences.

These labels – diary, autobiography, memoir, testimony – relate to notions of representation, and that space between event, word, image and memory. Anca Vlasopolos, of Romanian origin who emigrated to the United States, describes her book *No Return Address: A Memoir of Displacement* as a ' "fictionalised" autobiography' and in the preface asks 'where does the truth of an individual's history reside in a narrative labelled autobiographical?'[5] In *What a Nice World*, Daghani depicted himself with his hand raised as if taking an oath with the inscription 'The truth, the whole truth, nothing but the truth'. His diary thus becomes a testimony to what he witnessed, emphasizing the telling of truth. Perhaps the term 'life-testimony' would be more accurate. As Shoshana Felman defines it, 'A "life-testimony" is not simply a testimony to a private life, but a point of conflation between text and life, a textual testimony which can *penetrate us like an actual life*.'[6]

This term seems particularly appropriate for Daghani's diaries, as they are not just about what happened to him. Daghani was strongly motivated to continue reworking the texts for the sake of the other inmates. His duty as survivor was to tell about what happened in this and the other forgotten camps of this area in Ukraine, across the river Bug. Detail and accuracy were highly important for him. He made an image of how he imagined the final killings of the Mikhailowka inmates in 1943 but claimed that he destroyed it because it lacked authenticity: 'an illustration of a shuddering scene, not seen by myself' (Plate 21).[7] Instead, he narrated the episode in less direct ways: for example, 'So This is the End', a short story in *What a Nice World*, in which he imagined that he and his wife Anişoara were also killed. He reconstructed the events from his imagination and from the testimony of others, with the event remaining a void at the centre.

Diary, then, implies something written at the time, while testimony comes later and relates to memory and trauma. Daghani's written works were based upon a diary structure from the time of the event; later additions derived from memories, but also from later events, such as the court depositions, based on memories, but that shed new light on the original events. Memory was less of a structuring agent, as it would be in an autobiography or memoir, but one aspect of an ongoing multi-layered process.

LANGUAGE AND WRITING

The court proceedings had a significant impact on the structure of the diary, disrupting and fragmenting its temporal flow, and adding other voices to the narrative. Daghani gave a formal deposition to the Public Prosecutor in Lübeck, followed by depositions by employees of the engineering company as well as Nazi officers. However, after nearly ten years of investigations the proceedings were annulled as inconclusive for lack of evidence.

Daghani incorporated these depositions in varied ways, the most striking of which is in the typewritten manuscript *Let Me Live*. Here he added footnotes, some of which became so extensive that they dominate the space (Plate 22). The page was split into sections with coloured felt-pen outlines indicating the various sources of the material. This cumulative working process suggests the nature of history as a combination of sources, some presented as memory, others as fact. Points of view are offered as parallel accounts, simultaneously, providing a very postmodern reading. Hayden White asks: 'Can these events be responsibly emplotted in any of the modes, symbols, plot types, and genres with which our culture provides us for making sense of such extreme events in our past?'[8] Daghani's method seems to accept that no single response is sufficient nor can be fully representative. Rather, he can be seen as working around the events and his memories of them, incorporating various narratives in an openly fragmented format.

What was the language of Daghani's written diaries? Maurice Blanchot writes about *L'Écriture du Désastre* (The Writing of the Disaster), in which l'écriture has been interpreted as meaning both the physical activity of writing as well as the marks that are made (as opposed to *écrit* which refers to what is written).[9] Both aspects of Blanchot's *l'écriture* are important in Daghani's work as well as the language he uses. He often wrote in English. The first version of the diary from the camp was in English shorthand books and the published versions, including the Romanian edition published in 1947, were originally written in English. Subsequent versions were also written in English with some parts in German, for example from the Lübeck investigations. Why Daghani wrote in English is unclear; he was certainly an Anglophile, reading extensively in English even in Bucharest in the 1930s while working as a translator in an import–export company. He may well have hoped that English would reach a wider audience that would respond to what he had to say.

Daghani's diaries describe people and events that he witnessed, with lengths of entries ranging widely between a couple of lines and a few pages. The entries narrating the Daghanis' escape from Gaisin in July 1943 are particularly detailed and this change in pace adds to a heightened tension. He wrote of life in the camp, the other inmates, their work, living conditions, the guards and officers, the engineers, bringing the situations to life by recording conversations and observing the interactions between people. He added his thoughts, often by raising questions or ending a comment with three dots, thus not stating explicitly.

Daghani's writing renders his verbal works highly visual. For handwritten versions he employed a variety of calligraphic forms ranging from Old English to a Neo-Gothic style that he used most often. The pages and pages of this rather laboured, elaborate writing clearly convey the immense commitment he made to these projects, not least regarding the amount of time it would have taken to write so much by hand in this way (Plate 23). The sense of a personal endeavour is clear, while the use of handwriting seems to attest to the authenticity of the work: Daghani was there and this is what he witnessed. The old-fashioned style of the writing also seems to confirm the importance of these works, alluding to legal documents or religious manuscripts. He often decorated first letters as in illuminated manuscripts and used gold paint extensively. The sense of spirituality, biblical references and personal effort made by the artist, combine with these visual elements to make these diaries immensely potent works.

What of writing as an activity? Daghani seems to have seen himself primarily as an artist rather than as a writer, although in addition to the diaries he produced a number of poems, short stories and other pieces of prose, while written inscriptions often formed an integral part of his visual works. For Daghani, writing the diaries does not seem to have been a cathartic process; it seems to have been rather a circular activity in which writing led to more writing. Paul Celan wrote about writing as a means of working through: 'In this language [i.e. German] I have sought, then and in the years since then, to write poems – so as to speak, to orient myself, to explore where I was and was meant to go, to sketch out reality for myself [...] These are the efforts of someone [...] who goes with his very being to language, stricken by and seeking reality.'[10] Celan's experience of being 'stricken by' reality also provided a means of 'seeking' reality through language. As Shoshana Felman argues, 'it is to give reality one's own vulnerability, as a condition of exceptional availability and of exceptionally sensitised, tuned in attention to the *relation between language and events*' (italics in original).[11]

What was the aim of Daghani's writings, in particular the handwritten versions? When Daghani went to Lübeck to give his deposition he took *What a Nice World* with him, hoping to find a publisher for this bulky item with over 300 pages, weighing in excess of twelve kilograms. But who would publish such a thing and how? Practicalities would surely make it impossible or at least highly unlikely. In *L'Écriture du Désastre*, Blanchot makes the point that seems to reflect Daghani's activity too: 'Not to write – what a long way there is to go before arriving at that point [...] One must just write, in uncertainty and in necessity.'[12]

Thus Daghani's writings suggest both a personal fear of forgetting and a broader fear of the inmates and the camps in Ukraine being forgotten by history. As he carefully wrote and rewrote the events of those years, the process of making seems to have become as significant for him as the resulting works. Each time he wrote he recalled, and his guilt of surviving when others perished became intertwined with his anxiety about the impermanence of memory and the danger of forgetting. As his frustrations intensified at the lack of public interest in the camps in Ukraine, with all the attention focused on better-known camps such as Auschwitz, he felt ever more strongly that his account had to be heard, that victims deserve to be commemorated even if their death is undramatic. He commented, 'since Mikhailowka, Tarassiwka and other death-camps across the Bug did not boast of any furnace of cremation, a gas chamber and all the miscellaneous accessories, they are looked down upon by publishers and journalists'. However, at Mikhailowka and in similar places across the Bug, 'the inmate had to climb down into the grave and wait for the bullet. Then the grave was filled up and covered with lime. That at the time of the incinerator!'[13]

Daghani's rewritings and revisions may seem to contradict the authentic nature of diary writing, raising the question of whether a diary can be rewritten. However, his practice relates well to the Jewish tradition of Midrash in which biblical texts are continually reinterpreted over time and no single interpretation is regarded as primary. Midrash relates to a tradition of remembering, questioning and reconstituting the shared and subjective contexts that commemorate the past, and Daghani's accumulated footnotes and margin inscriptions correlate with this tradition of adding to and rewriting interpretations.

IDENTITY AND 'AESTHETIC DISGUISE'?

To what extent do these carefully constructed books and folios reflect a carefully constructed identity? To refer back to Paul Bailey, was Daghani in 'aesthetic disguise'? In his numerous self-portraits and reflections on his position and destiny as an artist, Daghani often seems to have carefully constructed his identity, attempting to ensure that his account and depictions would become known. This construction, however, is combined with a strong involuntary current that cuts through his experiences, haunting him with memories of the other inmates from Mikhailowka. Some diaries are never meant for publication but his clearly were, and he certainly intended to make an impression on his audience. The reader/viewer does not have the sense of discovering something in them about a person's private thoughts and emotions; this was not their aim. Daghani's words and images are highly valuable as source material and revealing of human relations in the most extreme conditions, while their subjectivity tells of the individual's experience, awareness and interpretation of history.

NOTES

1. P. Bailey, 'In the Waiting Room' [book review of Ned Rorem's *Lies*], *Times Literary Supplement*, 31 August 2001, p.17.
2. A. Daghani, *Groapa este în livada de vişini* (Bucharest: Socec & Co, 1947); A. Daghani, *Lasst Mich Leben* (Tel Aviv: Weg und Ziel Verlag, 1960); A. Daghani, *The Grave is in the Cherry Orchard*, published in M. Grindea (ed.), *Adam: International Review* (London) 29, 291–3 (1961). The German version was translated into the Hebrew by Leander Rosengarten, the sister of Heinz Rosengarten who perished in Mikhailowka, and published by her in Haifa in 2000; a copy is held in the Center for Advanced Holocaust Studies, United States Holocaust Memorial Museum, Washington, DC. The German version was republished with explanatory essays in 2002: F. Rieper and M. Brandl-Bowen (eds), *Lasst Mich Leben! Stationen im Leben des Künstlers Arnold Daghani* (Springe: zuKlampen Verlag, 2002).
3. A. Daghani, *A Pictorial Autobiography*, vols. I–III (1940–60; 1960–63; 1963–76), unpublished books, Arnold Daghani Collection, University of Sussex (hereafter ADC), C53–55.
4. A. Daghani, *Homo Ludens or The Most Personal Catalogue of Books etc.* (1949–82), unpublished book, ADC, C26.
5. A. Vlasopolos, *No Return Address: A Memoir of Displacement* (New York: Columbia University Press, 2000), p.ix.
6. S. Felman, 'Education and Crisis, Or the Vicissitudes of Teaching', in S. Felman and D. Laub, *Testimony: Crises of Witnessing in Literature, Psychoanalysis, and History* (New York and London: Routledge, 1992), p.2, italics in original.
7. See E. Timms, 'Accumulated Testimonies in the Arnold Daghani Collection' in this volume, for further discussion of this image.
8. H. White, *Figural Realism: Studies in the Mimesis Effect* (Baltimore, MD and London: Johns Hopkins University Press, 1999), p.28.
9. See translator's remarks in M. Blanchot, *The Writing of the Disaster*, translated by Ann Smock (Lincoln, NE and London: University of Nebraska Press, 1995), p.xiii.
10. P. Celan, 'Speech on the Occasion of Receiving the Literature Prize of the Free Hanseatic City of Bremen', in P. Celan, *Collected Prose*, translated by Rosmarie Waldrop (Manchester: Carcanet Press, 1986), p.34.
11. Felman, 'Education and Crisis', p.29.
12. Blanchot, *The Writing of the Disaster*, p.11.
13. A. Daghani, *What a Nice World* (1942–77), unpublished book, ADC, G1.041v.

1. Nanino at the window (in Czernowitz) awaiting full of apprehension my coming home. Too much of a risk in the streets…
(1942) in 1942 1943 And Thereafter (Sporadic records till 1977) (1942–77), ink and watercolour on paper
(G2.053r) (Arnold Daghani Collection, University of Sussex © Arnold Daghani Trust).

2. *Ivan, third sentry* (1943), watercolour on paper (Collection of the Yad Vashem Art Museum, Jerusalem © Arnold Daghani Trust).

3. Pieta (The death of Selma Meerbaum–Eisinger) (1942), pencil on paper (Collection of the Yad Vashem Art Museum, Jerusalem © Arnold Daghani Trust).

4. New Year flowers for Nanino (1943) in 1942 1943 And Thereafter (Sporadic records till 1977) (1942–77), ink and watercolour on paper (G2.060r) (Arnold Daghani Collection, University of Sussex © Arnold Daghani Trust).

5. *Camp interior* (1943) in *1942 1943 And Thereafter (Sporadic records till 1977)* (1942–77), watercolour on paper (G2.063r) (Arnold Daghani Collection, University of Sussex © Arnold Daghani Trust).

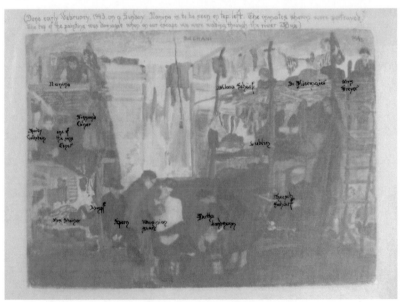

6. *Camp interior* (1943) in *1942 1943 And Thereafter (Sporadic records till 1977)* (1942–77), watercolour on paper with tracing paper overlay (G2.063r) (Arnold Daghani Collection, University of Sussex © Arnold Daghani Trust).

7. The stables at Mikhailowka (1942), ink on paper (Collection of the Yad Vashem Art Museum, Jerusalem © Arnold Daghani Trust).

8. *Portrait of Pita Mihailowski* (1942), watercolour on paper (Collection of the Yad Vashem Art Museum, Jerusalem © Arnold Daghani Trust).

9. *Work on the highroad* (1942), watercolour on paper (Collection of the Yad Vashem Art Museum, Jerusalem © Arnold Daghani Trust).

10. Eintritt *Verboten* (1942), gouache on paper (Collection of the Yad Vashem Art Museum, Jerusalem © Arnold Daghani Trust).

11. *Evening Prayer* (1943), pencil on paper (Collection of the Yad Vashem Art Museum, Jerusalem © Arnold Daghani Trust).

12. *The life-giving soup* (1943), ink on paper (Collection of the Yad Vashem Art Museum, Jerusalem © Arnold Daghani Trust).

13. *Against the wind* (1943), pencil on paper (Collection of the Yad Vashem Art Museum, Jerusalem © Arnold Daghani Trust).

14. *"Intestinal T.B."* (*Musia Korn, 18 years old*) (1943), watercolour on paper (Collection of the Yad Vashem Art Museum, Jerusalem © Arnold Daghani Trust).

15. Kaiser's room (1943), watercolour on paper (Collection of the Yad Vashem Art Museum, Jerusalem © Arnold Daghani Trust).

16. *One of the five tailors* (1943), watercolour on paper (Collection of the Yad Vashem Art Museum, Jerusalem © Arnold Daghani Trust).

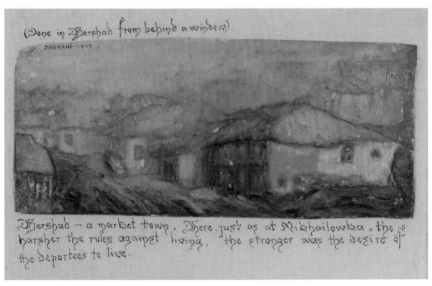

17. *The sight of Bershad* (1943) in *1942 1943 And Thereafter (Sporadic records till 1977)* (1942–77), watercolour on paper (G2.101r) (Arnold Daghani Collection, University of Sussex © Arnold Daghani Trust).

18. *Ghetto market, Bershad* (1943), watercolour on paper (Collection of the Yad Vashem Art Museum, Jerusalem © Arnold Daghani Trust).

19. *Mass graves, Bershad* (1943), watercolour on paper (Collection of the Yad Vashem Art Museum, Jerusalem © Arnold Daghani Trust).

20. *What a Nice World* (1943–77), spiral-bound sketchbook with mixed media (G1) (Arnold Daghani Collection, University of Sussex © Arnold Daghani Trust).

21. *Mikhailowka Camp* (1943) pencil on paper (Collection of the Yad Vashem Art Museum, Jerusalem ©
Arnold Daghani Trust).

Arnold Daghani as an Artist: Life and Representation

DEBORAH SCHULTZ

The work of Arnold Daghani reveals an artist who was both a witness to the world in which he lived, and a witness to his own life as an artist. His life and work were closely connected, with numerous self-portraits testifying to an ongoing examination of the dilemmas he faced as an artist and as a survivor. Memories of the slave labour camp at Mikhailowka continued to haunt his art, while his work after the war engaged with the challenge of Socialist Realism in Romania and the changing artistic styles of the Western world. He drew on the dominant forms of Modernism in works ranging from line drawings and watercolours to collage and assemblage, while adding his own innovative approaches too.

Daghani's eclectic range of artistic practices makes his overall achievement difficult to categorize. He also wrote extensively, in forms ranging from diaries, poetry and short stories to forensic accounts of legal investigations into the camps in Ukraine, from commentaries on artistic trends to reflections on contemporary events. Often these writings were combined with drawings, paintings and pre-existing objects, raising questions about aesthetic hybridity. His interdisciplinary approach, bringing together images with words, personal visions with historical documents, has meant that his work has only recently begun to receive sustained critical attention.

WATERCOLOURS THAT SAVED LIVES

Arnold Daghani was born into a German-speaking Jewish family named Korn in Suczawa, Bukovina, then on the eastern borders of the Austro-Hungarian

Empire. In 1918, the town became Suceava as the region was incorporated into Greater Romania. His parents encouraged him to study commerce and, apart from short periods in the late 1920s in Munich and Paris, he received virtually no artistic training, a factor that would play a significant part in his self-perception as an artist. When he moved to Bucharest in the early 1930s, he adopted a new artistic identity as Arnold Dagani. The name derived from 'dagan' (the Hebrew for Korn), a play on words that hints at the artist's sense of humour. While making his name sound less German (and, therefore, Jewish), it also indirectly affirms his Jewish identity. In 1959, in Israel, his name was misspelt with an 'h', but it was a variant that he decided to retain. A letter recalls his brother Manfred's suggestion that the 'h' might serve as an 'amulet', standing for 'Happiness, Hail, Hope, Harmony'.[1]

On 27 June 1940, Daghani married Anişoara Rabinovici, from Piatra Neamţ, whom he called Nanino and who was known by others as Anna. In the 10 November 1940 earthquake their home in Bucharest was badly damaged, and they relocated to Cernauţi, the regional capital of Bukovina (formerly the Austro-Hungarian city of Czernowitz, now Chernivtsi in Ukraine). The move would be a near-fatal mistake. For a while Daghani worked manually painting toys, but after the Germans passed through the region in June 1941, thereby returning it to Romanian control, Jews were only allowed to carry out menial tasks.[2] In June 1942, after months of uncertainty, they were deported to the slave labour camp at Mikhailowka, to work for the August Dohrmann engineering company, part of the Todt Organisation. Their work was on the Durchgangstrasse IV (or DG IV), a strategic supply road linking occupied Poland with southern Ukraine.

Daghani's record of events at Mikhailowka from 1942 to 1943 provides a fascinating account of life in the camp. His diary was published in Romanian in 1947, followed in 1960 by the German translation, *Lasst Mich Leben*. It was not until 1961 that the original English text was published in the Anglo-French literary journal *Adam* under the title *The Grave is in the Cherry Orchard*.[3] The Romanian and English versions included reproductions of a number of works Daghani had made in the camp. Indeed, it was his artistic skills that enabled him and Anişoara to escape. Ironically, he had been reluctant to take his watercolour box with him when they were deported. In *What a Nice World* (1943–77), an extensive collection of his writings and drawings bound together in book format, he recalls the scene when two plain-clothes policemen came to their room in Cernauţi to issue their deportation order. One of them noticed the box of watercolours and sketchbook that was being left behind:

> Why had we not packed them, too? he wanted to know. Seeing the shrug of my shoulder, he ordered me to open the rucksack and to put the colours and sketchbook in. I refused stubbornly, saying: 'We are being sent to death and you expect me to take them? To what use? No, I am not going to take 'em.' 'To what use?' he answered back. 'They might just save your lives; one never can tell.' As I went on being refractory, he made Nanino open the rucksack, and both sketchbook and colours were placed on top.[4]

Daghani emphasized that it was not his decision to take the watercolours with him, but in Mikhailowka he became known as an artist, commissioned by several of the guards to paint their portraits or interior scenes of their rooms. In some cases, as he records in his diary on 5 December 1942, he was offered bread or apples as a reward. A complex hierarchy meant that for lower-ranking guards he would have to make the works secretly. Paper was in short supply. Although a priest gave him writing paper to use for watercolours, a police sergeant was unable to buy paper in a local shop as it was reserved for officers. In the introduction to his diary, Daghani ironically observed: 'It is easy, it seems, to become a master over the lives and deaths of men: for that, the rank of a sergeant is sufficient – but it is not enough to enable one to buy writing-paper!'

In April 1943 the engineers Werner Bergmann and Josef Elsässer commissioned Daghani to make an eagle mosaic at their headquarters in Gaisin, a town at some distance from Mikhailowka. Daghani insisted that his wife should be his assistant. Bizarre as it seems, in the middle of the war, Daghani and Anişoara were commandeered to embellish the engineers' garden. No transport was available to take them there every day from the camp, so in June it was decided that they would stay in the headquarters' garage until the mosaic was completed. During those few weeks they came into contact with Abrasha, a shoemaker and member of the local resistance, who offered to help them escape. The Daghanis were hesitant, not believing escape was possible, and fearful of the consequences for their fellow inmates in Mikhailowka.

However, one night in mid-July the plan was carried out, described in dramatic detail in the diary. They were due to be sent back to Mikhailowka as the mosaic was complete, but at the last minute Bergmann asked Daghani to paint some parchment for a lampshade as a gift for Atti Grae, the secretary with whom he was romantically involved. Painting this gave Daghani and Anişoara an extra night at Gaisin. They hid that night in an empty building where they miraculously escaped being discovered by German soldiers. After spending the second night in a garden and the third in a potato field, they were given clothes by Abrasha so that they could dress like peasants and join a cart going to the nearby town, Sobelewka. There they met a guide whom they followed on foot for around forty miles. That night they crossed the river Bug and reached the Romanian-held territory of Transnistria and the relative safety of the ghetto in Bershad.

A few weeks later, Mikhailowka was attacked by Ukrainian pro-Soviet partisans. Some inmates escaped but the remainder were relocated to the nearby camp of Tarassiwka until early December when they were all killed. Daghani was deeply traumatized when he heard what had happened, and in memories and nightmares until the end of his life he recalled his fellow inmates. In this way, being an artist became intimately connected with his guilt at surviving the camp when the other inmates were killed. As he wrote many years later: 'Not to this very day have I been able to get rid of the horrifying thought how our fellow inmates were butchered one after another. By right we should have shared their fate.'[5] At the same time, however, they seemed to be fated to survive. When Anişoara's shoes needed mending, Stasia, a kitchen hand, had taken Daghani to Abrasha, rather than one of the other shoemakers in the town.

Daghani continued to draw and paint during the months of hiding in Bershad, depicting the small houses and witnessing everyday life in the ghetto's streets. In an unpublished interview Shoshana Nauman, who was a young girl at the time, remembered an artist, the 'stranger', who came once or twice and drew in her home. She recalled that she once also saw that stranger drawing in the central square of Bershad where the market was held.[6] Recording the camp or the ghetto without permission was considered a major offence, and those assisting the offence also faced punishment; it was a risk that, unlike many people in the ghetto, Nauman's family was prepared to take.

Daghani's respect for the dignity of the persecuted Jewish community is expressed in one of those works, a middle-distance view of the ghetto market, showing a crowd of men and women clustered around their paltry wares (Plate 18). The viewer might interpret this as a simple market scene, were it not for the threat conveyed by Daghani's inscription: 'Done clandestinely, from behind a window, in Bershad in the early autumn, 1943'. Another watercolour of that period, titled *The House We Found Refuge In – Against Payment* (Plate 24) conveys a greater sense of menace by means of spatial compression. This close-focus view of the cramped quarters in which he and his wife were hiding uses sombre colours and angular distortions to create a claustrophobic intensity. The inscription again draws attention to the risks of continuing to paint under such conditions: '"Caught in the act" would have entailed my facing the court-martial.'

In late December 1943, with the assistance of the Red Cross, Daghani and Anişoara were able to return to Bucharest, where they arrived in March 1944, a few months before Romania was 'liberated' by the Red Army. When Daghani was looking for a means to travel from Bershad to Balta, on their route to Bucharest, a ride by sleigh was offered, and then refused, by a man named Norn, secretary at the ghetto town hall, who panicked when he thought that they might be carrying those clandestine paintings with them. Daghani's comment is revealing: 'Now I knew where I was with him or with them: afraid to run into trouble on account of my works.'[7] When they found other means of transport, he sewed his artworks inside the lining of Anişoara's coat. In Balta they bumped into the secretary again. 'His first question was: "What have you done with your works?" "I've left them in Bershad", I answered hypocritically, patting at the same time Nanino's back inconspicuously, lest the works in her sheepskin coat should burst with laughter. "That was well done", Mr Norn said approvingly.'[8]

Such detailed observations bring Daghani's reminiscences to life, highlighting many unexpected moments. While only a short time previously they had been working as slave labourers in a camp and living unregistered in a ghetto, on the train journey to Bucharest a senior German officer offered Anişoara a seat. He remarked that 'among the senior officers there were two with the distinctive mark of the SS'. The situation became even more incongruous when one of the officers, 'on learning from Nanino that I was an artist, introduced himself to me as a fellow-artist of Bonn'.[9] Daghani recorded such encounters in straightforward language, with details that emphasize their unexpectedness. By means of such expressive anecdotes he succeeded in capturing, in both writings and paintings, the paradoxes of the Nazi era. He was well aware that the elegant German officers with their cultural aspirations could also be trained killers.

GENRE PAINTING IN THE NAZI PERIOD

In addition to artistic works 'commissioned' by the guards and engineers at Mikhailowka, Daghani secretly produced around fifty drawings and watercolours that give a sense of the inmates' life. These works have survived a long journey: hidden in a metal tube in the camp, carried in a sack above his head across the river Bug, then smuggled back to Bucharest. In a striking phrase in a diary entry dated 2 January 1943, he described these works as '"genre"-like'. They include portraits, interiors, and scenes of inmates at evening prayers, at work on the road and at the gravel pit.

The concept of 'genre painting' suggests scenes of everyday life, such as those painted in the Netherlands during the seventeenth century, or in France, England and elsewhere during the eighteenth and nineteenth centuries. It might appear incongruous to revive this idiom in the face of fascist oppression, when life was far from ordinary. However, Daghani's works demonstrate that even in the most desperate surroundings, familiar aspects of life continued: going to some kind of market, daily routines, spending time in domestic settings. The limited focus of the genre tradition was apt for an artist working in secret and Daghani's scenes of everyday life under German occupation have powerful resonances. The 'woman at the window' motif, rendered with serenity by artists like Pieter De Hooch and Jan Vermeer, becomes an expression of acute anxiety in *Nanino at the Window* (1942), where Daghani depicts his wife's shoulders tense with fear (Plate 1). In place of jolly peasants or leisure scenes, he shows us slave labourers with shovels shadowed by armed guards, or lines of famished figures queuing for a bowl of soup (Plate 12). In such politically calibrated scenes, visual understatement becomes a poignant expression of suffering. The narrative tradition of genre painting entirely suited Daghani's subtle and suggestive images, to which his inscriptions added further layers of meaning.

A heightened effect is achieved when particular incidents are endowed with Christian iconographic connotations, such as the woman giving birth in the stables. The scene after the death of Selma Meerbaum-Eisinger, as the body of the 18-year-old poet is reverently lowered from her bunk, acquires a strong religious resonance (Plate 3). Daghani was criticized, both by inmates, and by later viewers of his work, for not directly depicting the brutality of the camp. An extended diary entry dated 17 July 1943 reflects on this issue:

> I wonder what people at home would say about the works I shall show them. Will they react in the same way, or in about the same way, as some of the people in the camp? To Max, the convoy in one of my paintings if shown as going to the right would have been more effective, than going to the left. Likewise, the ex-journalist from Poland took exception to my showing the church opposite. To Selma the works looked tame, as according to her they did not show sufficient cruelty. While all I wanted to do was to depict life in the camp. Have I achieved it? Heaven knows.

In a later reflection, Daghani commented on how he heard Selma 'express her point of view that Art should, and even must be biased, if one wants to show the inhumanity we've been subjected to in the Camp'. But the artist responded: 'Is there any need to exaggerate, if reality itself has been showing us that the sky is the limit?'[10] Recalling Goya's *Disasters of War* and Manet's *Execution of Maximilian*, he argued that they acted primarily as artworks to which the atrocities are secondary. For Daghani, 'a person who looks at works which are said to depict the atrocity he or she has been through, wants a pictorial reflection of that exact feeling of reality. That standpoint is, of course, biased, but the "bias" is diametrically opposed to that voiced by Selma.'[11] His impulse was to emphasize the dignity of the inmates rather than portray them as victims. Despite the conditions in which they were forced to live, they took care, for example, to keep clean and arrange their living quarters as well as possible. Showing executions and beatings,

> would certainly lower the almost super-human dignity with which people [...] went to the grave [...] The mother removing her worn jacket, gives it to her son; a short embrace; the mother and aunt kissing Sally good-bye; the quiet prayers of the ninety-one-year-old and the blind man. Why cheapen that by atrocities painted or drawn, even if they surpass imagination and 'happen' to be true.[12]

The artist was selective in his representations while aiming 'to depict life in the camp'. Summing up his aims, he observed: 'I do not show crimes in the way of being committed, but martyrology of another kind.'[13] For him, art should operate within certain limits: 'Mozart said somewhere, even if music wants to depict the most horrible situations, it must never hurt the ear.'[14] Thus, genre painting of daily life, rather than dramatic or heroic renditions of major events, suited Daghani's visual style. He used a similar understated technique in depicting the room of Hermann Kaiser, one of the T.O. commanders (Plate 15). The simple design and delicate colouring look innocent enough until one notices the portrait of Hitler hanging in the top right corner, 'icon-like' as Daghani notes in his diary on 29 April 1943. Although the term 'genre' was originally used to distinguish such works from history paintings, it is precisely through the detailed and nuanced portrayal of everyday events that the artist conveyed the drama and complexity of human experience.

In Bershad the response to Daghani's works was again mixed. As he noted on 10 August 1943:

> I have shown my water-colours and drawings to a pharmacist today [...] I am determined not to show them any more. He has made me furious. Looking at them, he said contemptuously: 'Rot! What you have painted is small beer compared to our experiences. In fact, you don't show anything worth looking at. You ought to have been with us in the woods of Cosautz; there, mind you, things would have haunted you so much you would have had to paint them.' It's all in vain! We just do not understand each other. How curious it is to vie in outdoing one another in tales of misery and ordeal?

Lya Benjamin has commented that while responses to his works varied, from a German soldier voicing concern that the images could be used against them, to the inmates viewing them as objects for posterity, all considered them as documents rather than as works of art.[15] However, other early viewers were more sensitive to their aesthetic qualities. A number of the works from Mikhailowka and Bershad were featured by the Romanian Jewish cultural journal *Răspântia* (Crossroads) between 1944 and 1947.

In contrast with the visual works, Daghani's written diaries record more acts of brutality, although written in a straightforward narrative style, without graphic detail. Crucially, he wrote up the text from notes after he returned to Bucharest, whereas the drawings and watercolours were produced in the camp and ghetto. As Ziva Amishai-Maisels has indicated, prisoners tended to make rather objective recordings due to a necessary repression, for allowing their feelings to be fully expressed while in the camp would have made their traumatic experiences more difficult to survive psychologically.[16] While many artists did represent death and suffering, comparably understated images can also be found in the works of many other inmates.[17]

In portraying the inmates as dignified people rather than as victims, Daghani affirmed their existence as human beings. He treated them as individuals and recorded their characters with great warmth and perception in both images and texts. By doing so, he was able to give a more comprehensive picture of the interactions between individuals within these exceptional circumstances. He was also interested in the engineers for whom they worked, as well as the SS and SD officers running the camp. His treatment of them too as individuals indicates his strength of character and attempt to understand events from another's point of view.

During the 1960s, the German Public Prosecutor in Lübeck investigated war crimes in the slave labour camps in Ukraine for which Daghani's diary provided significant source material.[18] Formal legal depositions about events at Mikhailowka were given by Daghani, and by twelve employees of the August Dohrmann company, as well as several of the Nazi officers identified in his diary. These officers included SS-Unterscharführer Walter Mintel, a deputy camp commandant, who would claim that he had never been at Mikhailowka. In 1971 the investigations were annulled for lack of hard evidence. Daghani obtained transcripts of all of the testimonies and related documentation in four large files, from which he handwrote extracts into his albums and added sections to his revised diary. The investigations led the Daghanis to make contact with some of the August Dohrmann employees, namely the engineers Werner Bergmann and Josef Elsässer, and their former secretary Martha Fischer (née Grae). Daghani wanted to know more about their motives for being part of what he terms the 'extermination-cum-forced labour camp'. Perhaps surprisingly, they became friendly, met and corresponded until they died.

Daghani's tolerance reflects a great spiritual generosity reminiscent of that to be found in the diaries of Etty Hillesum, a Dutch Jew who died in Auschwitz. Hillesum recorded how she was asked by a friend, 'What is it in human beings that makes them want to destroy others?' to which she replied 'Human beings, you say, but remember that you're one yourself [...] All the appalling things that happen are no mysterious threats from afar, but arise from fellow beings close to us.'[19] A similar insight underlies Daghani's artistic decisions and his approach to people. The way he responded to his fellow inmates and captors, with gentleness and a wish to understand, directly informed the artistic decisions and the formal qualities of his works.

ARTWORKS AND MEMORY

The drawings and watercolours made in Mikhailowka and Bershad form a fragmentary visual diary. A particularly striking pair of images relates to the camp, escape and Daghani's later memories. The watercolour showing the interior of the prisoners' accommodation (Plate 5) is among the most elaborate of his genre paintings with its evocative detail: the colourful clothesline, the wobbly ladder, the woman rinsing a cloth in a bucket. What could be more homely than the figure of the barber in the foreground, shaving a seated man? But these are prisoners living in appalling conditions under the constant threat of death. On the upper margin, the artist noted the water damage that occurred when he and Anişoara were wading across the river Bug; thus, the highly significant point of crossing in their escape from Nazi-occupied Ukraine to the relative safety of Romanian Transnistria left its indexical mark on the image, an imprint to authenticate it. Some years later, he added a layer of tracing paper on which he noted the names of those depicted (Plate 6). This can be seen as a material metaphor for the layering of memory, but it also enhances the pathos of the scene. The female figure perched top left on an upper bunk is a portrait of Anişoara while the seated man in white who is being shaved by Herr Korn, the barber, is not a fellow prisoner, but one of the Ukrainian guards. It is a scene that can be read as a narrative of intimate oppression, highlighted by subtle colour coding (what prisoner could possibly possess such a white shirt?).

In this case Daghani's use of tracing paper to identify the characters of his dramatic scene was a practical solution. In other works he added semi-transparent paper with more elaborate inscriptions as a means of combining text and image. This practice recalls Charlotte Salomon's series of gouaches, *Leben? Oder Theater? Ein Singespiel* (1941–42), in which painted inscriptions over-lay images in a close integration of the two media. Geographically, these two artists were displaced to opposite ends of Nazi-occupied Europe, but aestheti-cally they were impelled towards the same conclusion. Their paintings required verbal amplification in order to do justice to an unprecedented emergency.[20]

In a self-portrait dated 1972, Daghani represents himself painting the same domestic scene (Plate 25). The artist is depicted from behind, as if in his memory he was watching himself working, or as if he was present as observer of a situation in which he himself had been an observer as an artist. Time becomes fragmented and interwoven; in this memory he does not recover the scene but adds himself to an enlarged field of vision. The earlier work may have prompted his memory to produce the later work, helping him to recall the occasion, while the relationship between them can be seen as indicative of the nature of memory. Even without such prompts, Daghani clearly had a remarkable memory, exemplifying what Lawrence Langer terms survivors' 'insomniac faculty' in which the process of remembering is not one of reviving decades-old memories which may be subject to inaccuracy as 'there is no need to revive what has never died'.[21]

The self-portrait of 1972 condenses time and reflects the involuntary nature of Daghani's memories. For while the artist is depicted working, the haunting faces of his fellow inmates, killed in the camp, are recalled in light washes, as if present in his memory. Although he stated beneath the image that 'The slaves shown are real portraits of them', the faces seem generalized rather than specific. This is also true for a number of other works in which faces are fragmented and layered, with interconnected frontal and profile portraits. Some faces are barely visible, ghostly, colourless shadows but whose presence seems clearly felt. Two Nazi soldiers were depicted with the inscription: 'At the place of execution, waiting for the slaves to arrive, as henchmen are apt to do' (Plate 26). In the grey space around the officers, Daghani drew the faces of those fated to die.

RELIGIOUS ICONOGRAPHY

Central to Daghani's practice as an artist lies his sense of spirituality. Although he and his wife were raised in Jewish families, he turned to both Jewish and

Christian iconography in order to depict and express his experiences. His fellow inmates were also Jewish and, as we can see in works such as *Evening Prayer* (Plate 11), some of them regularly took part in religious rituals. During the 1950s in Bucharest, he became close to Daniela Miga, a Romanian Orthodox poet and artist. From this period there are many depictions of Christ on the cross, Madonnas, Pieta scenes, monks and churches. A series of *Stations of the Cross* was exhibited in 1963 and later reproduced in a lithographic edition with an introductory text by Philip Rawson and a poem by Christopher Fry. In their abstracted essentiality focusing on elements of the cross and hands, and the use of black and white, they recall the series of Barnett Newman (1958–66).

Daghani's interest in Christianity was clearly profound and did not simply arise due to his circumstances. It seems to have been part of his complex and highly individual religious identity. It is suggested that at some stage he converted to Christianity, although it is unclear if this was carried out formally. There is a possibility that he became a Lutheran in Cernauţi in 1941, when it seemed that a baptismal certificate might provide protection against deportation. In his legal deposition given in Lübeck in 1965 he claimed somewhat ambiguously to have been a 'Protestant Jew' during the early stages of the war. However, in letters to Daniela Miga, in the archive of the Museum of Art, Constanţa, particularly those written in the late 1950s and 1960s from Israel and France, he wrote of how he was then considering converting to Christianity. Although his works on Christian themes were sometimes described as his best, he did not wish to be identified in narrowly confessional terms; 'I shouldn't like it', he asserted, 'since I never wanted to be unilateral.'[22]

Daghani's work is pervaded by religious iconography. The large works such as *What a Nice World* resemble medieval manuscripts in the use of calligraphy, gold paint and illuminated first letters. A 1954 gouache reworking of *Evening Prayer* indicates the way in which Jewish and Christian motifs were closely connected for him (Plate 27).[23] The painting is untitled but an inscription states that it is 'based on Evensong', the name for evening prayers in the Church. In the original drawing the men are separated from the seated figures; however, in the later painting men and women share a more intimate space. The ladder at the centre of the painting, a functional item within the living quarters, can also be seen as a religious motif. An important symbol both in Judaism, reminiscent of Jacob's ladder to heaven, and Christianity, with reference to the deposition from the cross, the ladder seems to highlight the way in which Daghani extended a drawing of every-day life into a painting with dual religious connotations.

In his diary he drew direct parallels between certain events in the camp and Christian narratives. His entry for '9th December' describes how:

> In the evening a woman is having labour pains. Cowering in her cage on the ground, her thirteen month old daughter is playing by her side, while her husband looks helplessly at his wife. In the other cages, life is going on as usual [...] In the welter of happenings, the event of the woman bringing forth the baby has passed unnoticed. As our doctor is coming in at the door, everything is all right. We have *increased* in number ...
>
> I can't help thinking of an analogous case which happened two thousand years ago. Then it was a publican's wretched deed and now it is a plurality's affair.

Daghani's account of this particular event gives a good example of his approach to representing life in the camp. No image of this scene was repro-duced in his original diary, but a 1955 pen and ink drawing seems to relate to the event, showing the baby being washed (Plate 28). The stillness and intensity of the scene, together with Daghani's commentary, lend the draw-ing a sacramental quality.

This may be contrasted with the entry in his original diary for 30 December 1942, when he was so moved by the religious implications of the scene after Selma's death that he responded to it both verbally and artistically: 'I have made a pencil drawing, fifteen by fifteen centimetres, having Selma being taken down on two ladders, as subject matter which I witnessed about a fortnight ago. It reminds me strongly of "Deposition from the Cross". Here we are, then, when Nativity and Pieta are presented again to our eyes. But do we really see?'

Daghani's perception of a Christian analogy in a camp scene raises the event above the squalor and brutality of life in the camp, portraying the inmates with great dignity and reverence. A pencil drawing made in the camp and reproduced in the *Adam* edition of *The Grave is in the Cherry Orchard* depicted the scene. It shows the body of Selma being passed down and a number of figures seated in the surrounding 'cages' (the term Daghani used to describe the small bunks) (Plate 3). A drawing of 1955 developed the religious feel of the scene by focusing more closely upon the central characters and by emphasizing the cross-section structure of the bunks (Plate 29). The biblical reference is made explicit by a sheet of tracing paper lying over the top of the drawing with the ink inscription from the Gospel of St John: 'Then took they the body.'

Daghani was, of course, not the first Jewish artist to draw analogies between the suffering of the Jews and of Christ. Works by Maurycy Gottlieb, Mark Antokolsky, and Marc Chagall, to name just a few examples, also made such an analogy: however, with fundamental differences. For these artists did so by emphasizing the Jewishness of the figure on the cross. In *White Crucifixion* (1938), for example, Chagall painted a prayer shawl wrapped around Christ's waist, and wrote 'Jesus of Nazareth, King of the Jews' in Hebrew letters above his head as well as the more conventional 'INRI' abbreviation. By contrast, Daghani's Christ was presented as a symbol of suffering, for both Jews and Christians. So although on the cover of a 1954–57 folio he portrayed a conventionally bearded Christ with the inscription 'My God, my God, why hast Thou forsaken me?', rather than make a more explicit self-portrait as in comparable works by Chagall, the voice is, in fact, Daghani's. The most accurate representation of his own suffering seemed to lie in identifying with Christ, while narratives from the New Testament related appropriately to the experiences of those around him.

This mixing of religions is central to Daghani's character, and a curious diary entry from the period spent in the ghetto at Bershad reflects his thinking. As they were not registered in the ghetto and not supposed to be there, he and Anişoara had to hide during the five months until they were able to begin the return journey to Bucharest in December. The paintings and diary entries, then, from this period were made from inside places of hiding. Within this context, just two weeks after arriving in Bershad, he made the following diary entry for 2 August 1943: 'Looking out of the room, Anişoara pointed out a man who was just passing. His ascetic figure made him look like Jesus Christ and I was anxious to meet him. Our landlady said she would invite him to come in: he is a Rabbi.' The text indicates a strong spiritual sensibility that foregrounded religious experience. That the man was, in fact, a rabbi, suggests the way in which the two religions were so closely interrelated for him, recalling the Jewishness of Jesus.

In a further drawing, dating from 1975, Daghani constructed a clear parallel between the suffering of the Jews in the camps and that of Christ.[24] In this rather crude drawing he wrote the names of all the camps in south-western Ukraine on a cross, around fragments of a figure, with the words 'I am the Light' in place of the torso. The inscription beneath the image reads: 'An appropriate monument to the victims of killing action, and to their murderers as a monument of shame: SS, SD, Police, Organisation Todt, Latvians, Lithuanians, Ukranians'.

The drawing acts as a monument both to the victims and to the camps which historical research has greatly neglected. While attention is focused on 'concentration' or 'death' camps such as Auschwitz, the numerous 'slave labour' camps in Ukraine have, until recent years, been virtually forgotten. However, as Daghani often pointed out, these designations are largely meaningless, for the majority of those at Mikhailowka were also murdered, and so it too could be termed a death camp. He was compelled not just to commemorate the other inmates, but to remind the world of the existence of these other camps where many died.

Why did Daghani feel that a cross would be 'an appropriate monument' to these Jewish victims? An explanation has been provided by Monica Bohm-Duchen: 'After the war, the analogy between the martyrdom of Christ and that of the Jews became almost a commonplace: indeed, when Dachau was liberated, the road through the camp was renamed "The Way of the Cross", while Pope John Paul II could refer to Auschwitz as "the modern Golgotha".'[25] Although this particular drawing was made by Daghani in 1975, he had also used the analogy earlier, while in the camp at Mikhailowka. Furthermore, his use of the analogy seems to be very personally felt, rather than as a public manifestation.

Did Daghani wish to imply that the suffering of the Jews in the camp would also lead to redemption? Franz Meyer, in a comment on Chagall's *White Crucifixion* that is equally relevant to Daghani's work, suggests that this Christ is not portrayed as redeeming the world: 'Here instead, though all the suffering of the world is mirrored in the crucifixion, suffering remains man's lasting fate and is not abolished by Christ's death. So Chagall's Christ lacks the Christian concept of salvation. For all his holiness he is by no means divine.[26] Daghani's Christ, as Chagall's, is depicted within specific historical circumstances, to represent Jewish suffering rather than redemption and a

147

particular religious faith.

Thus, although Daghani drew on religious iconography, he did not affirm one particular religion. A 1956 poem, in an unpublished book of writings and drawings, *A Large, a Big Question Mark*, reflects his universality, in which he wrote:

> Whether a Stupa we build,
> Or a Mosque;
> Whether a Cathedral we erect,
> Or a Temple;
> Whether prayers from a Chapel rise
> Or in a synagogue are chanted –
> It is You we praise.[27]

Daghani's commemoration took the form of personal interpretations based upon both Christian and Jewish traditions. Each Yom Kippur, in a personalized version of the Kaddish, the Jewish prayer for the dead, Daghani and Anişoara would recite the names of all their fellow inmates from Mikhailowka, a ritual that demonstrates the continued relevance for him of Jewish traditions. Moreover, he produced many works relating to Judaism, including drawings of Jewish prayers and rituals. Perhaps the most significant are his studies of a Passover Seder, showing his family gathered together in Bucharest. An ink drawing, dated 28 April 1954, titled *First Night of Passover*, accentuates the candles and other ritual objects on the table, while conveying the posture of the human figures of all ages in evocative outline (Plate 30).

Daghani's iconography seems to represent his own spiritual sensibility, which would lead him to perceive religious images in everyday scenes, and a sense of reverence and dignity with which he imbued his subjects. While other Jewish artists have employed Christian iconography to comment on anti-Semitism and the position of the Church during the Nazi period, Daghani does not appear to have had this motivation. Although the resonances of Christian iconography would enable the works to relate to a broader audience, his initial impulse seems to have been a visual response to specific scenes. It was only a short step for Daghani from genre scenes that simply depicted life in the camp to symbolic and spiritual images with broader and more resonant connotations.

POST-WAR ROMANIA

Daghani's self-identification with Christ related not only to his suffering due to his experiences in the slave labour camp and the fate of the other inmates, but also to his struggle as an artist, and the rejection he endured. When he wrote 'My God, my God, why hast Thou forsaken me?' in the mid-1950s, he did so at a critical moment in his life.

In late 1947, when the installation of a communist government became imminent, the artist and his wife were invited by Paul Celan to leave Romania for Vienna and then Paris. Daghani refused, for 'alas, much as we want to, we cannot, we have not the necessary means'.[28] However, soon afterwards, by when it had become more difficult to leave, Daghani and Anişoara began applying for passports.

The creation of the Romanian People's Republic in 1948 led to cultural life being dominated by the Soviet model of Socialist Realism, and until 1957, shortly before emigrating, Daghani refused to work in the officially prescribed style and did not join the Artists' Union. (He later claimed that he joined only on the insistence of the art critic Petru Comarnescu.[29]) He was, thus, unable to exhibit publicly; however, he continued to work actively as an artist while earning a living teaching English. His works from this period locate Daghani, once again, in the role of witness, with drawings of workers and peasants in the streets, as well as sites around Bucharest. In 1949 three of his drawings were published in the newspaper *Flacăra* (Flame). These depict men doing things – a writer, an engraver and a leather dresser. While the writer has an intellectual appearance (he wears glasses and the drawing is in a fine line), the engraver appears as a worker (drawn with a darker, heavier line). The focus of all the drawings is on the hands, actively writing, making and producing.

Daghani's work was rarely directly political. However, while drawing the Triumphal Arch, an illegal act as it was a (Cold) 'war target', he reflected upon how he still had to draw in hiding, as in the ghetto at Bershad: 'Things have, alas, not changed for me.'[30] Having rejected Socialist Realism, he felt artistically isolated; as he wrote on a 1949 self-portrait, 'I have been leading a secluded life, just working for myself. No guidance committee, no socialist realism, no toeing the party line.'[31] His hope was that by emigrating to Israel, by entering the 'Free World' to which he so often referred, his talent would be widely acclaimed, and success and critical recognition would follow.

149

Daghani began developing themes that would preoccupy him for many years, with many fine line drawings of female nudes, and works depicting theatre and circus scenes. He identified with the humorous and tragic clown, and presented his life as the 'Cirque Daghani'. He also produced a series of drawings and watercolours of traditional Romanian dolls in various settings. A notebook contains the signatures of numerous visitors to his home to see his work, including many of the leading figures in the Bucharest art scene of the time, such as art critics Petru Comarnescu and Eugen Schileru, and the artist and then director of the National Museum of Art, Max Herman Maxy. Daghani noted their strong support for his work and their encouragement to go abroad. As Comarnescu told him, 'Although it will be detrimental to our country, you must leave: Your place is in Paris or in New York!'[32]

By the mid-1950s emigration to Israel from Romania became possible and in 1958 Daghani and Anişoara received permission to leave. They had to renounce their Romanian nationality and were given a *certificate de voyage* to leave the country valid for only five days. They had to make their preparations hastily and left behind about 900 drawings and paintings, although for some years before emigrating from Romania, Daghani had been sending small collections of his works out of the country via diplomatic bags.[33] They would reach him, sometimes years later, and added to the vast accumulation of works he produced during the years in Vence and Jona.

EXILE AND ARTISTIC SUFFERING

Daghani soon became disappointed with the 'Free World', as he did not receive the attention he had hoped for or expected. Apart from an exhibition at the *Foyer Culturel* of the French Embassy, Tel Aviv, opened by the French Ambassador, the promised exhibitions did not materialize, and the art world became ever more inaccessible. It was difficult to find a place to live and Daghani and Anişoara were almost constantly on the move. They had embarked upon a long period of instability in exile.

In 1960, after less than two years, they left Israel and stayed temporarily in London with Anişoara's sister, Carola, a pianist, and her husband, Miron Grindea, publisher of the Anglo-French literary journal *Adam*, who introduced Daghani to many leading figures in the British art world, such as the architect Sir Hugh Casson, and Helmut Ruhemann, consultant restorer at the

National Gallery, who compared his work to that of Matisse, Picasso and Klee. They also stayed for a short while in the small town of Jona, Switzerland, near Zürich, where they were the guests of a wealthy friend, Lotte Stiefel, whom they had met in Israel. However, they were unable to obtain residence permits for either place. When the conditions on their Israeli passports expired they became officially stateless and Daghani wrote in despair, 'Which country will receive us? We have too long been standing on one leg. Like me, Nanino is waiting for a miracle to make its appearance round the corner.'[34]

They moved to the south of France, to Vence, where Daghani was initially supported by the Count Michael Károlyi Foundation, and where they stayed for ten years. There he hoped to become involved with the vibrant art scene, dominated by the leading Modernist artists whose work he admired such as Picasso, Matisse and Chagall. His output was mainly a mixture of nudes, portraits, landscapes, abstracts and works on musical and literary themes, and continued to develop in new directions, in many media. He commented on his experiences as an artist, often with black humour, and on contemporary life, particularly pop and hippie culture. He began making collages that he called 'alienations', in which parts of photographs, generally of female nudes, were transformed into figures and objects. These works range from the witty and ironic to the rather more sharply satirical, such as the series *Swinging Art in the Twentieth Century*, which was exhibited, together with the *Love* series, at the Institute of Contemporary Arts, London, in 1970. Daghani continued to combine the visual and verbal, bringing together drawings with poems and short texts in folios based around themes as varied as Ovid's love poems, eroticism, the circus, the Ten Commandments and the electronic space age. Some folios focus on particular figures who lived in the area, such as Katherine Mansfield, while a particularly striking folio follows scenographer Edward Gordon Craig (whom Daghani knew) through Vence, constructing a narrative around people and places he may have observed. He paid homage in portraits and copies of works to artists from Rembrandt, Vermeer, Ingres and Picasso to Mondrian, Beardsley, Ernst and Matisse. He depicted dancers and musical themes, from nudes playing piano to abstract compositions relating to the sounds of Schoenberg and Stravinsky.

It was while living in Vence that Daghani began to refer to the past. In Israel, he had donated a number of his works from Mikhailowka and Bershad to the Art Museum at Yad Vashem. The remainder he pasted into two large works, the book *What a Nice World* (1943–77) and the folio *1942 1943 And Thereafter (Sporadic records till 1977)* (1942–77), and added written commentaries to accompany the images. Thus these complex works contain words and images from the past interrelated with those from the 1960s and 1970s. Having aimed to put the past firmly behind him, he now returned to it and it came to haunt him. Pages and pages of these works are filled with ink wash drawings in which ghostly faces emerge from the shadows.

His work attracted some attention and, again, he received many visitors to his studio. Particularly enthusiastic was Joe Hollander, a local journalist who wrote in *Nice Matin* that 'Among the plethora of artists [...] who live, work and exhibit on this art-conscious coast, Daghani, to my mind, stands out head and shoulders above the rest [...] Daghani turns junk into jewels.'[35] Other friends also wrote encouraging letters that Daghani transcribed into books and albums. Ella (Mary) Leer wrote in 1967, 'I can't help feeling that things are bound to come out right for you, Arnold. I have such faith in you. If you weren't so talented you would have been more successful, you know. You are too versatile.'[36] Her analysis of Daghani's lack of success is supportive, but he undoubtedly would not have agreed with her advice. For, she continued, 'And if only you would be content to paint and let a business person look after all your interests for you. You must become more money-conscious, more prepared to paint for money and success and not to regard all your works as children you have conceived and borne.'

Unfortunately, the move to Vence did not greatly enhance Daghani's career. He quoted an art dealer's remarks to him: 'I like your work immensely, but you can't expect me to run the risk – you've got no name!'[37] He often wrote that his lack of traditional training meant that his work was immediately disregarded, while he frequently commented on a corrupt art world in which commercial concerns take precedence over quality of work. He felt ignored by critics, dealers and other 'sharks', and strongly distrusted anyone who made a connection between art and money. He set out what might be called his artistic creed in 1968 and repeated it many times in various sets of writings:

> I believe
> that art-dealers, journalist, and art-historians, as well as critics are to a great extent guilty of having degraded Art;

I believe

that, with few exceptions, the public is as guilty as the curators, com-
mentators, and collectors;

I believe

that art-dealers and promoters will sponsor, or destroy, in order to suit
their own purpose.

I believe

in the wickedness of false artists.[38]

Daghani became completely negative about commercial galleries and would
only consider a retrospective show in an exhibition: 'I want exhibitions at
Museums (first-rate) and connoisseurs to write about my work!'[39] By the late
1960s he had built up a large body of work which he wished to show as a
whole rather than in sections: 'I want an all-comprising show with its diver-
sity and versatility. A partial show without consideration of the variety and
many-sided abilities is like a body with a cut-off head and shoulder.'[40]

Daghani perceived and presented himself as powerless, as the victim of
circumstances. His experiences were not dissimilar from that of other artists:
unfulfilled promises, sales that are never concluded, and praise without material reward, in short, the difficulties of many modern artists working alone.
Furthermore, he was not quite as unsuccessful as his comments would imply.
Although support was fragmentary, in Romania he had received the attention
of some significant artists and art historians while during the Vence period he
had a circle of admirers. A number of prominent figures in the British art
establishment also indicated support for his work, although again this praise
did not result in any substantial public recognition. His response seems to
reflect not just the difficult experiences he was undergoing as an artist, but
also the suffering he endured in the camp and the fate of the other inmates
which continued to haunt him. Although temporally and geographically separated, these different periods of his life were intricately interrelated.

Meanwhile he received letters from Comarnescu who told him that back
in Romania he 'would be among the first and highest artists'.[41] But the
Daghanis were unable to return, and although legally they could stay indef-
initely in Vence, he could no longer bear the '*atmosphère artistique*'.[42] In 1970
they were granted permission to stay in Jona, but where there was no artistic scene and Daghani was at an even greater distance, both physically and in
terms of recognition, from the art world that he had now rejected.

Nevertheless, he continued to add to his by now enormous body of work, and welcomed visitors. Further folios follow his life there, commenting on contemporary society and on his experiences as an artist. He continued working on the large albums, and developed themes of work on music and literature, and portraits of contemporary figures, often drawn from the television or other reproduced sources.

FINAL YEARS

Having finally been granted residence permits, Daghani and Anişoara moved to Hove in 1977 where they remained until they died – Anişoara in 1984 and Daghani in 1985. By the time that they moved Daghani's health was worsening considerably. He suffered from depression, and from Parkinson's disease, evident in his increasingly shaky drawings and handwriting. He devoted much of his time to preparing his diary for publication, working on the typescript *Let Me Live* with the help of journalist Mollie Brandl-Bowen. He continued to fill small sketchbooks with drawings, and, as in previous homes, covered not only the walls of his apartment with his work but also the surfaces of furniture and lampshade as well as bathroom tiles and the glass windows of doors. Due to his often negative experiences with art dealers, by the late 1960s he had decided not to sell his work at all. He hoped that after his death his apartment in Hove would become a museum and a large collection of his work would remain intact. He felt strongly that individual works of his could not be understood properly in isolation.

Daghani's extensive body of work provides a unique and complex interweaving of documentation with art, personal experiences and memories. The artist acts as a double witness, both looking out at the world in which he found himself, and looking in at his own experiences and dilemmas. The combination of the historical with the personal, of the visual with the verbal, as well as the range of themes and media means that his works operate in the interstices between conventional categories. They raise questions as to how history and identity are constructed while signalling the significance of individual testimony. Their complexity highlights the problems of Holocaust representation.

NOTES

1. Letter from Daghani to Daniela Miga (3 June 1959), Museum of Art, Constanţa, Romania.
2. 'Zeugenschaftliche Vernehmung', Staatsanwaltschaft Lübeck bei dem Landesgericht, 2 P Js 1629/64, 9 June 1965: vorgeladen Arnold Daghani, p.2, Arnold Daghani Collection, University of Sussex (hereafter ADC).
3. A. Daghani, *Groapa este în livada de vişini* (Bucharest: Socec & Co, 1947); A. Daghani, *Lasst Mich Leben!* (Tel Aviv: Weg und Ziel Verlag, 1960); A. Daghani, *The Grave is in the Cherry Orchard*, in M. Grindea (ed.), *Adam: International Review* (London) 29, 291–3 (1961).
4. A. Daghani, *What a Nice World* (1943-77), unpublished book, ADC, G1.035r.
5. A. Daghani, *1942 1943 And Thereafter (Sporadic records till 1977)* (1942–77), unpublished folio, ADC, G2.113v.
6. Interview conducted by Petru Weber with Shoshana Nauman, 3 February 2004, Haifa, Israel; see Petru Weber, 'Beyond the River Bug: Mapping the Testimony of Arnold Daghani against other Sources' in this edition for further analysis of this interview.
7. Daghani, *What a Nice World*, G1.063r.
8. Ibid., G1.065r.
9. Ibid., G1.067r.
10. Ibid., G1.124r.
11. Ibid.
12. Ibid.
13. Ibid., G1.165r.
14. Ibid.
15. L. Benjamin, *Prigoǎna si rezistenţǎ în istoriǎ evreilor din România 1940–1944* [Persecution and Resistance in the History of the Jews in Romania 1940-1944] (Bucharest: Editura Hasefer, 2001), p.268.
16. Ziva Amishai-Maisels, 'Art Confronts the Holocaust' in M. Bohm-Duchen (ed.), *After Auschwitz: Responses to the Holocaust in Contemporary Art* (Sunderland and London: Northern Centre for Contemporary Art in association with Lund Humphries, 1995), p.50.
17. See, for further discussion, M.S. Costanza, *The Living Witness: Art in the Concentration Camps and Ghettos* (New York and London: Macmillan, 1982) and J. Blatter and S. Milton, *Art of the Holocaust* (London: Orbis, 1982). While the latter publication includes examples of Daghani's works, the camps of Ukraine and Transnistria are notably absent from a map showing the camps across Europe in 1943.
18. In addition to Daghani's diary, an eyewitness report written by Nathan Segall, representative of the Romanian Jews in Mikhailowka, and a letter from Heinz Rosengarten, fellow inmate of Segall and Daghani, written on 14 September 1943, also contributed to the investigations.
19. E. Hillesum, *An Interrupted Life: The Diaries of Etty Hillesum* (New York: Owl, 1996), p.72.
20. For further discussion see D. Schultz and E. Timms, *Pictorial Narrative in the Nazi Period: Felix Nussbaum, Charlotte Salomon and Arnold Daghani*, special issue of *Word & Image*, 24, 3 (July–September 2008).
21. L.L. Langer, *Holocaust Testimonies: The Ruins of Memory* (New Haven, CT and London: Yale University Press, 1991), p.xv. See also D. Schultz, 'Forced Migration and Involuntary Memory: the Work of Arnold Daghani', in Wendy Everett and Peter Wagstaff (eds), *Cultures of Exile: Images of Displacement* (Oxford: Berghahn, 2004), pp.67–86.
22. Letter from Daghani to Daniela Miga (3 June 1959), Museum of Art, Constanţa, Romania.
23. Daghani, *1942 1943 And Thereafter*, G2.070r.
24. Ibid., G2.098v.
25. M. Bohm-Duchen, *Arnold Daghani* (London: Diptych, 1987), p.59.
26. F. Meyer, *Marc Chagall* (New York: Harry N. Abrams, 1964), p.416.
27. A. Daghani, untitled poem (1956), in *A Large, a Big Question Mark* (1968), unpublished book, ADC, p.283.
28. Bohm-Duchen, *Arnold Daghani*, p.26.
29. Daghani, *What a Nice World*, G1.091r.
30. Ibid., G1.078r.
31. Bohm-Duchen, *Arnold Daghani*, p.73.
32. A. Daghani, *Matters of Ethics: Memoirs* (1979–83), unpublished book, ADC, C36.72r.
33. Daghani, *1942 1943 And Thereafter*, G2.106v.
34. Bohm-Duchen, *Arnold Daghani*, p.38.

35. A. Daghani, *Memoirs: Switzerland* (c. 1946–79), unpublished folio, C21.008r.
36. Daghani, *Matters of Ethics*, C36.04v.
37. A. Daghani, inscription on an untitled drawing (1967), ADC, A1004.
38. Daghani, *Matters of Ethics*, C36.83r.
39. Ibid., C36.72r.
40. Ibid., C36.72v.
41. Daghani, *What a Nice World*, G1.224r.
42. Bohm-Duchen, *Arnold Daghani*, p.40.

PART IV

TESTIMONY, JUSTICE AND RECONCILIATION

5

Accumulated Testimonies in the Arnold Daghani Collection

EDWARD TIMMS

Looking back on the terrible events recorded in *The Grave is in the Cherry Orchard*, Daghani felt he owed a duty to the dead to record further information about the fate they had endured. So committed was he to creating memorials for Mikhailowka that he never tired of re-transcribing the events that occurred there and reworking the most poignant pictorial images. The task of commemoration occupied him, intermittently, for forty years, and he was still working on a revised and expanded edition of his labour camp diary at the time of his final illness. The paradox of his camp diary is that its testimony gained weight as he repeatedly reworked his memories in narrative and pictorial form, expressing himself with increasing vehemence when the evidence which he presented was denied or ignored. This resulted in a highly original archive of commemoration with a multiplicity of layers.

For Daghani, it was not simply a question of recording his own sufferings. He was remembering for those who could not remember – the friends and neighbours who perished during the liquidation of the camp. In the diary their gestures are reverently picked out with a painter's eye, as in the scene in the stable after work with 'men swaying to and fro in the rhythm of their prayer' and the 'neighing horses behind the latticed partition' (2 September 1942). On 8 January 1943 he made a pencil drawing of this scene, entitled *Evening Prayer* (Plate 11). The drawings form a counterpoint to the narrative, endowing the sufferings he describes with a defiant human dignity. The two media function in divergent ways. The verbal accounts enact the role of witness historian, telling as directly as possible of the events in the camp, while the visual images achieve a certain aesthetic distance. The fascination of his work arises from the tension between the two modes.

In short, Daghani committed himself to the task of combining 'Memory and Creativity', the theme of Part III of this edition. It was this sense of the complementary character of text and image that led him to embark on the voluminous pictorial and calligraphic albums of his maturity, *What a Nice World* and *1942 1943 And Thereafter (Sporadic records till 1977)*. Perhaps the most compelling example is provided by the collage he based on the front page of the *Völkischer Beobachter* of 24 March 1933, with Hitler's profile superimposed and the swastika picked out in blood red (Plate 31). This is framed by a double caption: a press clipping added at the top, in which Hitler promises to annihilate the Jews of Europe; and Daghani's calligraphic inscription at the bottom, recalling that in January 1931 he had predicted Hitler's rise to power. Further examples of his work, accompanied by an ironic commentary, are reproduced in Daghani's three-volume *Pictorial Autobiography*, also in the Sussex Collection. The cumulative effect of these sequences of sombre images and calligraphic memorials is to convey a sense of inescapable oppression. Even when his theme is the miracle of survival, we cannot escape the shadow of the assassins and the memory of those who perished at their hands.

Daghani repeatedly returned to the mystery of why German soldiers, searching the building in Gaisin where he and his wife had taken refuge in July 1943, failed to check the one room in which they were hiding. This is the theme of one of his shorter albums entitled *The Building in which We had a Narrow Escape*. This album, too, concludes on a sombre note – with the evidence of those who witnessed the shooting of the Jews from Mikhailowka in December 1943, followed by the calligraphic portrait of a woman prisoner, incorporating the names and identities of more than 150 individual victims (Plate 32). They include, under the left eye, 'Anschel and wife', two figures who make a fleeting appearance in Daghani's diary, but are better known to posterity as the parents of Paul Celan.[1] The aim is to rescue even the most humble victims from oblivion and remind us that each of them had a human face.

TESTIMONY, GUILT AND DENIAL

Daghani was also remembering for those who preferred to forget: the perpetrators and the bystanders. During the 1960s and 1970s there was a series
of court cases in Germany, in which attempts were made to bring to justice
those war criminals who had eluded the de-Nazification measures of the
immediate post-war period. Daghani followed these cases with great interest, especially where the slave labour camps in the Ukraine were involved,
and accumulated a wealth of new material. He was infuriated to learn that
some of the perpetrators identified by name in his diary were entirely unre-
pentant about their crimes. This is the reason why he decided, during the
final decade of his life, to produce revised and expanded versions of his
diary. The version to be discussed here was identified by Daghani as the
'authorized manuscript' (abbreviated as AM followed by the page number).[2]

These unpublished memoirs, highly original documents of Holocaust
commemoration, consist of approximately 300 pages of typescript with
numerous hand-written additions and corrections. Inspired by the new evidence brought to light by the German courts, partly as a result of his own
efforts, Daghani revised and retyped the English text of his labour camp diary
and enriched it with a series of annotations. At certain points the annotations
are so elaborate that they run to several pages, and the narrative of the events
at Mikhailowka becomes intertwined with further encounters and discover-
ies dating from the 1960s and 1970s. A dozen pages are devoted to the text
of another eyewitness report about events at Mikhailowka, which a representative of the prisoners named Nathan Segall was able to record in October
1943, shortly before he and his family were shot.[3] Daghani notes the points
at which Segall's account diverges from his own, and his typewritten comments (which he later struck through in ink) suggest that he had doubts
about the accuracy of Segall's testimony (AM 196–207). The resulting form
of Holocaust commemoration owes its complexity to the interplay between
different perspectives, juxtaposing personal testimony against documentary
evidence and using collage techniques to undermine evasions and denials. This
polymorphous version of Daghani's memoirs converts the compelling narrative of his original diary into an unwieldy historical collage. A sample page,
reproduced in facsimile (Plate 22), shows how Daghani interpolated eleven
lines from the 'FINDINGS OF THE PUBLIC PROSECUTOR'S OFFICE' between
diary entries for 20 October and 21 October 1942. Coloured felt-pen lines

indicate the sources of the material, with highlighted sections distinguishing his diary text (in green) from the legal depositions (in red). Sensing that it would be impossible to find a publisher for such an unconventional document, he also prepared a more reader-friendly version of these expanded memoirs. In this task he was assisted, after the move to England, by Mollie Brandl-Bowen, an award-winning Jewish journalist based in Hove.[4]

These expanded versions of the diary enrich the personal memoir with elements of a legal deposition. Daghani's involvement with court proceedings dates from the publication of the German edition of his diary in 1960. This version, translated by another Jewish survivor from the Bukovina named Siegfried Rosenzweig, was published by a German-language press in Tel Aviv under the title *Lasst Mich Leben*. Daghani was dissatisfied with the quality of the translation and particularly objected to the Foreword, as is clear from his handwritten comments on the copy at the University of Sussex. Rosenzweig's view of the crimes committed in the camps is that 'only German hordes were eagerly at work' and Daghani's portrayal of their cruelty towards Jews reveals 'the true German character'. Daghani struck this whole foreword through in black biro and added (in German) the handwritten comment: 'I disagree with the foreword; it is contradictory to my conception.'[5]

It was not Daghani's aim to make general statements about the 'German character'. His narrative of events at Mikhailowka reveals a spectrum of personality types among the Germans, from sadists like Mintel, Maass and Kiesel, capable of shooting Jews without compunction, to professional engineers like Elsässer and Bergmann, who showed some sympathy for the prisoners. At the same time he makes it clear that fanatical Nazis found willing collaborators among the Lithuanian and Ukrainian guards, some of whom were just as sadistic as their German superiors. It was by no means 'only' Germans who were responsible, just as it was not only Jews who were victimized. His diary entries about the ghetto at Bershad record that Jewish militia men colluded with the system of oppression (31 July 1943). Daghani is equally careful not to idealize the various groups of Jewish prisoners. His account of the courage with which they endured their sufferings does not prevent him from indicating that they are ordinary men and women with familiar human failings. There is an undercurrent of irony in the references to the self-appointed Jewish spokesman, Nathan Segall, who enjoyed certain privileges. And it is clear that well-educated German-speaking Jews from Romania felt reluctant to associate with Jews from more primitive communities in the Ukraine.

This expanded version of Daghani's camp diary is a work that combines documentary weight with narrative complexity, offering a differentiated account of situations, actions and characters which avoids sensationalism. His writings about the camp, like the paintings he completed there, constitute an art of understatement. He was determined not to exaggerate or embellish his account: 'I never used a hyperbole, and everything related was founded on facts.' (AM 183) He was reluctant to draw any scene which he had not seen with his own eyes. There is just one pencil drawing in the collection of the art museum at Yad Vashem, dated 1943, which seems to contradict this statement (Plate 21). In the authorized version of his diary, Daghani mentions an image showing 'Ukrainian Jewish slaves before their execution and the SS-Unterscharführer Walter Mintel in the middle of the screaming, crying multitude holding in one hand a whip, in the other a gun' (AM 195). Although the drawing at Yad Vashem does not show a 'multitude', it fits the description in every other way. Daghani claimed that he had destroyed the drawing because it was based on 'hearsay'; it would have been 'an illustration of a shuddering scene, not seen by myself' (AM 195). Perhaps this is a preliminary sketch for a drawing that was indeed destroyed for the reasons given. The style is clumsy and the effect melodramatic, lacking the subtlety of his other works. In repudiating this spectacular style in favour of an art of understatement, he affirms the integrity of his personal vision. He was sensitive to what has become known as 'Holocaust kitsch', lurid representations of cruelty and suffering designed to appeal to predictable emotions. Such images might have had greater popular appeal, but would have been a betrayal of his artistic conscience.

Avoiding such melodramatic effects, Daghani uses irony and understatement, in both texts and images, to accentuate the cruel absurdity of the regime in a slave-labour-cum-extermination camp. A passage dated 14 September 1942 describes the scene at morning roll-call when twenty-five slave labourers were selected to be taken away and shot. This leads to the following reflection on returning that same evening to their quarters in the stables: 'August Dohrmann Co. seems to own the horses as well, but we have the odds against us, for it is unlikely that they will kill the horses.' (14

September 1942) The understated style of the narrative is one of its finest qualities, and yet one of the reasons for its relatively unenthusiastic reception. It is significant that the original English edition of *The Grave is in the Cherry Orchard* appeared in magazine form, and that the task of finding a publisher for a new book edition has proved so time-consuming. There are 'too few atrocities', a literary agent observed in 1960 after reading the English typescript.[6] This miniaturized account of events in an obscure slave labour camp in a remote corner of south-east Europe has little to offer to those who envisage the Holocaust as a tragic drama enacted on a grand stage. Indeed, the main reason why Daghani quarrelled with Yad Vashem is that the committee responsible for inscribing the names of Nazi death camps on the floor of the museum refused to include Mikhailowka. It was, after all, only a forced labour camp, and the liquidation of its inmates took place elsewhere.[7]

Despite these difficulties, the German translation of Daghani's book made a significant impact, precipitating a judicial inquiry into the crimes committed in the slave labour camps of the Ukraine. On 16 May 1960 the Chief German Prosecutor in Ludwigsburg wrote to thank Rosenzweig for sending him a copy of *Lasst Mich Leben* and asked for Daghani's address (AM 256). It took several years for a formal investigation to get under way, but on 5 April 1965 Daghani received a letter from Dieter Joachim, the Public Prosecutor in Lübeck, asking him to make a formal legal deposition (AM 256–7). Daghani travelled to Lübeck, taking with him the album *What a Nice World*, the pictorial and calligraphic chronicle of events in the labour camp on which he was working at the time. He was hoping that the importance of his testimony would at last be recognized and that he would succeed in finding a publisher for *What a Nice World*. On 18 July 1965 the Swiss newspaper *Die Tat* published a detailed appreciation of the album by Hugo Debrunner, praising him as an artist who had had the strength to remain creative amid the oppressive horror of an extermination camp.[8] However, no publisher was willing to accept such an unconventional work.

During two-and-a-half days of discussion in Lübeck with the Public Prosecutor and his Assessor, a twenty-four page stenographic transcript of Daghani's testimony was prepared. This 'Zeugenschaftliche Vernehmung' (abbreviated in what follows as ZV followed by page number) provides formal confirmation for many of the crimes recorded in the diary, adding further significant details. The involvement of Walter Mintel in the shooting of

107 Ukrainian Jews is again described, even though Daghani concedes that he did not witness this atrocity with his own eyes. And the criminal activities of Bernhard Maass, an officer who makes only fleeting appearances in the diary, are particularly emphasized. Maass is now described as 'the most important person' at Mikhailowka, and it is clearly suggested that he was responsible for the shooting of between fifty and fifty-five prisoners on 26 April 1943 (ZV 9–12).[9]

According to Dieter Joachim, the Public Prosecutor, it was due to Daghani's diary that the events in the 'ghost-world' of the south-western Ukraine had come to the attention of the German courts. 'In fact', Joachim is recorded as saying, 'it descended upon us like an avalanche.' He now had hundreds of names in his card index and a map on the wall showing where remote labour camps like Mikhailowka, Krasnapolka and Ivangorod had been located. Tarassiwka was such an obscure place – perhaps merely a collective farm – that its location at first seemed undiscoverable (AM 259–61). However, following the leads provided by Daghani, the prosecutor soon succeeded in tracing eyewitnesses to the Tarassiwka massacre.

English translations of their testimony are incorporated in the memoirs. Werner Bergmann confirmed that between 400 and 450 Jews were shot dead by German police, supported by Lithuanian auxiliaries, under the command of a German officer who was unknown to him. Russian troops were advancing and 'we apprehended that one would kill the Jews in Tarassiwika before evacuation' (AM 230). Josef Elsässer's account is more circumstantial. On the previous day SS-Hauptsturmbannführer Christoffel, the new camp commander, had led him to believe that no action against the Jews was impending. He was thus astonished when he arrived at Tarassiwka the following morning:

> I became aware that most of the Jews of the camp had already been shot dead, their bodies in two mass graves. As I got nearer, the SDs and the Lithuanian auxiliaries were just going to shoot dead the last Jews. Among those still alive were two young girls who were calling out to me to help them, but I could do nothing. I saw how they together with the others were shot dead. They had to strip naked and lie prone on the bodies in the mass grave. Then they were killed by an SD with a machine-gun in the back of their heads. (AM 231–2)

The abbreviation SD refers to the Sicherheitsdienst, a Nazi organization responsible for mass shootings of both Jews and partisans.[10] This testimony, together with that of another Dohrmann employee, Hermann Kaiser, suggests that the order for the killings could only have come from Christoffel, who was allegedly then in command of the camp (AM 234). The actual shootings were carried out by two unidentified SD-men, about whom another witness observed: 'I vividly recall two SDs who after the action were quarrelling which of them had aimed better. I later looked at the open graves. I heard isolated groaning in the graves.' (AM 237) A total of twelve pages are devoted by Daghani to statements describing the massacre at Tarassiwika by eleven different witnesses, mainly Dohrmann employees. There could be no more compelling confirmation of the stark horror which he had recorded in the final pages of his diary twenty years earlier.

Daghani now became as a kind of Simon Wiesenthal figure, a writer whose testimony made it possible to bring specific criminals before the courts and confront their accomplices with the consequences of their actions. On 7 April 1967, the *Jewish Chronicle* carried the following report:

> Luebeck prosecutors are inquiring into the activities of 39 people suspected of complicity in the shooting in 1942 of about 25,000 Jews building a road from Lemberg (now Lvov in the Soviet Union) to Stalino. The Jews were shot in 84 separate mass executions ...
>
> Investigations were opened after publication of a book, *Let Me Live*, in English by Arnold Daghani, a Rumanian painter.
>
> About 1,500 people are reported to have been interviewed in West Germany and about 100 Jewish survivors in Israel.

Actually, it was the German edition of the diary that prompted the opening of investigations, but the *Jewish Chronicle* correctly gives Daghani the credit. Several of the Nazi officers identified by name in Daghani's text were interrogated by the courts, notably Walter Mintel. And it is clear from the archival materials at the University of Sussex that the artist followed the proceedings with close attention, obtaining transcripts of the court hearings and making English translations of the most revealing passages. In November 1971 Dieter Joachim sent him four voluminous files totalling 741 pages, entitled 'Investigations versus Friese and Others for Murder' (AM 268).[11]

The investigations dragged on for almost ten years. On 10 November

1971, as Daghani records in his typewritten account of the proceedings, he received a letter from the Public Prosecutor in Lübeck informing him that it had proved impossible to identify those responsible for the annihilation of the slave labourers from Mikhailowka, which took place in Tarassiwka on 10 December 1943. Hence 'the proceedings were annulled'. On 8 March 1972, as Daghani records, he was interviewed at his home in Switzerland by Hans-Joachim Röhse, Counsel for the Hamburg County Court, and Frau Dr Sarembe, the Public Prosecutor investigating the charges against Walter Mintel. The court officials were accompanied by Mintel's own lawyer. 'The lawyer put to me the question, whether I had seen the graves, and had it not been possible that the selection had as aim, to transfer the people to other camps? There were no witnesses to sustain the charges against his clients for murder.' On 14 March 1976 Daghani finally received a letter from Röhse, now President of the Hamburg Court, informing him that the proceedings against Mintel had been quashed, since the evidence obtained by Dr Sarembe from Daghani and other witnesses was insufficient to obtain a conviction (AM 219–21).

Daghani was determined that the perpetrators should be named and shamed, even if they could not be convicted and imprisoned. His interest in the case of Walter Mintel was reawakened by an article by Jürgen Serke, published in the German magazine *Stern* on 8 September 1980. This eight-page article, which was entitled 'ICH WILL NICHT STERBEN. NEIN.' ('I do not wish to die. No.'), paid tribute to the poet Selma Meerbaum-Eisinger, who had been imprisoned in Mikhailowka and died there on 16 December 1942 at the age of 18. Serke records that when Selma contracted typhoid fever, she was nursed during her final illness by Daghani's wife Anişoara. After her death, Daghani made the drawing entitled *Pieta* (see Plate 3), depicting the scene in which Selma's body, wrapped in a blanket, is reverently lowered from the bunk bed in which she had died. The final page of Serke's article pays tribute to his work of commemoration:

> Were it not for Arnold Daghani, we would not know what fun the SS had at Mikhailowka in picking out a few Jews, time and again, and shooting them dead ...
>
> In Daghani's diary ... one name repeatedly occurs which caused fear and terror among the prisoners: SS-Unterscharführer Walter Mintel, the camp commandant ...

Walter Mintel, father of eight children, who married his second wife in 1971, became a foreman after the war and is 73 years old today. As an accused man he testified that he was never at Mikhailowka.

Daghani responded to this article by writing a letter dated 29 September 1980 addressed to Herrn Walter Mintel, Schanzengrund 29, Hamburg-Hausbruch, West Germany: 'May I help your memory?' he politely inquired, after quoting from *Stern* Mintel's declaration 'that he was never at Mikhailowka'. And he went on to list the eighteen dated entries from his diary in which Mintel's activities are recorded, including the entry for 12 November 1942 when 'one hundred and seven slaves having no room left for them, were by SS Unterscharführer Walter Mintel's order shot dead' (AM 296–7).

Over eighty pages of the expanded version of Daghani's diary are taken up by English translations of German court reports and witness statements. At one point he inserts a 'ROLL-CALL' – a list of all the friends he remembers who were killed at Mikhailowka, Tarassiwka or one of the other slave labour camps in the Ukraine (AM 246–52) (Plate 33). Their fates are recalled as if they were answering at the roll-call in their own voice. The complete list of 250 people, including many children, is reproduced at the end of the present volume. According to Mollie Brandl-Bowen, reciting the names of the dead became a solemn ritual, repeated by Daghani and his wife every year at Yom Kippur.

RECONCILIATION

A key question raised during the investigation into the slave labour camps was the role of German civilians – 'those who participated in the crimes, or tacitly tolerated them', as Daghani puts it (AM 258). He notes that security in the camps (including the liquidation of unwanted Jewish slave labourers) was the responsibility of the Commander of the Security Police in the Ukraine ('Kommandeur der Sicherheitspolizei und des Sicherheitsdienstes', AM 123). By contrast, the road-building operations were controlled by Organisation Todt, the German public works unit, whose officials wore uniforms and held quasi-military rank, but were not technically members of the police or the armed forces.[12] On one occasion, as his original diary records with astonishment, Werner Bergmann appeared at the camp 'dressed in a fashionable light grey flannel suit'. This brought it home to Daghani that he and his fellow labourers were not prisoners of war, but 'slaves owned by a road-making company, with a death sentence over our heads' (10 June 1943).

However, asked in 1965 by the German Public Prosecutor whether he personally had anything with which to reproach representatives of the Dohrmann construction company like Bergmann and Elsässer, he 'answered in the negative' (AM 263). Indeed, both in the diary and in the stenographic transcript he reports that on one occasion, in May 1943, Elsässer and Bergmann may have intervened to prevent an 'extermination action', and that they were recompensed by the prisoners with money and valuables (ZV 21). Given the vehemence of his polemic against perpetrators like Walter Mintel, the tone of Daghani's comments about bystanders is remarkably restrained, although not without irony: 'From the moral, ethical point of view the firm DOHRMANN, like all the other road-making companies, should not have lent a hand in the use of forced-labour, and their extermination.' (AM 263–4)

The most original dimension of Daghani's memoirs, in their expanded form, is the theme of reconciliation. During the early 1970s he decided to resume contact with some of those who had participated in events at Mikhailowka, while not being directly involved in crimes. In *The Grave is in the Cherry Orchard*, the consideration shown by some Dohrmann employees, including female personnel like Martha Fischer (née Grae), forms an ambiguous counterpoint to the brutality of the camp guards. In revisiting these ghosts from the past, Daghani's primary motive seems to have been to discover the precise roles and motives of people who had been involved in the 'Forced labour cum-annihilation-Camp' – and yet had shown a certain humanity. This 'research work', he reflected, 'has its own rewards' (AM 269). After learning that key officials from the Dohrmann company had been traced by the Public Prosecutor and interviewed as witnesses, he wrote a series of letters which were forwarded to them. A copy of the German translation of his diary, *Lasst Mich Leben* (1960), had meanwhile been obtained by the Dohrmann company and read by several of its former employees.

On 23 January 1973, Daghani records, three letters were delivered simultaneously to his home at Jona in Switzerland – replies from Werner Bergmann in Freudenstadt, Martha Fischer in Mainz, and Josef Elsässer in

Remscheid. Anişoara burst into tears as she started reading the letters. All three expressed pleasure at knowing that the Daghanis had survived. They also began to describe in some detail their own memories of events in the Ukraine, as the Germans were forced to retreat, the slave labour camps were abandoned, and the prisoners liquidated. 'Unfortunately, neither Mr. Elsässer nor I could do anything for the rescue of the Camp of Mikhailowka', wrote Bergmann. The civilians, he claimed, had to be very cautious, since they were 'not well thought of by the SS' (AM 269). Elsässer's letter went even further, since he evidently felt that he deserved some credit for allowing the Daghanis to escape. He recalled that he 'intentionally did not fix a padlock to the door of the garage' where they were supposed to be confined overnight while working on the mosaic (AM 272). He also emphasized how frightened he had been that the SS might suspect he was colluding with the prisoners.

During the following years the Daghanis, in an act of unprecedented generosity, made friends with their former captors. A total of twenty-six letters were exchanged with the Bergmann family and thirty with the Elsässers (AM 286). The tone of these letters is surprisingly cordial, although on several occasions Daghani presses his correspondents to justify their conduct during the war. Elsässer had read *Lasst Mich Leben* with close attention, and in a ten-page letter, parts of which are reproduced in the memoirs in English translation, he challenges Daghani's account at certain points. Under 'Fact One', Elsässer insists the Dohrmann company did not undertake its operations in Russia voluntarily, but was acting under duress. Under 'Fact Two', he disclaims responsibility for the use of slave labour:

> The firm had no influence at all with regard to manpower. We were supposed to build roads with POWs, whom we did have in Worowoniza. Should you, Mr Daghani, have been present when we were informed that we had to build roads with women, sick men and even children! I had a head-on discussion with Mr Bergmann, but, alas, without success. I wanted to rejoin the Wehrmacht.

Challenging the diary entry for 14 September 1942 about prisoners being treated like horses, Elsässer insists, as 'Fact Three', that 'the firm August Dohrmann did never own a single horse in Russia'. And he goes to great lengths to deny that he and Bergmann accepted bribes of dollars and jewellery in October 1943, when they drove by lorry to collect supplies from

some of the prisoners' families in Czernowitz. While admitting that he witnessed executions, Elsässer claims that his own attitude towards the slave
labourers was humane:

> Again and again I used to warn our column-leaders: 'Don't hit, don't
> vex, and what's most important, don't you kill!' We were only given
> the task, to employ you as manpower. What was on the whole hap-
> pening in the camp after leaving off work was a matter for the police.
> I knew the Lithuanians and they knew me; they were aware that I high-
> ly disliked them. And even when the SD-man came and you write that
> such and such O.T.-man aided and abetted the SD-man, the question
> arises: 'What were Mr Mühl in Tarassiwka, Kaiser in Mikhailowka,
> Peter Höller to do, when that regular demon was raging in the camp?
> Nothing.' (AM 273–4)

This argument attempts to draw a clear line between the allegedly correct
treatment of labour detachments by the Dohrmann officials attached to
Organisation Todt and the brutality of the security police and the Lithuanian
guards. Daghani, as we shall see, remained unconvinced.

In his self-appointed mission of creating a comprehensive memorial to
Mikhailowka, Daghani felt compelled to extend his investigations through
personal discussion. Together with Bergmann, Elsässer, Martha Fischer and
their families, he and Anişoara embarked on an extraordinary effort of collective memory retrieval, which is reflected in the plural narrative of his
memoirs. About the interpretation of certain events there could be no con-
sensus: this was precluded by the bad conscience of the bystanders, as well
as the fallibility of their recall. But the process nevertheless proved therapeu-
tic. Martha Fischer, accompanied by her husband Karl and her daughter, visited the Daghanis in March 1973. After 'three interesting and instructive
days' spent in their company, she wrote to say how impressed she was that
'you were feeling no hatred for your tormentors'. As a token of friendship,
Martha presented the Daghanis with the original set of Rosenthal porcelain
which had caught the artist's imagination on the eve of their escape from
Gaisin.[13] In May 1973 the Daghanis also visited Werner Bergmann and his
wife in Freudenstadt, taking *What a Nice World* to show them. After a long day
spent talking through the past, Bergmann saw them off at the station. It was
clearly a very emotional experience, as Daghani records: 'Neither of us

THREE, that is he, Nanino and me had been able to hide emotion as we said "good bye" to each other. To me it was, as if I was taking leave of an elder brother. Nanino and I have reconciled ourselves with the past.' (AM 279)

Finally, on 22 August 1974 they had a visit from Josef Elsässer. Anişoara viewed the approaching visit with some apprehension, since Elsässer's ten-page letter of January 1973 had shown him 'walking clumsily over the past'. But Daghani was 'dying to know the answer to some questions'. When Elsässer arrived, accompanied by a friend named Friedrich Mayer, there was some hard talking, since Daghani refused to accept his argument that the Dohrmann company was acting under duress. He explained that there is a great difference between military conscripts and civil contracts. The latter involves 'a mutual arrangement based on an agreement between the parties' (AM 281). During the ensuing discussion Elsässer once again tried to explain his conduct during the trip to Czernowitz. And he claimed credit for having tried to arrange decent accommodation for the Romanian Jewish workers, ensuring that they would 'not be penned together with the already crawler-infested Ukrainian Jewish slaves'. Once again, Daghani was sceptical, since he recalled that it was the leader of the Romanian Jews, Nathan Segall, who was responsible for their accommodation.

This may appear a trivial discrepancy, but from Daghani it provoked the following reflection: 'Is it really important, to know which is which? Perhaps for historical reasons, but, alas, there can be no AUDI ALTERAM PARTEM, for the other part was extinguished by a bullet in the nape of the neck.' (AM 282) Segall was among those shot by the Germans at Tarassiwka in December 1943. The 'stimulating conversation' continued after lunch, with Elsässer identifying himself as 'one who shudders speaking about the horrible crimes of which he never approved'. The Daghanis found it difficult to square this claim with the disclosure that Elsässer still kept his sandy-coloured Organisation Todt uniform in his wardrobe.

Both Bergmann and Elsässer were well advanced in years at the time of these conversations. Bergmann died on 25 March 1977 at the age of 70, while Elsässer died on 31 May 1979 aged 81. The funeral notices, received from their families, are incorporated in Daghani's memoirs together with photographs of the two men. It is clear that the Daghanis felt shocked to hear of the death of Bergmann: 'The news hit us like a thunderbolt.' (AM 286) But their feelings towards Elsässer were more ambivalent. Towards the end of

1979, sorting through the letters he had received, Daghani began to suspect that Elsässer had been less than frank during their conversation and correspondence. He was particularly puzzled by Elsässer's reluctance to explain how he originally obtained a copy of *Lasst Mich Leben* (AM 290). More significantly, the circumstances surrounding Elsässer's visit to Czernowitz in October 1943 remained a mystery. According to testimony which Daghani later obtained from Mrs Ernestine Rosengarten, Elsässer had tried to impress his contacts in Czernowitz by posing as a lieutenant in the SS (AM 289). Even more disturbing was an allegation which Daghani unexpectedly discovered in the file of the Public Prosecutor from Hildesheim – he gives the reference as 9 Js 521/60, Sonderordner I. According to this testimony Josef Elsässer had actually participated in the killing of Jewish forced labourers (AM 290). During their meeting in Switzerland in 1974, Elsässer had recalled that he had been wounded in battle near Lemberg during the early stages of the war and that he dreaded the idea of being sent back to the front (AM 281). No wonder Daghani and his wife started to have second thoughts about him.

Elsässer's claim that 'Dohrmann never owned a single horse in Russia' was now seen as a characteristic evasion:

> I never affirmed [Daghani writes in a note dated 10 June 1980] that the firm Dohrmann owned any horses in Russia (in addition to several hundred Jewish slaves!), but the entry of 24 HUMAN BEINGS killed on that day in connection of which I made the remark referring to the horses he [Elsässer] deliberately passed over, or rather reduced to the satisfactory comment that the firm Dohrmann never owned a single horse in Russia. (AM 291)

Despite the clumsiness of Daghani's syntax, his analysis of Elsässer's evasiveness is clear. 'The more I think the more revealing is my suspicion that Elsässer's part in the camp was more than fishy', he concluded (AM 291). It is clear that Daghani never succeeded in resolving his perplexity. At the bottom of page 293, which appears to be the final page which he added to this version of his memoirs, there is a note in the shaky handwriting that is characteristic of the artist's old age: 'I have given it up, since it is to no purpose. My aim was and has been, that what happened to the slaves on the DG IV should be known!'

CONCLUSION: MIKHAILOWKA AS A MICROCOSM

The significance of Daghani's Holocaust testimony remained virtually unrecognized for over fifty years. Long before Daniel Goldhagen, he demonstrated that a close analysis of the workings of the slave labour camps may provide crucial insights into the whole Nazi system. But by contrast with Goldhagen, he insists that the most careful discriminations are necessary if we are to understand the complicity of ordinary German citizens in the programme of extermination. It is instructive to compare Goldhagen's description of the Lipowa Labour Camp in Lublin with Daghani's account of Mikhailowka. The Lipowa Camp, which produced shoes and clothing for the armed forces, was operated by the Deutsche Ausrüstungs-Werke (DAW), an SS economic enterprise. For Goldhagen it provides a clear picture of the brutality of 'the Germans' and their 'cruel treatment of Jews'. Although there can be no doubt about the cruelty of the Lipowa regime, Goldhagen obscures the workings of the labour camp system by attributing almost every act of cruelty to the collective action of 'the Germans'. He does mention in passing that the German personnel at the camp included technicians and women clerical workers, but he has nothing to say about the behaviour of these groups. If he had given further thought to the matter, he might have been obliged to discriminate between different behaviour patterns and modify his generalizations about the 'pervasive cruelty' of 'the Germans' and the 'genocidal eliminationist antisemitism' which allegedly motivated them.[14]

Daghani, by contrast, knew from first-hand experience that there was little to be gained from generalizations about the 'German character' or about 'German hordes' engaged in mass murder. His diary portrays a whole spectrum of attitudes both among the German personnel and among their Lithuanian, Ukrainian and Romanian allies. To indicate that not all Germans were anti-Semitic, he also records a conversation with a soldier who criticized the persecution of Jews (6 June 1943). And in the expanded version of the diary he includes as report that the Dohrmann staff felt such sympathy for the slave labourers that they sent them 'a large box of marmelade [sic]' (AM 186). Daghani recognized that some of those involved in the running the camp were decent human beings. The news that a German police-sergeant named Louis Glasbrenner had met a violent death at the hands of Ukrainian partisans filled him with regret: 'He was decent while commandant of Mikhailowka, as far as I knew or could judge.' (AM 186) In Daghani's testimony to the Lübeck Public prosecutor, the word *anständig* (decent) is also applied to another camp commander, Willi Buder. During his term of duty (1 December 1942 to 14 February 1943) no acts of violence against Jewish prisoners occurred (ZV 6–7). While emphasizing the brutality of individual German commanders, Lithuanian guards and members of the SD and the SS, he does not portray the Dohrmann employees as aggressive or anti-Semitic.

The Dohrmann company nevertheless plays the crucial role in Daghani's sequence of narratives. Standard accounts of the German war economy tend to focus on large industrial enterprises and centralized political and military controls. Daghani's memoirs remind us of the significance of small family firms. The contribution of such firms to the German war effort has received little attention, even though they too were involved in the processes of rationalization which resulted in the 'production miracle' of the years 1941–44.[15] Daghani reverts to the question of these family firms at a crucial point in his memoirs, compiling a list of half-a-dozen construction companies which ran labour camps in the southern Ukraine: 'MIKHAILOWKA owned by August Dohrmann; NEMIROW owned by Fix & Stöhr; KIBLICZ owned jointly by KAISER & UFER; KRASNAPOLKA owned by ERAS, Nürnberg; BEREZOWKA owned by Stöhr KG, München; NARAEWKA owned by Karl Kaiser, Hanau; BRACLAW owned by Horst & Jüssen' (AM 252). The employees of such companies constituted the civil arm of the slave-labour-cum-extermination camps.[16] Without their participation, the system could not have functioned. They designed the roads, operated the telephones, typed the letters and ran the transport system.

Daghani shows how such people sustained the war effort even after they became aware of its criminal consequences. His memoirs make it clear that the Dohrmann staff lived a double life. They may claim to have maintained professional standards during working hours, doing their best to ensure that the work force were not unduly harassed by their armed guards. But in reality they knew that while they were supervising work on road construction or in the gravel quarry, groups of 'expendable' slave labourers were being executed back at the camp. The following passage, to which Daghani gives prominence in the introduction to *The Grave is in the Cherry Orchard*, makes this point clear:

> With the road-building companies, the one essential thing was that work should go on smoothly: not only were the contractors profit-making

concerns, but the work on the main road provided their own staff with an excuse for staying behind the front line. This desire that everything should go forward as efficiently as possible became evident in a conversation I had one day with a T.O. camp-führer, Karl Ulrich. He asked me if I had not been wondering over the fact that for a long time past executions had ceased to take place on the actual working-plot. In fact, I had not given it a thought; the decrees of those who owned our lives were too unfathomable for any of us to question them, even in our minds. The T.O. man, however, insisted on offering his explanation. The company, August Dohrmann Arbeitsgemeinschaft, had protested against any execution taking place on the working-plot on the grounds that it would have an unfavourable effect on the fellow-workers of those shot dead. The manager, therefore, expressed his opinion that any 'purge' carried out well away from the highway would have a far less depressing effect on our zest for work.

The same point is reiterated with even greater force in the expanded version: 'The members of the Organisation Todt (some of the members were murderers themselves) knew well enough the final fate of the disable-bodied and able-bodied Jews in the forced-labour-cum-extermination-camps, owned by the road-building firms and companies respectively.' (AM 288)

It was this preoccupation with the road-building companies that led Daghani, towards the end of his life, to start a correspondence with the new owner of August Dohrmann, Dr Walter Spelsberg, son-in-law of the late Paul Dohrmann, one of the owners during the war. Unlike the directors of more famous German enterprises, Dr Spelsberg did not attempt to deny his firm's involvement. In his letter of 20 December 1979, as transcribed by Daghani (AM 288), he wrote: 'From discussions with Mr Elsässer, who died a few months ago, I have learned of the shattering, inhuman occurrences at the time of the operation of our firm in the Ukraine. Those occurrences put us Germans deeply to shame.'[17]

The exemplary theme of Daghani's diary is the collusion between decent blokes, capable of feeling shame, and sadistic thugs, wielding sub-machineguns. It was this combination (sometimes within a single personality) which made the system work. Werner Bergmann exemplifies the paradox with which Daghani tries to come to terms in the expanded version of his memoirs: 'I cannot understand how a person, decent as he may be, can accept the idea of having slaves, who are doomed to extermination, for the simple reason that the Führer has so decreed.' (AM 127) Another passage about Bergmann reflects on the psychological implications: 'He may be decent, but will he ever be able to whitewash his conscience that we were slaves, who ultimately were shot dead?' (AM 124) Bergmann, Elsässer and the other Dohrmann employees who watched in December 1943 as the Jewish slaves, some of whom were their friends, were taken to the cherry orchard to be shot, may have felt that they were helpless bystanders. But as Elsässer later acknowledged, they had made a pact with the devil: 'What were Mr Mühl in Tarassiwka, Kaiser in Mikhailowka, Peter Höller to do, when that regular demon was raging in the camp?' (AM 274) They knew what was happening and they accepted it, even though in their subsequent testimony they disguised their thoughts behind abstractions and evasions.

It is the role of these accomplices which make the slave labour camps so revealing. The structure of collusion which sustained the German war effort can be seen in microcosm at Mikhailowka. The Dohrmann company were apparently conscientious employers. 'We have seen one of our owners for the first time. August Dohrmann's brother came on a lorry to pay wages to the overseers', Daghani notes on 7 September 1942. But only two days earlier one of the workers at the gravel quarry, a girl of 18, had been beaten and shot dead. In a laconic aside, Daghani insists that it would have been possible for the Dohrmann company to refuse the offer of Jewish slave labourers and insist on employing Ukrainian workers instead, who would have had to be 'paid and fed, and, of course, not shot dead'. His final judgment is clear: 'Indirectly, executions will always be linked with the firm DOHRMANN, at least in the mind of the fugitives.' (AM 160) And if the war ends with an Allied victory, he would 'like the roadmaking companies brought to trial' (AM 169).

Daghani could argue, with some justice, that the slave labour camps of the Ukraine were – in their own way – just as significant as Auschwitz, because at Mikhailowka the links with German civil society were so transparent. In this sense, the system of slave labour was more representative of Germany at war than the extreme case of the extermination camps. The testimonies of Auschwitz survivors, as influential studies have shown, record atrocities and humiliations that are beyond comprehension. Acknowledging that the values of western civilization 'collapsed on the ramp at Auschwitz', we enter 'a realm of unreconciled understanding, where events remain permanently unredeemed and unredeemable'.[18] By contrast, Daghani's memories of Mikhailowka retrieve a past in which we can discern the all too human impulses of conquest and domination, resistance and solidarity. A new order was being constructed in the Ukraine, in which German settlers would be dominant, while other ethnic groups would be eliminated or reduced to the status of serfs. Slave labour was essential to this system of political domination. Why then, Daghani asked himself after reading one of the standard accounts of Nazi war crimes, were the labour camps being ignored: 'twenty-odd forced labour-cum-annihilation Camps vanished into thin air' (AM 267). Nothing infuriated him more than the failure of Yad Vashem to acknowledge the existence of the camps beyond the river Bug. He became a kind of local patriot for Mikhailowka, cherishing the memories of what had occurred there all the more intensely when they were ignored.

In 1973 he reflected in his memoirs: 'Just an idle question: What force, obsession or otherwise has been driving me to allow my mind for twenty-nine years (after our return to Bucharest from Modern Hell – Forced labour-cum-annihilation-Camp) to be bent on what took place there?' His answer is: 'There have been published umpteen books about the camps, but none to my knowledge about the camps in South-Western Ukraine. On the map hanging on the wall in the Wiener Library, London, not a single camp of the ones in the South-Western Ukraine, that is, across the river Bug.' A few years later he added three further sentences in manuscript: 'Why this neglect? Are they considered to be no match for the aristocratic Auschwitz? Exactly as the late poet wanted that his parents should have had the respectable end in Auschwitz?' (AM 269)

Here, as at other points in his memoirs, he is alluding to reports about the death of the parents of Paul Celan – Leo and Friederike Antschel. He particularly resented references in the German press which suggested that they perished at Auschwitz, when in fact he knew only too well that they had been fellow prisoners at Mikhailowka (AM 34–5). However, his criticism of Celan for suppressing the information about his parents' experiences in Mikhailowka was based on a misapprehension. On 21 October 1959 Celan did write a commemorative poem about Mikhailowka, but the subject of his parents' death was so painful that he could not bring himself to publish it. It did not appear until 1997, long after Celan's death, and was translated into

English by Michael Hamburger.[19] The title is 'Wolfsbohne' – 'Wolf's-Bean', a popular name for the flowers better knows as lupins:

> Weit in Michailowka, in
> der Ukraine, wo
> sie mir Vater und Mutter erschlugen: was
> blühte dort, was
> blüht dort? ...

> Far away, in Mikhailovka, in
> the Ukraine, where
> they murdered my father and mother: what
> flowered there, what
> flowers there? ...

These lines provide an appropriate epitaph for Daghani's lifelong effort to ensure that the questions raised by memories of Mikhailowka should not remain unanswered. The artist's work reminds us that certain human values did flower among the ruins.

NOTES

1. Paul Celan's family name was actually Antschel, and his parents Leo and Friederike Antschel were both briefly imprisoned in Mikhailowka, before being taken away and shot. For further details, see I. Chalfen, *Paul Celan: A Biography of his Youth*, translated by M. Bleyleben (New York: Persea, 1991), especially pp.150–7.
2. References to the 'authorized manuscript' of this expanded version of Daghani's diary, entitled *Let Me Live*, are identified by the abbreviation AM followed by the page number. This typescript has the catalogue number H5 in the Arnold Daghani Collection, University of Sussex (hereafter ADC).
3. In autumn 1943 Segall was permitted to accompany two Organisation Todt men who were travelling to Czernowitz to obtain supplies. While in the town of Moghilew, he found an opportunity to record an eyewitness report of his experiences in Mikhailowka: N. Segall, 'Gedächtnisprotokoll eines Augenzeugen', 21 October 1943 (six-page typescript; copy in the ADC).
4. Daghani admired Mollie Brandl-Bowen as a radical journalist with a strong record as a campaigner against racism and neo-Nazism. He entrusted her with the task of editing the extended version of his memoirs, and after the artist's death she worked tirelessly on his behalf, preserving valuable papers in her own collection. It was largely due to her efforts that a new German edition, based on the extended version, has been published: F. Rieper and M. Brandl-Bowen (eds), *'Lasst Mich Leben!' Stationen im Leben des Künstlers Arnold Daghani* (Lüneburg: zuKlampen Verlag, 2002), 352 pages.
5. A. Daghani, *Lasst Mich Leben*, translated by Siegfried Rosenzweig (Tel Aviv: Druckerei 'Eylon', 1960), copy with handwritten corrections by the author, now in the ADC. Daghani's comment is unambiguous: 'Bin mit dem Vorwort nicht einverstanden; widerspricht meiner Auffassung.'
6. 'Too Few Atrocities' is the title of Miron Grindea's introduction to *The Grave is in the Cherry Orchard* in *Adam: International Review* (London) 29, 291–3 (1961), pp.4–6.
7. A short account of events at Mikhailowka is included in *Pinkas Hakehillot* (Jerusalem, 1969), the

Hebrew Encyclopaedia of Jewish Communities published byYadVashem (transcript in English in the ADC).

8. H. Debrunner, 'Künstlerisches Dokument eines Schicksals – Arnold Daghani, Vence: "What a Nice World"', in *Die Tat*, 18 July 1965, p.10.

9. 'Zeugenschaftliche Vernehmung', Staatsanwaltschaft Lübeck bei dem Landesgericht, 2 P Js 1629/64, 9 June 1965: vorgeladen Arnold Daghani. A carbon copy of the twenty-four-page transcript of this testimony is now in the ADC. References to this document are identified by the abbreviation ZV followed by the page number.

10. The full name of the SD was Sicherheitsdienst des Reichsführers SS. According to I. Gutman (ed.), *Encyclopedia of the Holocaust* (New York: Macmillan, 1990), the section of the SD responsible for Jewish affairs had a central role in organizing and implementing the Holocaust (pp.1337–8) and carried out mass shootings in the Ukraine (p.1528).

11. These files, with the German classmark 3 Js 1428/65 StA Itzhoe, are in the ADC.

12. OrganisationTodt, named after its founder Dr FritzTodt, was responsible for large-scale military construction projects in Nazi Germany and the occupied territories. By 1944 the number of OT employees had reached 1,360,000, including about a million foreign workers and PoWs and 20,000 prisoners from concentration camps. See Gutman (ed.), *Encyclopedia of the Holocaust*, pp.1095–6.

13. Part of this porcelain tea set is now in the private collection of Carola Grindea (London).

14. D.J. Goldhagen, *Hitler's Willing Executioners: Ordinary Germans and the Holocaust* (London: Little, Brown, 1996), pp.295–300, 320–2.

15. For an account of the 'production miracle', see R.J. Overy, *War and Economy in the Third Reich* (Oxford: Clarendon Press, 1994), pp.343–75. Overy concentrates on large-scale industrial production, virtually ignoring the significance of smaller firms.

16. For an incisive account of the slave labour camps, see D. Bloxham, '"Extermination through Work": Jewish Slave Labour under the Third Reich', *Holocaust Educational Trust Research Papers*, 1, 1 (London, 1999–2000).

17. 'Aus Gesprächen mit Herrn Elsässer, der vor wenigen Monaten verstorben ist, weiß ich um die erschütternden, unmenschlichen Geschehnisse während des Einsatzes unserer Firma in der Ukraine. Diese Geschehnisse sind für uns Deutsche zutiefst beschämend.' From the signed letter of 20 December 1979 from Dr Walter Spelsberg, August Dohrmann KG Bauunternehmen, 5630 Remscheid, Salemstraße 19, to Mr Arnold Daghani, 1 Palmeira Square, Hove (copy in the ADC).

18. L.L. Langer, *Holocaust Testimonies: The Ruins of Memory* (New Haven, CT and London: Yale University Press, 1991), pp.199–200.

19. *Times Literary Supplement*, 16 May 1997.

Sunday-October 18th:

land

Selma Eisinger, eighteen-year-old, promised to ~~led~~ me "THE HOME
AND THE WORLD", in its German translation, the only book she has brought
with her. It is now with Edy Weiss. Sir Rabindranath Tagore's book has
come into a strange environment. It was, I think, in "LADY WINDERMERE's
FAN", that Oscar Wilde coined 'We are all of us in the gutter, but some
will still look at the stars above."

Lawyer Arieh Zuckermann has suggested I had better go tomorrow
to the gravel-pit instead of to the "Strasse", in fact, he will see to it
that I get on the list, for ALIOSHA WISOTZKAS seemed to have looked at me
very long, ~~just~~ as the convoy had arrived back at the stable. Is it that
I did not shave yesterday and the day before ? At any rate, he was very dis
pleased that I should have pulled the shawl over my head. And of course I
look my worst.

Monday - October 20th: Misha

From the returning convoy I learn that ~~Misha~~, the deputy-spokesman
for the Ukrainian Jewish slaves, was shot dead by ALIOSHA WISOTZKAS right
on the toiling-plot. Misha, physically still fit, was said to have been
ordered by ALIOSHA WISOTZKAS to follow, but he succeeded in snatching the
gun away from the latter, and to fire at once. WISOTZKAS was slightly
wounded. Meanwhile, a villager-guard took aim at Misha who fell on to the
ground relaxing the grasp that was holding the gun. WISOTZKAS seized the
gun eagerly and pulled the trigger. Misha was of about 24.

FINDINGS OF THE PUBLIC PROSECUTOR's OFFICE: Vol.7.p.1627; vol.18,pp.4210.
4215: According to the witnesses Marian and Pepi Dolberg, Ephraim Fruch-
tel, Dr.Bernhard and Mizzi Locker, and Arieh Zuckermann, the Ukrainian
Jew Misha was on tje 19zh of October,1942,removed from his post as
spokesman for the Ukrainian Jews. He had to join on the 20th of October
his fellow-slaves on their way to work. While he was working,WISOTZKAS
picked him out from the group. The Jew Misha attacked him and tried to
snatch away from him the rifle. It came to a mêlée, at which WISOTZKAS
got wounded. Another guard came to WISOTZKAS' assistance, he aimed,
wounded Misha and thus gave WISOTZKAS the opportunizy to shoot dead Misha
~~WISOTKAS~~ with his own hand... WISOTZKAS is dead.

back

Tuesday-October 21st:

Disquieting news. The O.T.-man WILLI KUSTIN is reported to
have remarked to the slave Mr.Stammler (The sons of the couple were at
the outbreak of the German-Russian War called up to the Soviet Army)
that we are going to be kept here during the winter;our work will consist of clearing the snow off the "STRASSE". Is the O.T.-man really
in the know ?

22. A page from Let Me Live (1980s), typewritten manuscript (H5, p. 49) (Arnold
Daghani Collection, University of Sussex © Arnold Daghani Trust).

Rumanian Gendarme

... became arrested

... a box of watercolours and a sketchbook on top of the world ... we are to be left with the other things behind. Why had we not spotted them too? he wanted to know.

Seizing the string of my shoulder-bag, he started me to open the rucksack and to put the colours into sketchbook in. It refused stubbornly, saying: 'We are being sent to death and you expect me to write then? To what use?' So I am not going to take 'em. 'To what use?' he asked back. 'They might just save your life!' was, one never can tell. As I kept on being refractory, he undid the strings open the rucksack and both sketchbook and colours were placed on top.

When I went out into the kitchen to leave a message with Mrs. Goldenberg for Professor Grigorescu, she told me whispering ... as if anything mattered now, that the neighbour down in the courtyard, one Mr. Fundel or the like — I never got his name properly — stealthily pointed up to our door as the two men and the gendarme came to look for us. Why stealthily, I wondered, or was it because he himself was a bearer of the Yellow David-star, and what might have happened had he not directed them to our door? One only day, and it would have meant a world of difference, for Professor Grigorescu is coming tomorrow. But, of course, except of the neighbours' making.

Before we left home, Mrs. Goldenberg made Nanino and me ... have some hot milk she had built for us.

Out in the street — the two men had left up — the gendarme looking at the wedding ring on Nanino's finger, said full of compassion: 'The Germans surely will cut off your finger, to take the ring; you'd better give it to me' for all his insolent show of compassion. Nanino did not want to oblige.

Six o'clock in the afternoon — Herded to the station in a long column of about two thousand and five hundred deportees, it was the grin of some on-lookers that saw us off; others were looking at us as if it were just part of a pageantry. It is absurd but I was feeling self-conscious. Poor Nanino, wished to me only for the worse it seems

Half past seven — A Rumanian colonel, I could not make out of which army, called out to the assembled mass of people that each head of family would be distributed a loaf of bread, free of any charge, once we were in the freight-train. It is interesting to note that the word used by the colonel for 'gratis' was a crude one, just the term by which the master would address himself to his serfs. Perhaps, to him we just were the scum, the dregs. Hitler's slogan meant for the nation 'Freedom and Bread' applied to the deportees used in the goods-train underwent a change. 'Bread and no-freedom'.

A quarter past eight. The doors of the goods train were heard being locked from without.

Twelve midnight —— The goods train pulled out of the station. 'Volksgarten' ...

Ghostland Trans-Dniestre

June 11th – Thursday

... and disgorged its human load before a blown-up bridge. After the train was emptied of its freight, the gendarmes boarded it again. Pulling back, the train soon vanished. We had been left to ourselves at a deserted quarry on the river Bug. The name of the river some of us had from the gendarmes, the only clue for our whereabouts. The ten little bungalows, some will have it, served as housing for convicts working at the quarry before the territory was overrun by the invading German and Rumanian armies.

A few hours later, a civilian, in his native clothing, turned up and pasted an order on — bungalow number ten, the biggest of all the bungalows. As the proclamation or whatever it was had been worded in Ukrainian, I could not read its contents — nor did I care to know. I understood that he was headman at a neighbouring (at what distance, I wonder?) village. The man lacked friendliness.

July 4th – Tuesday

Neither at the quarry nor here, at Labryhino, have the Rumanian authorities ever made available any other food except a bread-ration, nor have they given any means to the deportees to make a living. And yet 'life' has been going on, but how long will it go on in this improvised Gypsy-like camp on the outskirts of not the village?

23. A page from *What a Nice World* (1943–77) including *Romanian gendarme* (1963), ink on paper (G1.035r) (Arnold Daghani Collection, University of Sussex © Arnold Daghani Trust).

24. *The house we found refuge in – against payment* (1943) in *1942 1943 And Thereafter (Sporadic records till 1977)* (1942–77), ink and watercolour on paper (G2.103v) (Arnold Daghani Collection, University of Sussex © Arnold Daghani Trust).

25. *Sunday morning* (1972) in *1942 1943 And Thereafter (Sporadic records till 1977)* (1942–77), ink on paper (G2.062r) (Arnold Daghani Collection, University of Sussex © Arnold Daghani Trust).

At the place of executions, waiting for the gloves to arrive as hangman are apt of make

26. *At the place of execution* (n.d.) in *1942 1943 And Thereafter (Sporadic records till 1977)* (1942–77), ink on paper (G2.044v) (Arnold Daghani Collection, University of Sussex © Arnold Daghani Trust).

27. *Based on Evensong* (1954) in *1942 1943 And Thereafter* (*Sporadic records till 1977*) (1942–77), gouache on paper (G2.070r) (Arnold Daghani Collection, University of Sussex © Arnold Daghani Trust).

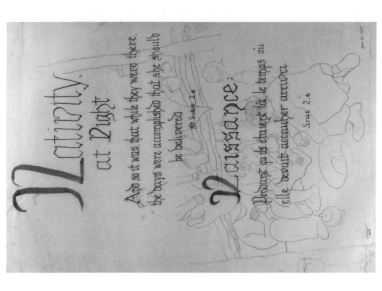

29. *Then took they the body* (1955) in *My God, my God, Why hast Thou forsaken me?* (1954–57), ink on paper with semi-transparent paper overlay (D29.10r) (Arnold Daghani Collection, University of Sussex © Arnold Daghani Trust).

28. *Nativity at night* (1955) in *My God, my God, Why hast Thou forsaken me?* (1954–7), ink on paper with semi-transparent paper overlay (D29.09r) (Arnold Daghani Collection, University of Sussex © Arnold Daghani Trust).

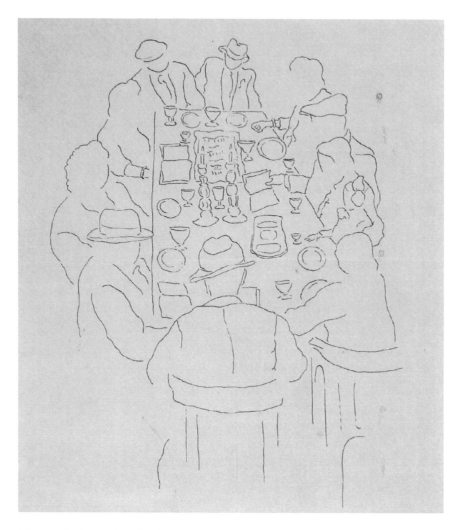

30. *First Night of Passover* (1954), ink on paper (A2) (Arnold Daghani Collection, University of Sussex ©
Arnold Daghani Trust).

31. *Völkischer Beobachter* (1974) in *1942 1943 And Thereafter (Sporadic records till 1977)* (1942–77), ink and facsimile on paper (G2.008r) (Arnold Daghani Collection, University of Sussex © Arnold Daghani Trust).

32. Woman wearing headscarf of names (1975) in The Building in which We had a Narrow Escape (1974–78), ink on paper (C45.46v) (Arnold Daghani Collection, University of Sussex © Arnold Daghani Trust).

Roll-Call:

(It is, alas, a less than tiny fraction I have been able to assemble for these

Commemorative Leaves

33. Roll-Call (1960s–70s) in 1942 1943 And Thereafter (Sporadic records till 1977) (1942–77), ink on paper (G2.117r) (Arnold Daghani Collection, University of Sussex © Arnold Daghani Trust).

34. Bershad interior (1943), ink on paper (Collection of the Yad Vashem Art Museum, Jerusalem © Arnold Daghani Trust).

35. Flowers from Bergmann (1973) in 1942 1943 *And Thereafter* (*Sporadic records till 1977*) (1942–77), ink and gold paint on paper (G2.097r) (Arnold Daghani Collection, Special Collections, University of Sussex © Arnold Daghani Trust)

6

Beyond the River Bug: Mapping the Testimony of Arnold Daghani against Other Sources

PETRU WEBER

> When the survivors of the deportation will have disappeared, the archivists of the future may dispose of a few more documents, which still remain hidden today, but they will lack the principal source: the living memory of the witnesses.
>
> Michael de Boüard[1]

On 16 August 1941 the German Ministry for the Occupied Eastern Territories ordered all Jews between 14 and 60 years of age to be subjected to forced labour. In February 1942 the leader of the SS, Heinrich Himmler, charged the commander of the SS in Ukraine and southern Russia with the construction of a highway, the Durchgangstrasse IV (DG IV). In turn, SS commander Hans-Adolf Prützmann passed the order on to the Organisation Todt (OT), which carried out infrastructure work, to organize the labour and to provide equipment for its construction. Manpower was provided by both the SS and the OT and consisted of local Jews and later of Romanian Jews since there was not enough local slave labour power.[2] This strategic highway linked occupied Poland with southern Ukraine. It commenced at what was then Polish Lwów (now Ukrainian Lviv) and ended at Stalino, the main gateway to Stalingrad and the Caucasus. At certain points the route came close to the eastern bank of the river Bug. Labour camps surrounded by barbed wire were set up about ten to fifteen kilometres apart along the length of the highway at places including Gaisin, Ivangorod, Uman, Kirovgrad, Mikhailowka, Tarassiwka and Nemirov. They were guarded by armed Ukrainian militiamen and regiments of Lithuanian volunteers.

The OT made the plans for the highway and was responsible for its construction as well as for the personnel needed for the project. It contracted German building companies that brought their own engineers, workmen and even guards to the Ukraine where they taken over by the OT and, therefore, considered members of the Wehrmacht, although they were not subordinated to the SS. The task of guarding the slave workers was the duty of the so-called 'Polizeisicherungsabteilung DG IV' set up in March 1942 in Berlin. The commander of the slave labour camps belonged to this police department and employed Ukrainian, Lithuanian, and Latvian guards from the Schutzmannschaften-Battaillon.[3] The SS units in the region were mainly composed of local ethnic Germans and their task was to procure the labour power. Due to the extremely difficult conditions in the camps, a large number of the local Jewish detainees perished. In order to supply the lacking workforce, SS detachments crossed the river Bug to 'recruit' about 4,000 Romanian Jews. The Jewish ghettos on the western bank of the Bug, that is, in Transnistria, administered by the Romanian authorities, were the main source of this manpower.[4] The Romanian authorities, including the civil governor of Transnistria, Professor Gheorghe Alexianu, and the head of state in Bucharest, Marshal Ion Antonescu, agreed to this 'trade' of Romanian Jews. Their initial plan was to 'evacuate' all the deportees from Bukovina and Bessarabia across the Bug, but the Germans agreed to take only as many as they needed.[5] Aside from the DG IV, Romanian Jewish deportees, many of them natives of Bukovina, had to work on other projects run by the OT such as the construction of a bridge on the Bug between Trihati and Ochakov connecting Transnistria with the German-controlled 'Reichskommissariat Ukraine'.

Only at the end of 1942 did the SS leadership realize the necessity of improving the work and living conditions in the camps, since the high mortality rate of the slaves could jeopardize its economic plans.[6] In spite of this, units of local ethnic Germans and of the SS continued to organize mass killings of Jews, even of those needed for work. On 6 November 1942 a wave of killings engulfed many slave labour camps beyond the Bug. Thousands of Jews, many of them natives of Romania, were killed in the camps of Brailov, Gaisin and Bar. By September 1943 only about 1,500 Romanian Jews were still alive out of those handed over by the Romanian authorities for building the DG IV. Between 10 and 18 December 1943 the

SS killed the majority of those who remained. In all, only 150 Romanian Jews used on the construction of the highway survived.[7]

LEGAL INVESTIGATIONS

The trial in Ulm in 1957–58 of members of Einsatzgruppe A and Gestapo responsible for crimes in Lithuania had drawn attention to the crimes committed by Germans in the occupied territories in Eastern Europe. Due to this trial, Ministers of Justice and judicial senators decided to set up in Ludwigsburg, on 1 December 1958, the Central Office of the County Courts Administration for the Elucidation of Nazi Crimes (Zentrale Stelle der Landesjustizverwaltungen zur Aufklärung nationalsozialistischer Verbrechen).[8] Therefore, from the end of the 1950s through to the 1970s, a series of investigations and trials concerning crimes committed by SS, SD, police, auxiliary personnel and German civil authorities were carried out by German prosecutors and judges. After former survivors brought charges and made legal depositions against those responsible for the suffering and death of hundreds of people, the German public prosecutor's offices initiated a larger investigation in order to bring to court those responsible for the killings and mass executions in the slave labour camps of south-western Ukraine.

Through the translation of his diary into German in 1960 under the title *Lasst Mich Leben* (Let Me Live), Daghani made it also possible that the crimes in Mikhailowka and Tarassiwka would be included in this larger investigation. It is uncertain whether it was just a coincidence or it was his deliberate decision to publish his diary in German at that particular time; however, it played a decisive role in widening the investigations. The translator, Dr Siegfried Rosenzweig, who lived in Munich, sent a copy of the diary to the Chief German Prosecutor, E. Schule, in Ludwigsburg.[9] Dr Rozenzweig also sent copies to others figures in Germany, including the Catholic prelate of Heidelberg, Dr Hermann Maas, who considered it 'a historical document about the most awful renunciation of God and about the most dreadful sins', as well as 'a call to the Germans whose tyrants and their subjects had committed such shameful deeds'.[10] Thus, after almost twenty years, the crimes of Mikhailowka and Tarassiwka became known in Germany through the translation of Daghani's diary.

After the Central Office in Ludwigsburg decided that the incriminatory material was sufficient, the investigation was forwarded to the Federal Court, which distributed it to the County Public Prosecutor Offices, to which the accused persons belonged according to their place of residence. In their turn, these Public Prosecutor Offices had to decide whether all conditions were appropriate for a detailed investigation. Therefore, from the summer of 1960, the Public Prosecutor Offices in Hildesheim, Koblenz and Lübeck opened investigations regarding mass executions and Nazi crimes carried out under SS and SD command in south-western Ukraine.[11]

The Public Prosecutor's Office in Lübeck was led by Dr Dieter Joachim, who, during the investigation built up close contact with the Daghanis, even visiting them in 1974. After the investigation was officially opened, it took years for the Public Prosecutor's Office to collect sufficient material and data relating to the suspects and eyewitnesses. The documentation contained hundreds of names, classified in card indexes as well as maps, showing where the slave labour camps had been located.

By 1965 the collected material seemed to be sufficient to begin the recording of testimonies and Daghani went to Lübeck in June in order to make a formal legal deposition. It was his first official appearance before representatives of the German Court. He must have had the feeling of being on the right track in his pursuit of justice, even though it had taken more than twenty years. He was surprised to learn new facts about the case. What he believed about the DG IV as being just a connection between Gaisin and Uman, turned out in fact to be a much larger project on which thousands of slave labourers had a similar fate to the inmates of Mikhailowka.

EYEWITNESS TESTIMONY AS A SOURCE OF HISTORICAL ANALYSIS

Although the number of historical publications concerning the fate of about 250,000 Romanian Jews during the Second World War has increased considerably due to the work of researchers such as Jean Ancel, Randolph L. Braham, I.C. Butnaru and Radu Ioanid, the written and audio-recorded testimonies of eyewitnesses who directly experienced deportation and detention in Transnistria have barely been used as historical sources. Many of these eyewitness testimonies were published only in the last ten years; some of them are still manuscripts waiting to be published, and oral history, especially in Romania, is still a relatively young branch of historical research. Such testimonies present the personal experiences of ordinary people directly involved in major political events, and provide numerous details undetectable in official files.

The slave labour camps were in Ukraine, rather than Transnistria, and not under Romanian authority. However, what the detainees experienced there can be regarded as part of the Transnistria memorial. After thousands of Romanian Jews were handed over to the Germans by the Romanian authorities with the assent of Marshal Antonescu, those slave labour camps beyond the river Bug became part of the ordeal endured by Transnistrian deportees and, therefore, part of Romanian history too.

One can distinguish two main categories of testimonies:

1. Those which were the result of simultaneously writing down the experienced events in the period during which they took place.
2. Those which resulted from a process of remembrance several years after the experienced events (the memoirs).

Within the first category a distinction must be made between diaries written on the spot (for example, Mirjam Bercovici-Korber, *Jurnal de Ghetou: Djurin, Transnistria, 1941–1943*) and diaries written months or a few years after the personal experience, but based on notes made while in the labour camp (for example, Daghani's *The Grave is in the Cherry Orchard*). Of the second category, one could also make a distinction between two kinds of testimonies. On one hand, those which, in spite of being written from remembrance, contain exact names and data related to people, places and dates (for example, Ruth Glasberg Gold, *A Survivor's Memoir: Ruth's Journey*). On the other hand there are testimonies based mainly on remembrance, written from memory. In both cases of this second category, the narration could have been influenced and completed by additional knowledge, gained by the author due to his/her own research regarding the historical upheavals of the period (for example, Felicia (Steigman) Carmelly, 'Childhood Robbed' in the volume *Shattered! 50 Years of Silence: History and Voices of the Tragedy in Romania and Transnistria*).

Within the first category of testimonies set out above, a distinction must be made concerning the age and place of detention of the author. Two examples, namely the teenage girl Mirjam Korber and the artist Arnold Daghani in his 30s, illustrate this difference well. Korber spent those critical years in the ghetto of Djurin in Transnistria. Unlike Daghani, Korber started to keep a diary without thinking that her notes could ever be read by anybody else: 'What I am writing here is in vain. Nobody will ever read it and if I get away from here I will burn all that is related to these cursed times in Djurin. But in spite of this I continue to write.'[12] Even if in her vision the events and stories she described seemed to be meaningless and monotonous, she continued to record moments of ghetto life for her own spiritual need. She began her diary shortly after the 'evacuation' from the Bukovinian Kimpolong (Câmpulung) on 4 October 1941 and kept it until October 1943. Thus, over two years she caught the main aspects of the everyday life of the deportees in the ghetto of Djurin. Sometimes her entries follow on at intervals of two or three days, but at other times of weeks, depending on her mood that could have been influenced by the events and news in the ghetto.

Most of the entries date from the first year of her deportation,[13] while she had to adjust herself to conditions and situations she could never have imagined before: 'I start only today to describe, rather to sketch again the monstrosities we experienced, and who knows whether something more horrible isn't in store for us.'[14] The alternation between hope and disappointment caused by the rumours about repatriation led Korber to make more frequent entries in her diary.[15] In an entry dated Thursday, 2 September 1943, she wrote, 'Why did I start to write again? Because our return home has become very acute. There are for three weeks rumours that we will go home. Because these rumours are nothing new to us, I did not pay any attention to them. But now it seems to be something real.'[16] Rumours regarding new laws or regulations concerning the deportees often reached the ghettos and the labour camps quite distorted, thus causing confusion. The agitation aroused by the rumour during the first weeks of September 1943 that the 'first deportees from Southern Bukovina' would be allowed to return to their homes can be explained by the readiness of the Romanian government to repatriate the Dorohoi Jews deported in 1941 'by mistake' and the orphans up to the age of 15.[17] Korber mentioned in her diary that the reason for a possible permit to return home could be an amnesty decree issued on 6 September by Marshal Antonescu. However, it is not known if any Jews were repatriated as a result of this decree. Many events of the Second World War are also reflected in Korber's diary such as the participation of some Italian divisions on the eastern front as allies in the German–Romanian coalition.[18] The Italian soldiers left a positive impression, as they showed compassion for the deportees. Similar appreciations about the Italian soldiers in Transnistria were recorded also by other deportees.[19]

Korber was only 18 years old when she started to keep her diary. Her vision of what was worth writing down was different from Daghani's very deliberate intention to note aspects and details, including names and ranks of the camp guards and officers in order to publish them or even to use them for bearing testimony in a court of law. The conditions from one camp or ghetto to another also varied. It is hard to imagine that Daghani could have been able to keep a diary like Korber, since he had to hide his shorthand notes.[20] Unlike Daghani, Korber, fearing repression, probably avoided registering in her diary details about the Romanian soldiers, Ukrainian and Jewish militiamen as well as about the only Romanian gendarme who guarded the ghetto.[21] But the fact that Korber's notes could scarcely have been used as incriminating testimonies in a court of law does not disqualify her diary as historical testimony. On the contrary, her diary contributes to a better understanding of the life of deportees in Transnistria, expressing the particular fears and concerns of an 18-year-old girl.

NATHAN SEGALL'S REPORT

Although Daghani can be considered the chronicler of Mikhailowka, another detainee also left behind a testimony from the camp in the shape of a report compiled two months before the inmates were executed. Nathan Segall was the prisoners' spokesman at Mikhailowka and dictated his report in October 1942.[22] Since Daghani escaped the camp before this report was written, he learnt about its existence only in 1961. Daghani considered the report 'untrustworthy', finding several inaccuracies in it, and had serious doubts as to whether it could ever be used as a historical document of reference. The confrontation between Segall's testimony and Daghani's raises questions over the historical interpretation of individual accounts based on personal experience. This is not a singular case since often people who experienced the same occurrences remember them in different terms.[23] In this case one might also take into consideration the fact that Segall's position as spokesman was different from that of Daghani. However, despite its deficiencies, the report contributes to a better understanding of the oral and written testimonies provided by the victims of the Holocaust. Daghani considered it

187

necessary to correct Segall's errors, writing a six-page-long footnote to it. The report also contains sentences accepted by Daghani which are worthy of being taken into consideration.

The report brings us back to 18 August 1942 when SS officers came to the quarry (Cariera de Piatră) near Ladijin (Ladyžino), under Romanian authority on the western bank of the river Bug, in order to take Jewish deportees for slave labour on the DG IV. According to Segall, people were taken indiscriminately: old men and women, sick people, children. This is an important detail confirmed by Daghani, and contrasts with the usual German policy. Were those unfit for work from the very beginning 'sentenced' to death in the labour camp of Mikhailowka, with the tacit consent of the Romanian authorities? When the deportees arrived on the bank of the river Bug, there was a ferry waiting for the women and children, while the male deportees had to swim across. Not all of those 'recruited' from the quarry were transported to Mikhailowka, with some sent to other slave labour camps in the region such as Krasnapolka, Tarassiwka, Ivangorod and Gaisin. The brutality of the German and Lithuanian guards at Mikhailowka seemed to outdo the arbitrariness of the Romanian soldiers in Transnistria. Weekly raids on Sundays by the SS served to intimidate the people, depriving them of their last personal belongings. The Lithuanian guards in particular turned out to be frightening because they were 'illiterate, certainly former peasants at any rate, degenerated individuals for whom a human life did not matter'.[24]

Segall's report reveals a painful aspect of camp life: Jewish policemen. As elsewhere in the ghettos, labour and concentration camps, the oppressing authorities established a Jewish 'police'. In many cases Jewish councils were charged with organizing such a police, although there was no tradition in their communities of having this kind of internal security organization. The Germans laid down some criteria for the selection of Jewish 'police' members, but these were often neglected. It was more important for them to create a small group of Jewish men ready to obey their orders. At the same time the Jewish committee or ghetto leaders tried to assign reliable men in the Jewish 'police' so that they should serve the Jewish community and not the Germans.[25] Although Segall was spokesman for the entire camp, including the Ukrainian Jews, he had less authority among the latter group. There were two policemen, aged 22 and 24, who served in the section for Ukrainian Jews, one of whom was known as a brutal executor of SS orders, in spite of his Jewish origin: 'These two Jews belong to the darkest chapter of our dark life there.'[26]

Segall used the first person plural in his report, including himself amongst all the detainees sent to work at the gravel pit and on the highway. Daghani was irritated by this, for, as long as he was at Mikhailowka, Segall was only once told to work on the highway.[27] Analysing Daghani's comments on the report, one could conclude that Segall tried to prepare a positive image of himself for the time after the war, in case of an Allied victory over Nazi Germany. Daghani doubted the merits Segall ascribed to himself in rescuing people from executions or taking care of the detainees' health. He was certainly disappointed by the report, not only because in his view Segall distorted the truth, but also because there was almost nothing new that he could learn from it, as he initially had hoped, especially because in his position Segall had more access to information than others. The most sensational discovery was a note on the daily ration of food, which, according to Segall, consisted of twenty grams of meat. As Daghani, his wife and a former inmate who visited them in 1973 remembered, they saw meat in their soup only once.[28]

Segall's report represents that of an individual torn between his duty towards the sufferings of his fellow inmates and the temptation of using his position for personal advantages once the war was over. The value of this document consists of reflecting the terrible psychological pressure of persecution. Even if Segall might have felt a certain keenness to become spokesman and assume a leading position in the camp, he testified to the difficulty of his position. Often he had to decide about life and death as the SS instructed him to draw up lists of those who were to be selected for execution. He strove as much as he could to put on the list the sick and elderly, thus those who had fewer chances of survival.

Segall was murdered together with the inmates removed to the labour camp of Tarassiwka after Mikhailowka was dissolved.[29] When in November 1943 he accompanied a representative of the Dohrmann Company to Transnistria, he had the opportunity to escape but returned to Tarassiwka. The execution of the detainees in Tarassiwka took place, according to Daghani, on 10 December 1943. However, a document issued in March 1944 by the Jewish Head Office in Bucharest mentioned that 'across the Bug about 438 Jews are working in a camp called Tarasivca supervised by

Germans where on 3 December (1943) Natan Segall, native from Dorohoi deceased'.[30] This formulation gives the impression that Segall died of natural causes one week before the executions.

MEMOIRS: NARRATIVE AND ARTISTIC TESTIMONIES FROM
BEYOND THE BARBED WIRE

One can divide the memoirs related to Transnistria into two categories: memoirs written shortly after the war (for example, E. Muniu, *Pogromurile din Basarabia şi alte Câteva Întâmplări*, published in 1947) and memoirs written in the 1990s (the collection edited by Felicia (Steigman) Carmelly: *Shattered! 50 Years of Silence*, 1997; Ruth Glasberg Gold, *A Survivor's Memoir*, 1993). Felicia Carmelly's project provided much significant material from this forgotten region of the Holocaust. The volume contained thirteen accounts of Transnistria survivors, together with her own, thus considerably increasing the research basis of the topic. These memoirs contribute to the understanding of those aspects of the Transnistria ordeal which would be difficult to trace only by processing official files in archives. How was it possible that so many people could be humiliated and dispossessed of their human dignity and how could they come to terms with their fate, which changed so radically from one day to the next? What was their reaction and attitude?

A first finding from reading the memoirs is that the Jewish families affected by deportation were not aware of the real danger that they faced. The lack of information and the belief that in the modern world an extreme right-wing ideology would not be able to reawaken an 'obsessive hatred and blood thirst toward innocent people' led them to neglect the ominous threat.[31] Although anti-Semitism was an open state policy since 1938 and became more oppressive after 1940, people still believed that it did not threaten their lives. Even after the pogroms in Dorohoi (1 July 1940) and Iaşi (29 June 1941) people kept their hopes alive for better days.

Since September 1941, there were rumours about deportations of Jews from Bukovina and Bessarabia, but it was impossible to get more information since the plan to do so was kept secret. In some cases, Bessarabian Jews were driven across the river Dniester into the territory of the future Transnistria, which, until the agreement of Tighina, was controlled by the German Army.[32] Some news about this action could have reached Bukovina as rumours of possible deportations. The actual deportations commenced during the second half of September in Bessarabia and during the second week of October 1941 in Bukovina. Generally, deportation orders were given from three days to just a few hours before the deportation took place, so that people often had scarcely enough time to prepare themselves for the long journey. They were not informed for how long and under what conditions they would be deported. One rumour was that, once 'relocated', Jews would be given a piece of land to cultivate; another was that Jews would be deported to be killed. In the Cernauți area, the ghettoization of the Jews was the first sign of future deportation, although people could still scarcely believe that they would indeed be deported.[33] Since bribery became a practice to escape deportation, Jews believed that the authorities 'are playing tricks' in order to take their money but in the end would not deport anybody.[34]

The official terms used for deportation were those of 'evacuation' and 'displacement', giving a harmless connotation to deceive the deportees. People 'evacuated' during the first wave believed that they would be back soon.[35] The deportees were also quite confused about the reason for their deportation. As the anti-Semitic laws and the press campaigns grew worse, they became aware that the authorities and part of the population with extreme right-wing convictions would like to get rid of them. The accusation that Jews, especially those from Bukovina and Bessarabia, were pro-Soviet was often repeated in the newspapers. The authors of memoirs refer almost without exception to the attitude of the Bukovinian and Bessarabian Jews towards the Soviets. They hoped for a better future under a Soviet regime after the experience they had under Romanian governments, but many of them were disappointed during the Soviet occupation. Romania, an ally of Nazi Germany, seemed to them a more serious threat and some of the Bessarabian and Bukovinian Jews preferred to flee with the Soviets when the Romanian and German armies launched their attack for the 'liberation' of Northern Bukovina and Bessarabia.[36] Those who were unable to leave Romania before the attack on the Soviet Union, but submitted applications for that purpose to the Soviet consulate, were also deported regardless of their place of residence after the applications fell into the hands of the Romanian Security Police (Siguranța).[37]

There were cases when Romanians, who had better information channels and could learn more about the 'displacement' of the Jewish population, warned the Jews. A gentile gesture even came from a servant of the regime, the prefect of Dorohoi, Barbu Stroici, who summoned the leaders of the Jewish community to inform them about the anti-Jewish measures planned by the Antonescu regime and to assure them that he would protect his Jews from hooliganism, vandalism, violence and other crimes.[38] In some special cases, non-Jewish neighbours were ready to help Jews, to hide them to escape murder and deportation.[39] However, most memoirs mention the rather hostile attitude of the non-Jewish population living in the same town or village, when the Jews were marched to the railway stations to be deported. Instead of compassion, some Romanians and Ukrainians profited from their deportation. While the first transport of Jews was on its way to Transnistria, many Romanians swarmed to Bukovina to enrich themselves by looting Jewish properties, the so-called 'gold-rushers'.[40]

During the deportation, people became more aware of the cruelty that surrounded them. For many of them, crossing the river Dniester was the first shock, when they were deprived of their identity papers and exposed to the arbitrariness of gendarmes and local peasants.[41] Deportees started to realize that without their papers they no longer had an identity and no one would be able to search for them if they disappeared.[42] Some more courageous people in the first groups of deportees who witnessed tragic scenes attempted to escape. Many were shot; others were caught and sent back with the next convoys. Consequently, among the next groups of deportees, rumours were spread that they would be shot near the river Dniester or thrown alive into the river. In one case, a convoy of Bessarabian Jews was shot after they were ordered to cross the Dniester, despite bribing the Romanian commanding officer who took their money, promising to let them live.[43] Once beyond the Dniester, the gendarmes who guarded the convoys did not find it in themselves to tell the deportees that they were sent to Transnistria 'to die of cold and hunger'.[44]

The ways in which the authors describe the living conditions in the ghettos and labour camps of Transnistria are very similar. Words like typhoid fever, starvation, cold, dirt and death can be found in each narrative characterizing the everyday life of the deportees. Thus, the Romanian authorities created conditions that inevitably led to the 'natural' death of tens of thousands of people.[45]

Conditions varied between a ghetto and a concentration or labour camp.

The most evident contrast could be drawn between the ghetto in Ladijin, described by Isak Weißglas as a 'Jewish paradise' and the concentration camp in Vapniarca. The latter functioned as a typical concentration camp, surrounded by three barbed wire fences with watchtowers every fifty metres. Unlike other camps in Transnistria, people deported to Vapniarca were regarded as 'political detainees', and not only Jews but many Ukrainian and some Romanian 'opponents' were detained there. The most numerous was the group of Ukrainian Jews deported from Odessa after the massacre from 23 to 25 October 1941. They were soon joined by several hundred Jewish deportees from Bessarabia and Bukovina. In August and September 1942, a contingent of 722 Jewish deportees from a number of Romanian cities, arrested for various alleged offences, was brought to Vapniarca.[46] Besides harsher detention conditions, Vapniarca can be compared to German extermination camps but here, instead of using the more expensive Zyclone B gas, pea cattle fodder was introduced as meal for humans. It was a slow but efficient extermination of the deportees, many of whom died after becoming sick of lathyrism.[47] After three months, the 'action' was stopped due to the courage with which doctor detainees managed to inform, through Romanian train personnel and civilian functionaries, their colleagues and the Jewish community, who interceded on behalf of the detainees.

Although surveillance was very strict, detainees were able, while risking their lives, to establish contact with people willing to relay their suffering. Examples of humanitarian gestures even came from some Romanian officers.[48] The most important thing for detainees was to get information to relatives in Romania, who might send them money and other necessities. Often these helpers were military and railway employees, who travelled regularly between Romania and Transnistria. Some commanding officers with acquaintances among deportees also provided similar important services at great personal risk. They carried messages sent from deportees to their families, to the Central Jewish Committee and other organizations.[49] One of these humane officers was Colonel Motora who after the war was awarded the distinction 'Righteous Gentile' for saving the lives of 450 Jewish deportees during their march towards Romania in March 1944.[50]

THE ARNOLD DAGHANI COLLECTION

Arnold Daghani and his wife Anişoara (or Nanino, neé Rabinovici) were deported from Cernauţi on 7 June 1942 to the eastern edge of Transnistria, near the river Bug, to Cariera de Piatră (the quarry). The first record in his diary dates from 18 August 1942, two months and a week after their deportation. It was the day when German soldiers came to 'recruit' Transnistrian deportees, taking them over from the Romanian military authorities across the river Bug for slave labour in the territory under German rule. Owing to the testimony of another deportee at the quarry, Isak Weißglas, father of the poet Immanuel Weißglas, we can approximately reconstitute the detention conditions that Daghani experienced. About twelve kilometres from the quarry was the village of Ladijin (Ladyžino) with a large Jewish ghetto, to which deportees from the quarry were sometimes sent. Both Weißglas and Daghani were sent to Ladijin and from there, together with 480 other deportees, they were taken by the Germans to Mikhailowka.[51] Daghani was not impressed by the conditions in the ghetto: 'Neither at the Quarry nor here, at Ladyshino (Ladijin), have the Rumanian authorities ever made available any other food except a bread-ration, nor have they given any means to the deportees to make a living. And yet "life" is going on, but how long will it go on in this improvised Gypsy-like camp on the outskirts of the village?'[52]

The commemorative-artistic legacy of Arnold Daghani consists of the diary evoking the daily routine and the tragic end of the deportees in the slave labour camp of Mikhailowka and the ghetto of Bershad; of the paintings and drawings he secretly produced in the camp and ghetto; and of the albums containing additional literary and artistic works related to his experience as a deportee, which he wrote and made during the rest of his life. In addition, Daghani left behind his correspondence during the 1960s and 1970s with the former representatives of the August Dohrmann Company involved in the construction of the DG IV, with the prosecutor who led the investigation into the killings at Mikhailowka, and with various other people and institutions involved in his fight for justice.

The Arnold Daghani Collection also contains copies of the files of the Court Investigation in Lübeck including Daghani's testimony given in June 1965 about the killings committed in Mikhailowka.[53] Based on his diary, Daghani described the circumstances of the crimes and their perpetrators. However, he was not eyewitness to all of the murders. Most of them were described to him by his fellow inmates who witnessed them. Murders occurred quite seldom in Daghani's presence although he witnessed several times how the incriminated guards selected and dragged off their victims to the place of execution.[54] Generally, shootings of prisoners selected for this purpose took place outside the camp, out of sight of the other detainees. Only those who had to bury the victims had direct knowledge of how the executions took place and who exactly the executioners were. They told their fellow inmates what they witnessed and therefore the information was recorded by Daghani.[55] Owing to Daghani's diary, the names of those involved in this kind of killing could be revealed during the court investigation. Friese, Maass, Mintel, Wisotzkas, Zelinkas, Sukerka and Strijenskas spread fear and terror around them in Mikhailowka, being responsible for the death of hundreds of victims. There were also exceptions among those who had power over the slave labourers, like Willy Buder, the commander of the camp between 1 December 1942 and 14 February 1943. He came from Erfurt and was a bookbinder, then a policeman before the war. Daghani described him as an 'honest, kind-hearted' person, stating that as long as he was the camp's commander no actions of violence against the Jewish inmates took place.[56] Daghani testified to Buder's good intentions regarding the detainees by mentioning that on New Year's Eve he wished them a healthy new year and that they should all be back home in the year 1943.[57]

Due to the fact that the events related by Daghani occurred only sixty years ago, the historical investigation of his writings can be expanded by means of oral history based on interviews with persons who shared similar conditions in the camp at Mikhailowka or the ghetto at Bershad. The search for survivors led to three persons: Philipp Kellmer, Tvi Zemmel and Shoshana Nauman.

ORAL HISTORY: THE TESTIMONY OF PHILIPP KELLMER

Philipp Kellmer was born in Cernauți and deported with his family in June 1942, when the Daghanis were also deported.[58] Like the Daghanis, they also escaped the first wave of deportation in October 1941. There is no evidence of how Daghani and his wife were able to do so, but their situation might have been similar to that of the Kellmer family.[59] Philipp Kellmer's father managed to obtain a 'permit to remain' through a local Jewish lawyer who knew his former teacher, Professor Banațeanu, who was in close contact with

Stere Marinescu, the cabinet chief of General Calotescu, the governor of Bukovina. Through close and reliable acquaintances, or by bribing the authorities, many Jews were able to remain in Cernauţi after October 1941, even if they did not belong to those professional categories that the authorities officially permitted to stay.[60]

Kellmer was 18 years old when he met Daghani in Mikhailowka. In spite of the age difference between them, they became friends, a friendship that became closer after Kellmer caught Daghani secretly making notes in a small scruffy book.[61] This might have been one of the two practice books for English shorthand in which Daghani made notes about events, dates and people in the camp, from which he was able to compile his diary in a more polished form after the war.[62] Daghani was afraid, even of his fellow inmates, and asked Kellmer to keep quiet about it. It is still uncertain to what extent Daghani made these notes in English or Romanian. There are no doubts that he could speak English well since he worked before the war as an English–Romanian translator in a clerical position in Bucharest. According to Kellmer, he made notes in Romanian, the language he also used when speaking to his wife Anişoara. Other sources indicate that his notes were in English, taking into consideration his caution and anxiety that somebody, even a fellow inmate, could discover and read the lines he wrote.[63]

As in the play *Ghetto* by Joshua Sobol, many of the detainees had a particular 'role' to play, but in a much bloodier 'play'. Whereas Daghani was the artist of the camp, Kellmer was one of the two policemen for the Romanian Jews, as recommended by Nathan Segall after Edy Weiss, one of the two previous policemen, became ill. The Jewish police had very limited authority. Kellmer's duty was to wake the Romanian prisoners at 5 or 6 a.m. for work and they had to leave the barracks in fifteen minutes. Ukrainian Jews were housed separately.

Kellmer lost his father in the camp as he was ill, despite being only 42 years old, after he was put on the 'death list' by Nathan Segall. Kellmer was aware that Segall had no choice because the execution quota prescribed by the SS had to be fulfilled.[64] The matter of killing people was a daily concern and nobody could feel safe, due to the unpredictable mood of the SS officers, Lithuanian guards or even some of the OT men.

Kellmer survived due to the partisan attack on Mikhailowka and sought safety in the ghetto of Bershad. When he met Daghani there, he told him what had happened. According to Kellmer, when the pro-Soviet Ukrainian partisans liberated the camp on 7 August 1943, there were only two SS soldiers and a few guards around. The attack took place at midnight. The guards were quickly disarmed without shedding much blood; only one of them was killed during the operation. The partisans entered the stables where the deportees were sleeping and told them that they were free. They opened the gates of the camp but only a few of the deportees left. They were confused because the front line was far away, the surrounding area was full of German units and all around was a foreign environment. During the whole night they discussed what they should do. Only a few of them decided to leave the camp. Segall argued that either everybody should leave the camp or no one, as the retuning SS could subject those who stayed to harsh reprisals. Finally they agreed that there were few chances of survival by hiding in the surroundings and, therefore, the majority decided to stay.[65] The following morning SS troops came to the camp with the Obersturmbannführer Maass, who could not believe his eyes seeing almost all the detainees still there, and that, in spite of the open gates, so few had left the camp.

Two aspects of this unusual liberation puzzled Daghani: why were the Ukrainian partisans so keen to liberate a Jewish slave labour camp? And what prompted Segall to act in the way he did? Only decades later, after examining all the sources available, did Daghani and Anișoara realize that Segall probably wanted to prevent a trap into which the detainees could have fallen by fleeing en masse through the open gates.[66] Some years later, Daghani learnt from Kellmer some further details about that night. Kellmer's explanation for why the camp was liberated that night and not earlier seems to be based on the very personal motive of one of the villager-guards in the camp named Vanka or Vasia, who became a spy for the partisans. Allegedly, he felt in love with Henia, one of the detained girls, and wanted to liberate her with the help of the partisans. Her family also decided to escape and fled to Bershad.[67]

In 1943 the Jewish ghetto of Bershad became a shelter for those who managed to escape the slave labour camps run by the Germans.[68] Barbarism and art tried to live together in ghettos like Bershad where there was an amateur theatre with performances almost every Saturday in the early afternoon.[69] In the ghetto of Shargorod young people initiated a clandestine literary newspaper, with copies produced by hand. Intellectuals in particular sought a spiritual release from the everyday sorrow they experienced in the ghettos through creative activities. When the Soviet Army approached the river Bug, the Romanian authorities decided to repatriate all the Jews deported from Bukovina, Bessarabia and the rest of Romania. However, their plan could not be carried out because of the rapid advance of the Soviets.[70] Under these circumstances the Romanian authorities tried to give the world the impression of rescuing the Jewish deportees they had oppressed for three hard years in the ghettos of Transnistria.[71]

The Daghanis were not the first detainees from Mikhailowka to find shelter in Bershad. Months earlier other inmates managed to flee and had lived there since then.[72] Others, like Kellmer, arrived in Bershad two months after the Daghanis, together forming a group of refugees from Mikhailowka. The improvement in living conditions and the lenient treatment of the deportees in Transnistria, compared to that in the camps beyond the river Bug, did not guarantee their lives. They just had a better chance of surviving.[73] Eyewitness reports of the survivors show how differently they experienced life in these ghettos. There were substantial differences from one place to another, and the living conditions of the deportees often depended on the predisposition of the local commander. Research related to the ghetto of Bershad also reflects differences in how those who lived there perceived their own situation. Kellmer, for instance, called Bershad 'our paradise' just as Isak Weißglas had described the ghetto in Ladijin as a 'Jewish paradise'.[74] It was certainly easier to survive in Bershad than in the slave labour camps and it is very likely that those who escaped from Mikhailowka appreciated this chance.

THE TESTIMONY OF TVI ZEMMEL

Tvi Zemmel is known in Daghani's diary as Zwie Herschel Semmel, the son of Benedykt Semmel, who manufactured for Daghani the tin tube in which he kept his drawings and paintings. Zemmel was born in Cernauţi in 1920 from where he was also deported, together with his family, in June 1942. When he was interviewed in February 2004, in Haifa, Israel, he was in hospital, and his health condition seriously affected his capacity to remember things from the past.[75] However, he could not forget his terrible experience in Mikhailowka[76] and the pain of losing his mother and sister under tragic circumstances. The latter happened on 26 April 1943 when fifty-five inmates were loaded on a lorry and transported to the place of execution. Zemmel was one of the few detainees at Mikhailowka who did not obey Segall's order and, together with his father, escaped the camp when it was attacked by partisans. He joined the partisans and became a Soviet soldier, later returning to Transnistria in order to find his father. After the war they emigrated together to Israel. Tvi Zemmel died in Haifa in 2008.

THE TESTIMONY OF SHOSHANA NAUMAN

Shoshana Nauman (née Rosa Brenner Engelberg) was one of the Transnistrian survivors who lived with her mother in the ghetto of Bershad. During the time of Daghani's stay there she was only 10 years old. However, she remembered the 'mysterious' painter she saw several times on the streets of the ghetto and who once even made a drawing in the room where she lived with her mother.

Nauman was born in 1933, also in Cernauți, into a modestly religious Jewish family. When in October 1941 the Romanian authorities started to deport Jews from the ghetto of Cernauți, her family was unable to procure a 'permit to remain' and was among the first Bukovinian Jews deported to Transnistria. The deportees believed they would be given land in Ukraine, moving into the houses of Ukrainians and Jews who fled before the Romanian and German armies occupied the territory. Once in Mărculești, on the western bank of the river Dniester, the deportees realized what the authorities had in store for them. Gendarmes started to mistreat them, depriving everybody not only of their valuables, but also of their documents. Those who refused to hand them over were shot on the spot.

Nauman arrived in Bershad together with her mother, father, sister and brother on 16 December 1941, but due to the widespread typhoid fever, she soon experienced the death of her father, sister and brother: 'While beyond the Bug people were shot dead, in Bershad they died from themselves.'[77] Men were taken for work, and that was the only way to gain some food. In Bershad there were also groups of German military forces whom Nauman often saw on the streets. They even ran a brothel. There were very few local Jews; the majority of the ghetto inhabitants were deportees from Bukovina and, since they were all directed to Bershad, the ghetto became very crowded. Before the war about 4,000 Ukrainian Jews lived in Bershad, whereas in 1942 the number of Jews exceeded 10,000.[78] The ghetto was also overcrowded because during the military operations in the summer of 1941 many houses were destroyed. Only due to the deaths of hundreds of victims of the typhoid epidemic did living conditions in the ghetto became bearable. By the time Daghani and his wife found shelter there, accommodation space was available. They could rent a place to live for ten Marks (probably RKKS[79]) and, like everybody else in the ghetto, they had to wear the Star of David.[80]

Nauman discovered the identity of the 'mysterious' artist, who drew in the rooms where she lived with her mother, after visiting the museum at Yad Vashem, Jerusalem. She had started to paint in the 1970s, decades after her experiences as a young girl. She felt it her duty to show the world the ordeal of her family and of the other Transnistria deportees. For Nauman, it was also a way of coming to terms with her painful memories. She produced several paintings depicting her family's deportation, the living conditions and the atrocities she witnessed in Bershad. She worked only from her own memory and painted as trustworthily as possible all those images that she still had very vividly in her mind. She never painted things she had not witnessed with her own eyes.[81]

Before the Russians liberated the ghetto, there was an attempt by the Jews living there, in collaboration with Ukrainian partisans, to get rid of the German and Romanian guards. The military authorities discovered the plans and ordered reprisals. Ukrainian partisans were hanged on the streets of Bershad. About 250 Jews, among them members of the Jewish militia, were locked in a wet, flooded bunker. They were kept there for more than a week until they died of cold and exhaustion. Nauman depicted people being forced into the bunker.[82]

On her visit to Yad Vashem she accidentally caught sight of a picture that closely resembled one of her own that she had painted from memory in 1973 (Plate 34).[83] It depicted the same interior with two entrances, a wooden bed, smoking stove, and a rack stretched along the wall on which food used to hang so that rats could not reach it. In the centre of Daghani's picture is the outline of a young girl; Nauman realized that was herself.

The testimonies and memoirs of those who experienced the camps and ghettos of Transnistria provide valuable material on this forgotten region of the Holocaust. They give the reader a better understanding of the actual conditions in which people fought for survival and the ways in which they dealt with the daily rounds of persecution and humiliation. They offer an insight into the lasting impact of such experiences and the role played by memory in analysing the past. It is often in the small and seemingly unimportant details of such writings that the impact of historical events is made evident on human lives.

In March 1944 Daghani and his wife Anişoara arrived in Bucharest after a long and dangerous journey. Nobody was waiting for them, but they had survived ... survived to bear witness in both words and images. *Mass Graves* (1943) is the title of one of Daghani's most poignant watercolours from Bershad (Plate 19). It forms a unique visual monument to the experiences of a land of terror that he was later to synthesize in the memorable sentence: 'The ghost-territory which no geography book ever mapped or listed, yet, although unmentioned and outside any normal world, the cradle of a collective traumatism, has disappeared altogether after two years and seven months [...] only mass graves bear witness to the Inferno that existed during that period.'[84]

NOTES

1. Michael de Boüard was a French historian, member of the Resistance, deportee to Mauthausen, member of the Committee for the History of the Second World War from 1945 to 1981, and a member of the Institut de France: see P. Vidal-Naquet, *Assassins of Memory: Essays on the Denial of Holocaust* (New York: Columbia University Press, 1992), p.13.

2. H. Kaienburg, *Die Wirtschaft der SS* (Berlin: Metropol, 2003), p.448.

3. Ibid., p.449.

4. Although situated on the western bank of the river Bug, a camp under German control was also set up at Braslav, as the highway route crossed the Bug there for a few kilometres. See also R. Ioanid, *The Holocaust in Romania: the Destruction of Jews and Gypsies under the Antonescu Regime, 1940–1944* (Chicago, IL: Ivan R. Dee, 2000).

5. Report of a Romanian officer of 11 October 1941: 'All the Jews from Bessarabia and Bukovina have been evacuated into the region west of the Bug where they will stay during this autumn until, according to the convention concluded with the German state, it will be possible to push them eastwards across the Bug.' Centrul pentru Studierea Istoriei Evreilor din Romania (hereafter CSIER) (Centre for the Study of the History of the Romanian Jews), file III 1045/14, p.14.

6. Such improvements 'according to the available possibilities' meant on paper: a 'more tasty' meal, permission to receive parcels from relatives or international organizations, better distribution of the workload according to the physical capability of each detainee, resting hours during the day for those who had to work in the night and the abolition of corporal punishments that could influence the efficiency of the worker. H. Kaienburg, *Vernichtung durch Arbeit: Die Wirtschaftsbestrebungen der SS und ihre Auswirkungen auf die Existenzbedingungen der KZ-Gefangenen* (Bonn: J.H. Dietz Verlag, 1990), p.328.

7. All of these figures are confirmed by Jean Ancel with reference to the Odessa Archives and the investigations of the lawyer Matatias Carp carried out shortly after the end of the war, when he published his *Black Book* on the Romanian Holocaust: J. Ancel, *Contribuţii la Istoria României: Problema Evreiasca 1933–1944*, vol. 2, part 1 (Bucharest: Editura Hasefer, 2003), p.310.

8. The use of the terms 'war crimes' and 'war criminals' by Allied courts, and the continued use of these

terms by the press, has complicated discussions about Nazi criminality. The German courts have always used the terms 'Nazi crimes' and 'Nazi criminals', dropping the adjective 'war', because the overwhelming majority of Nazi crimes were legally unrelated to wartime conditions. The war was used by the Nazi leaders only as an excuse, and by their apologists today as a rationalization, to hide the ideological basis of their crimes. See A. Rückerl, *NS-Verbrechen vor Gericht: Versuch einer Vergangenheitsbewältigung* (Heidelberg: Müller, 1982).

9. F. Rieper and M. Brandl-Bowen (eds), *Lasst Mich Leben! Stationen im Leben des Künstlers Arnold Daghani* (Springe: zuKlampen Verlag, 2002), p.211.

10. Ibid., p.212.

11. In January 1964, the office of Hildesheim transferred its competency regarding this investigation entirely to the office in Lübeck.

12. M. Bercovici-Korber, *Deportiert: Jüdische Überlebensschicksale aus Rumänien 1941–1944: Ein Tagebuch* (Konstanz: Hartung-Gorre Verlag, 1993), p.109.

13. Ten entries were made during only the first two months in comparison with thirty-three during twelve months in 1942 and only seven during 1943 (one in March, five in September and the last one on 10 October).

14. Bercovici-Korber, *Deportiert*, p.55.

15. The entire ghetto was in preparation fever to leave Djurin. People continued to spread all kind of hope with rumours that in Lipnik they would be given carts and supplies for the journey, sent by the Jewish Central Office from Bucharest. Ibid., p.113.

16. Ibid., p.111.

17. Because of the advance of Soviet troops in autumn 1943, there was a shift in the Romanian Government's attitude towards the deportees. Following negotiations with representatives of the Jewish Community and International Red Cross, in December 1943 the Dorohoi Jews were allowed to return to Romania and a few month later about 5,000 orphans left Transnistria for Romania. F. (Steigman) Carmelly (ed.), *Shattered! 50 Years of Silence: History and Voices of the Tragedy in Romania and Transnistria* (Scarborough, ON: Abbeyfield, 1997), p.123.

18. Bercovici-Korber, *Deportiert*, p.94.

19. J. Prutschi, 'Frozen Silence' in Carmelly (ed.), *Shattered!* p.358.

20. E. Timms, 'Arnold Daghani's Original Diary', pp.4 and 9 in this volume.

21. Bercovici-Korber, *Deportiert*, p.10.

22. Segall dictated his 'Gedächtnisprotokoll eines Augenzeugen' to a fellow detainee named Gerda Brüll on 21 October 1943. An English translation of the report, titled 'Record from Memory of an Eyewitness', with Daghani's remarks, is available in the Arnold Daghani Collection. It is contained in the file *Let Me Live*, a typescript of 300 pages on which Daghani and Mollie Brandl-Bowen worked in the 1980s, with the intention of publishing a revised and extended edition of the diary, *The Grave is in the Cherry Orchard*. (References to this 'authorized manuscript' are identified by the abbreviation AM followed by the page number. This typescript has the catalogue number H5 in the Arnold Daghani Collection, University of Sussex.) See the published report in German in Rieper and Brandl-Bowen (eds), *Lasst Mich Leben!* pp.179–87.

23. Rebecca L. Golbert has recently carried out research on how eyewitnesses have narrated the same event differently; see R.L. Golbert, 'Holocaust Sites in Ukraine: Pechora and the Politics of Memorialisation', *Holocaust and Genocide Studies*, 8, 2 (2004), pp.205–33. See also E. Tonkin, *Narrating Our Past: The Social Construction of Oral History* (Cambridge: Cambridge University Press, 1992) and L.L. Langer, *Holocaust Testimonies: The Ruins of Memory* (New Haven, CT and London: Yale University Press, 1991).

24. To this assertion made by Segall, Daghani gave his opinion against such kind of generalizing, remarking: 'That does not mean that all illiterate peasants are murderers.' AM 202.

25. Candidates for the Jewish police had to be healthy, with military ability and higher education; see *Enzyklopädie des Holocaust: Die Verfolgung und Ermordung der europäischen Juden*, Band II (Munich and Zurich: Piper, 2002), p.699.

26. AM 198. Philipp Kellmer also confirmed in his interview the brutal character of at least one of the Ukrainian Jewish policemen.

27. AM 203.

28. The former inmate from Mikhailowka who visited the Daghanis in July 1973 in Switzerland was Mizzi Locker who also managed to escape before the camp was exterminated. AM 200.

29. At that time there were 178 Bukovinian and 170 Ukrainian Jews in the camp. See N. Segall,

'Gedächtnisprotokoll eines Augenzeugen', 21 October 1943, p.5.

30. Report on the situation of the Jews in Transnistria, 1944: CSIER, file III/309, p.28. The Jewish Head Office probably had no idea in March 1944 that the camp of Tarassiwka had been liquidated in December 1943. Doubts persist as to whether the person in the document dated March 1944 was Segall and whether the mentioned date was accurate. According to Daghani, Segall was still alive on 4 December 1943 when, with Heinz Rosengarten, he visited the ghetto of Bershad, collecting food and clothes supplies for the inmates in Tarassiwka (Rieper and Brandl-Bowen, *Lasst Mich Leben!* p.198).

31. In a transport of deported Jewish people, some of them were discussing why Jews did not resist all the measures taken against them; see R. Udler, 'The Cursed Years' in Carmelly (ed.), *Shattered!* p.395.

32. Due to the agreement of Tighina signed on 30 August 1941 between Germany and Romania, the latter was allowed to establish, in the territory named Transnistria between the rivers Dniester and Bug, an administration in order to 'exploit economically the region'. A. Angrick, 'Rumänien, die SS und die Vernichtung der Juden' in M. Hausleitner, B. Mihok and J. Wetzel, *Rumänien und der Holocaust: Zu den Massenverbrechen in Transnistrien. 1941–1944* (Berlin: Metropol, 2001), p.130.

33. The ghettoization was part of the deportation plan issued by the Supreme Headquarters of the Romanian Army 'in accordance with instructions by Marshal Antonescu'. R. Ioanid, 'The deportation of the Jews to Transnistria' in Hausleitner, Mihok and Wetzel, *Rumänien und der Holocaust*, p.88.

34. R. Glasberg Gold, *Ruth's Journey: A Survivor's Memoir* (Gainesville, FL: University Press of Florida, 1993), p.44.

35. Carmelly (ed.), *Shattered!* p.223.

36. L. Hoffer, 'Ordinary People in Extraordinary Times' in Carmelly (ed.), *Shattered!* pp.272, 350.

37. See also the report of Magdalena Kuhn whose family was deported in September 1942 from Timişoara 'to the river Bug', then handed over to the Germans who eventually shot them. M. Kuhn, 'Timişoara' in Carmelly (ed.), *Shattered!* p.426.

38. M. Leib, 'It began in Dorohoi' in Carmelly (ed.), *Shattered!* p.288.

39. Emma Lustig, a survivor of the carnage in the village of Milie, mentioned in her account how a non-Jewish peasant neighbour offered to hide her family in his home for the night while other local peasants, together with the *Banderovtzes* (pro-German Ukrainian paramilitary bandits called after their leader Bandera), slaughtered the entire Jewish population of Milie; see Gold, *Ruth's Journey*, pp.39, 280.

40. Gold, *Ruth's Journey*, p.38.

41. In the transit camps from Transnistria, gendarmes randomly picked on some of the deportees and brutally beat them up for no apparent reason. Those beatings were intended to intimidate and break the spirit of the deportees in order to prevent any future attempt at resistance. Leib, 'It began in Dorohoi', p.296.

42. H. Rubinger, 'The Bridge Over Troubled Waters' in Carmelly, *Shattered!* p.438.

43. Gold, *Ruth's Journey*, p.55.

44. F. Rosenblatt, 'How I envied the dog' in Carmelly (ed.), *Shattered!* p.370.

45. In a report of the Gendarmerie Legion of Prahova about the circumstances in which forty Jews died on one of the 'death trains' from Iaşi, it was very important for the rapporteur to emphasize that they died because of 'physical weakness' and that 'no violence contributed to the death of the above-mentioned'. In fact, people were locked in overcrowded, stifling freight wagons driven in the torrid sunshine of July in temperatures of over 30°C; see the report of the Gendarmerie Legion Prahova in Carmelly (ed.), *Shattered!* pp.40–1.

46. They were alleged Socialists, Communists, Zionists and members of Jewish organizations, deported after the police had created files on them indicating that they were suspicious. This wave of deportations affected entire Jewish families in Arad, Timişoara and other Romanian cities. I. Benditer, 'Cattle fodder for the victims', in Carmelly (ed.), *Shattered!* p.187.

47. On the suggestion of the German Gestapo representative, the Romanian Ministry of Internal Affairs ordered the introduction of dried peas as food for detainees; it was used as cattle fodder and had a toxic effect on humans. While this solution was initially used as a cheap way of feeding the detainees, it shortly became a criminal act. The measure of the Ministry of Internal Affairs might have had caused the death of the detainees through the accumulation of toxins in the body. Ibid., p.189.

48. One of them was an officer in the ghetto of Shargorod, who helped and supplied the author of an eyewitness testimony with food, as she was still a child, effectively saving her life. Ibid., p.241.

49. Benditer, 'Cattle fodder for the victims', p.190.

50. When troops of the pro-German army wanted to kill by machine gun the convoy consisting of 450 Jews, Colonel Motora prevented the massacre, ordering the Romanian soldiers to close ranks around the convoy and to march faster in order to leave the danger zone as soon as possible. Owing to his energetic intervention, he saved the lives of the 450 deportees. When Colonel Motora learnt that, on the following day, the administration of Transnistria would be transferred to the Germans, and becoming aware of what that could mean for the deportees, he took care that the people would immediately cross the Dniester to Bessarabia. Ibid., p.201.

51. I. Weißglas, 'Ghetto und Deportation' in H. Wiesner (ed.), *In der Sprache der Mörder: Eine Literatur aus Czernowitz, Bukowina* (Berlin: Literaturhaus, 1993), p.143.

52. A. Daghani, *What a Nice World* (1943–77), unpublished book (Arnold Daghani Collection, University of Sussex), p.64.

53. Besides Arnold Daghani's diary, the eyewitness report of Nathan Segall and a letter of Heinz Rosengarten, a fellow inmate of Segall and Daghani, written on 14 September 1943, were also starting points for the prosecution.

54. 'Korn suddenly felt faint [...] Wisotzkas might have observed this because he went to him and ordered Korn to follow him. He followed Wisotzkas. Shortly after that I heard a shot.' 'Zeugenschaftliche Vernehmung', Staatsanwaltschaft Lübeck bei dem Landesgericht, 2 P Js 1629/64, 9 June 1965: vorgeladen Arnold Daghani. Arnold Daghani Collection, University of Sussex (hereafter ZV followed by page number), 20.

55. 'When we returned in the evening to the camp, I learnt from the shoemaker called Fleischer that he had the duty, similar to other inmates, to fill the grave in which these 25 Ukrainian women were thrown. The grave was situated in a glade near the camp. While he approached the mass grave, Fleischer heard whispering voices coming from the grave. The watching officer Strijenskas immediately shot in the direction where the voice came from and gave the order to fill the grave.' ZV 15.

56. ZV 6.

57. ZV 7.

58 During the first days of the deportations many Jews tried to escape by hiding. According to a nominal list issued by the Romanian police there were 338 persons who did so only during the 'evacuation' of 28 June 1942. Many of these Jews were caught or they even surrendered some days later. Among the names was that of Heinz Rosengarten, an engineer from Cernauti, who was with the Daghanis at the quarry and in Mikhailowka. CSIER, file 397/8.

59. After escaping the deportations of October–November 1941, Daghani and Anişoara were allowed to leave the ghetto. They were able to move back into the town owing to a 'provisional residential permit signed by the mayor, Dr Traian Popovici'. Daghani, *What a Nice World*, p.60.

60. Some of those who managed to get the 'permit to remain' even had the possibility of emigrating to Palestine through Romanian tourist agencies such as Romania, which, in May 1942, had a list of ninety-eight persons with permits for emigration. The first emigrants left Cernauţi on 20 June 1942 during the second wave of deportation. However, on 23 June 1942 the Ministry of Internal Affairs annulled their transportation 'until new regulations' were in place. Therefore, those who were waiting to emigrate, but had not yet managed to do so, were deported to Transnistria. Center for Advanced Holocaust Studies, United States Holocaust Memorial Museum, Washington, DC (hereafter USHMM), RG-31M/307, Cernovtsi Regional Archive, reel 9, pp.1-6, 42.

61. Interview conducted by the author with Philipp Kellmer, 16 October 2003, Paris. A tape of the recorded interview together with a typed summary of it can be found at the Centre for German-Jewish Studies, University of Sussex, Brighton.

62. Timms, 'Arnold Daghani's Original Diary', pp.4 and 9 in this volume.

63. Ibid. See also Rieper and Brandl-Bowen, *Lasst Mich Leben!* p.321.

64. Interview with Philipp Kellmer.

65. Interview with Philipp Kellmer.

66. Rieper and Brandl-Bowen, *Lasst Mich Leben!* p.91.

67. Vanka or Vasia arrived after the war in the Soviet-controlled Cernauţi to marry Henia. However, Henia's parents were against the marriage. When the frontier to Romania was reopened, Henia and her family moved to Bucharest and soon after emigrated to South America. AM 193.

68. Shortly after the Daghanis' arrival in Bershad, five children also managed to flee from the German-controlled territory to Bershad. AM 173.

69. Daghani, *What a Nice World*, p.108.

70. According to an order of the General Headquarter of the Gendarmerie based on the decision of the Romanian government, four transit points were planned on the river Dniester where the deportees could enter Romanian territory. The gendarmes received the order to let Jews cross, but only those with certificates that proved that they were Romanian natives. CSIER, file III/932, p.46.

71. The Headquarter of the Gendarmerie in Odessa sent a telephone message to its subordinates based on a telegram from Marshal Antonescu: 'Please take all measures for the evacuation of the Romanian citizens regardless of their origin and be careful that certain deeds committed against Poles and Jews in Transnistria should not be ascribed to us.' CSIER, file III/932, p.118.

72. Ibid., p.119.

73. In January 1944 a delegation of the International Red Cross, accompanied by members of the Romanian Red Cross, was allowed to make an inspection of the Jewish ghettos of Transnistria. A confidential report stated that 'although the living conditions have improved considerably in comparison with January 1943, they are still not good enough'. CSIER, file III/361, p.65. In December 1943, the State Department in Washington had learnt that 'the conditions of the Jewish people in Transnistria are reported to be in course of substantial improvements'. CSIER, file III/361, p.73.

74. Interview with Philipp Kellmer.

75. Interview conducted by the author with Tvi Zemmel, 4 February 2004, B'nei Zion Medical Centre, Haifa, Israel.

76. One of the Lithuanian guards ordered Zemmel and another inmate to dig out the head of a dead man lying in a mass grave and to remove the golden crowns from his mouth. Rieper and Brandl-Bowen, *Lasst Mich Leben!* p.72.

77. Interview conducted by the author with Shoshana Nauman, 3 February 2004, Haifa, Israel.

78. Ibid.

79. Reichskreditkassenschein was the official currency not only in the so-called 'Reichskommissariat Ukraine' beyond the river Bug but also in Transnistria.

80. Rieper and Brandl-Bowen, *Lasst Mich Leben!* p.173.

81. Interview with Shoshana Nauman.

82. Ibid. In his testimony E. Muniu, who was also detained in the ghetto of Bershad, mentioned a mass killing of about 250 Jews in January 1944. E. Muniu, 'The Mărculeşti ghetto and beyond' in Carmelly (ed.), *Shattered!* p.431.

83. Although Shoshana Nauman referred to a painting that she had seen, this ink drawing from the collection at Yad Vashem comes closest to her description.

84. AM 128.

7

Memories of Mikhailowka Recorded in Legal Depositions and Personal Letters

The publication in 1960 of a German translation of Daghani's diary, Lasst Mich Leben, prompted the Public Prosecutor in Lübeck to investigate war crimes in the slave labour camps in Ukraine. Legal depositions were made by Daghani and twelve employees of the August Dohrmann construction company, as well as suspected war criminals identified in his text. In 1971 the investigations were shelved for lack of conclusive evidence, but Daghani refused to abandon the pursuit of justice. He obtained transcripts of the testimonies in four bulky files running to several hundred pages, now in the Arnold Daghani Collection at the University of Sussex. His aim was to incorporate the most revealing passages in the expanded version of his memoirs, so as to name and shame the perpetrators and their accomplices. This was followed by a remarkable exchange of letters between Arnold and Anişoara Daghani and those who had earlier been among their tormentors. Excerpts from those testimonies and letters are reproduced below, translated by Edward Timms (with explanatory comments in parentheses).

WERNER BERGMANN

In autumn 1943 the Jews were transferred from the camp at Mikhailowka to the camp at Tarassiwka, so that about 400 to 450 Jews must have been there at the time. In December 1943 these Jews were shot not far from the camp by a unit of the SD [Sicherheitsdienst – the Nazi Security Service]. I heard about this from Joseph Elsässer, who called at my office in Gaisin one morning in a state of great agitation. We immediately went by car to Tarassiwka, but the killing action there was already complete. The SD unit was just withdrawing from Tarassiwka. It consisted of some SD men and some Lithuanian volunteers. The unit was commanded by an SD officer who was unknown to me and whose name I also failed to discover. From my own people [employees of the August Dohrmann company]. I then learnt that the SD unit had arrived early in the morning and surrounded the camp. They then divided the Jews into two large groups and shot them group by group behind the camp, after ordering them to undress completely.

I have no knowledge who ordered this operation. In my opinion SS-Hauptsturmführer Christoffel must have been involved with this operation. At that time it was generally known that the territory had to be abandoned because of the advancing Russian troops. We feared that the Jews at Tarassiwka would be killed before this happened. On the day before the killing operation Elsässer told me he had heard from Christoffel that no action was planned against the Jews. But as the killing operation was carried out the very next morning, I assume that Christoffel carried out a strategy of deception. Obviously the aim was to give the Jews a sense of false security, so that the killing operation could be carried out according to plan. I have no knowledge whether Christoffel, Friese and Maass [three camp commanders who feature prominently in Daghani's diary] were present during the killing operation. In any case I didn't see them when I arrived at Tarassiwka.

JOSEF ELSÄSSER

On the day before [the killing operation] SS-Hauptsturmführer Christoffel gave me a letter in Gaisin and asked me to deliver it to Police Sergeant Laubach in Tarassiwka. Laubach's address was typewritten on the envelope. The letter was sealed. Since I suspected that an operation was to take place against the Jews and assumed that the letter contained details about some such action, I decided to open it. At my quarters, I steamed the letter open, damaging the envelope in the process. There was a note in the envelope with the simple words: The operation will not take place. There was no signature underneath. Then I took a similar envelope and retyped the address of Police Sergeant Laubach on it. Then in Tarassiwka I gave Laubach the letter. I then conveyed to Mühl and other people from the Dohrmann Company who were based in Tarassiwka that no action against the Jews was to be expected. I knew they would pass this information on to the Jews. All the greater was my amazement next morning when I arrived at Tarassiwka and became aware that most of the Jews in the camp had already been shot dead, their bodies in two mass graves. As I got nearer, the SDs and Lithuanian auxiliaries were just going to shoot dead the last Jews.

Among those still alive were two young girls who were calling out to me to help them, but I could do nothing. I saw how they together with the others were shot dead. They had to strip naked and lie prone on the bodies in the mass grave. Then they were shot in the back of the head by an SD man with a sub-machine-gun. An estimated 425 Jews (men and women) were killed on that day in Tarassiwka. Even a little boy about 2 years old is said to have been killed.

I don't know who it was that carried out this operation. The only name I heard that day was the name Fröhlich. That must have been the name of one of the SD commanders.

HERMANN KAISER

In December 1943, based on the fact that Laubach had several deep ditches dug by Jews in the vicinity of the camp, we guessed that the Jews of Tarassiwka were going to be killed. Earlier Laubach had tried to get us construction workers involved in digging the ditches, but we refused because we sensed that something was wrong.

Some days later, after the ditches were ready, a truck arrived in Tarassiwka carrying a SD detachment, early in the morning just as we were marching the Jews off to work. The unit consisted of two SD men in field-grey SD uniforms and about twenty Lithuanian auxiliary policemen. They were accompanied by a civilian who was probably the commander of the unit. The Jewish camp was surrounded by the Lithuanians. Then they drove all the Jews out of the camp and marched them to the aforementioned ditches. There the Jews had to take off their clothes and were then shot by the two SD men. I wasn't present during the executions, but from a considerable distance I heard the salvoes of shots from the sub-machine-guns that were carried by the two SD men. On that morning all the Jews who were in the Tarassiwka camp were killed. It was announced that 350 Jews were involved. After the execution the clothes of the Jews were loaded on to a truck by the Lithuanians and driven away. After the detachment had left we went to look at the nearest of the graves and saw that it was filled with dead bodies. I no longer remember who it was who covered the graves with earth.

The identity of the two SD men and the unit commander is something of which I have no knowledge.

I never discovered who ordered the killing operation, but it is my opinion that the order to carry out this action can only have come from SS-Hauptsturmführer Christoffel who was in charge of the Jewish camp at Tarassiwka.

Although the Public Prosecutor failed to identify those responsible for these crimes, his investigations had the indirect consequence of putting Arnold Daghani and his wife in touch with employees of the August Dohrmann company, responsible for road construction at Mikhailowka. This led during the 1970s to a remarkable exchange of letters, which ended on a note of reconciliation. The letters reproduced below, addressed to Daghani in Jona (Switzerland), are a short selection from an extended correspondence. They attempt to clarify certain questions raised both in his letters and in his diary, which his correspondents had read in German translation.

From: Werner Bergmann, D 7290 Freudenstadt, Bahnhofstrasse 60
21 January 1973

Dear Mr Daghani,

I have received your friendly letter of 10 January 1973, for which warmest thanks. When at the beginning of September 1972 I was asked by the Public Prosecutor in Dortmund whether they could give you my address, your name meant nothing to me despite intensive reflection. Now that I have your picture in my hands, I remember you well. May I take the opportunity to congratulate you long after that event on your successful escape. Many of your fellow sufferers had such an opportunity, but unfortunately very few of them made use of it. I did not report your escape, so only a chance discovery would have endangered or terminated it. Unfortunately, neither Mr Elsässer nor I could do anything for the rescue of the camp at Mikhailowka, we had to be very cautious because we were not well thought of by the SS.

During our retreat we travelled through Braclaw and saw that the camp there, for which we had once been responsible, had not yet been liquidated. However, it could only be a matter of time. From our first resting place – I don't recall the name – I drove back to Braclaw during the night with Friedrich Mühl, the excavation foreman, in a one-and-a-half-ton Ford truck. Since no sentries were to be seen, we unlocked the gates and gave the inmates their freedom, which I hope enabled them all to reach their old homes in good health. We loaded the elderly and disabled on to our truck and drove them back to our quarters, where we placed them in the care of an unguarded ghetto that was there. Unfortunately I have not heard anything further about the liberated inmates of the Braclaw camp, though it would have interested me very much to hear what happened to them. Perhaps, dear Mr Daghani, you may have heard something about your fellow countrymen?

Now to your questions:

(1) I can no longer definitely remember who it was that commissioned you to decorate that lampshade. But if you say that it was I who arranged for you and your wife not to be sent back to the camp at Mikhailowka, but allowed you to have extra time that evening, then that must be correct. Since being transported back to the camp that evening no longer occurred, it gives me great pleasure even today to know that I thereby indirectly helped to protect you and your wife from a terrible fate.

(2) As I already mentioned, it was impossible for me and Mr Elsässer to intervene to save the Mikhailowka camp, not even with money, gold or other valuables. About those events I heard for the first time from Mr Elsässer last year during his visit to me. He was asked about those events during one of the legal interrogations.

(3) The claim by Nathan Segall [the Jewish spokesman at Mikhailowka] that he and his family would be protected from execution, cannot be true and is sheer invention. The terrible fate of the Mikhailowka camp proves this.

Dear Mr Daghani, I hope that my comments have been able to help you in your quest for truth so that you can complete the chapter in your autobiography entitled 'Twenty-eight years ago'. In conclusion, may I ask you on the first occasion that brings you to Germany and the Black Forest, to join me for an hour over coffee. You and your wife are both warmly invited.

With cordial greetings to you and your wife

Werner Bergmann.

From: Josef Elsässer, Remscheid
21 January 1973

Dear Mr Daghani,
Dear Mrs Daghani,

So pleased to receive from you a personal sign of life. Please forgive the lateness of this reply. Before writing this letter, I read your book *Lasst mich leben* through again.

To come straight to your request:

The reaction in various quarters on the morning after your escape. On the previous evening I said to Mr Bergmann: 'It wouldn't surprise me if tomorrow morning the two of them have disappeared.' He laughed, and so did I. Mr Bergmann and I didn't mention this to anyone, for if the SS had heard about it, there would have been no saving me – because of aiding escape and sabotage. After a few days I discussed the matter with Mr Segall, and he told me that he admired your courage. I'd already suggested escaping to Mr Segall, Mr Rosengarten and Mrs Pepi, but Pepi was the only one among them to attempt it. Rosengarten said he felt a sense of great responsibility for the camp, and when I said to Segall in Tulcin in Romania that he could stay there, he explained to me that this was impossible without his wife and children.

After all, I intentionally did not fix a padlock to the door of the garage, and for this reason it would have been easy for the SS to make me responsible for allowing you to escape.

Enough of that, it is really gratifying that the trials and tribulations you experienced were rewarded by the fulfilment of freedom. Unfortunately I don't any longer have a photograph of that room. Nor do I have that lovely letter you wrote me in Gaisin on the evening before your escape, and for what reason? After the camp at Tarassiwka was liquidated, I was scared that the SS would discover photographs among Mr Rosengarten's possessions showing me with his parents in Czernowitz. If as a result a house-search had been made in my quarters and your letter had fallen into their hands, I would have been unable to defend myself, for this reason I destroyed the letter.

Now to another question.

In your book *Lasst mich leben* there are passages that don't always correspond to the truth, even though you may have received those details from other people. First on page 8:

Fact Number One is that the August Dohrmann Company did not voluntarily go to Russia, but was drafted there.

Fact Number Two is that the firm had no influence at all with regard to manpower. We were supposed to build roads with prisoners-of-war, whom we did have in Worowoniza. Should you, Mr Daghani, have been present when we were informed that we had to build roads with women, sick men and even children! I had a head-on discussion about this with Mr Bergmann, but alas, without success. I wanted to rejoin the Wehrmacht.

Fact Number Three: You even claimed that the August Dohrmann Company cared more about horses than human beings. The August Dohrmann Company did not own a single horse in Russia.

A further point about the journey to Czernowitz.

Nathan Segall and Heinz Rosengarten, Fredy and Pepi came to the entrance of the Mikhailowka camp and spoke to me as follows. After a sleepless night they had a great request to make to me: Couldn't I see whether it was possible to travel to Czernowitz and obtain for the prisoners winter clothing and everything else that was needed. I asked for time to think the matter over and then said: That is a good idea.

I went to Mr Bergmann, he sent me to Mr Stracke, then I had to go to the SS. Mr Stracke then gave me written confirmation, and with that confirmation I first had to go to the German–Romanian liaison officer in Odessa to obtain permission to enter Romania. He said I should travel via Tiraspol, but I persuaded him to allow me to cross the river Dniester at Moghilew where the roads were in better condition. Mr Segall, the driver and I then drove to Czernowitz. In Moghilew the Romanian army took Mr Segall into custody, he had to remain there in the ghetto until I returned from Czernowitz. From there we drove back to Tarassiwka. You will understand that this was easier said than done. But I vehemently deny that Mr Bergmann and I demanded jewellery and dollars in return. I never made such a demand for anything. That kind of attitude has no place in my whole life.

One more point: Again and again I used to warn the column-leaders: 'Don't hit, don't vex, and what's most important, don't you kill!' We were only given the task to employ you as manpower. What was on the whole happening in the camp after leaving off work was a matter for the police. I knew the Lithuanians and they knew me; they were aware that I highly disliked them. And even when the SD-man came and you write that he was aided and abetted by such and such an O.T.-man [Organisation Todt, the military construction corps]: The question arises: What were Mr Mühl in Tarassiwka, Kaiser in Mikhailowka, Peter Höller supposed to do when that regular demon was raging in the camp? Nothing.

When I witnessed the first executions in Worowoniza, I spoke to Mr

Schweser of Krasnapolka the following words: '*Under no circumstances do we have the right to win the war.*' He looked at me with a worried face and said that was something I should never say again. A short time later, after he had a similar experience, he admitted that I was right.

Dear Mr Daghani, I'm not trying to justify anything in this letter, just to state the facts. If only we could arrange a time to meet somewhere, many things could be clarified.

Cordial wishes to you and your wife

from Josef Elsässer.

From: Werner Bergmann, D 7290 Freudenstadt, Bahnhofstrasse 60
14 May 1973

Dear Mr and Mrs Daghani,

Many thanks for your friendly letter of 10 May. I am delighted that you are now planning to visit us on 25 May, but in my opinion you shouldn't simply say 'Good Day' and then continue your journey without even a brief glimpse of Freudenstadt. Hence my suggestion:

We would like to invite you very warmly to arrive here on the Thursday, 24 May, on the same train at 10.56. You could then continue your journey to Mainz on the Friday at 15.52, as planned. That would give us the opportunity for an extended conversation and we could show you something of Freudenstadt.

Please will you let me have an affirmative answer, a refusal will not be accepted.

Cordial greetings from

Werner Bergmann and his wife.

Daghani and his wife found the visit to the Bergmanns, who welcomed them at the railway station with a bunch of flowers, such a moving experience that he made a delicate flower painting to commemorate the encounter [Plate 35]. Recording this visit in his extended memoirs, he concluded: 'Nanino and I have reconciled ourselves with the past.'

Although Daghani recognized that Bergmann and Elsässer deserved some credit for aiding their escape, he remained fiercely critical of the criminal actions of the SS and SD men in charge of the slave labour camps in Ukraine. Moreover, his self-appointed mission of commemorating their victims led him to create the following Roll-Call, recording the fate of fellow prisoners whose names still resonated in his memory. The list names 250 persons in all, including many children. A specific identity is indicated even at the points where Daghani and his wife could no longer remember a personal name: 'Young Ukrainian Jewish mother from TEPLIK or UMAN with babe newly born in the camp'. Memory, for Daghani, meant affirming individuality, defying the tendency to reduce the Holocaust to statistics. He attached such significance to this Roll-Call that in the folio 1942 1943 And Thereafter (Sporadic records till 1977) he devoted five pages to a reverently calligraphic version of the names and responses of those who perished. Reciting the names of the dead became a solemn ritual, repeated by Daghani and his wife every year at Yom Kippur. The limitations of the written record were transcended as the names were liturgically recited within the framework of an age-old religious tradition.

8

Roll-Call: Memorial List of those who Perished in Mikhailowka

ARNOLD DAGHANI

This Roll-Call was hand-written by Daghani in the folio 1942 1943 And Thereafter (Sporadic records till 1977) (1942–77) Arnold Daghani Collection, University of Sussex, G2.117r.

It is, alas, a less than tiny fraction I have been able to assemble for these [Commemorative Leaves].

Mr Leo Antschel:	present	We were transferred on the 17th and 20th Sept., 1942, from
Mrs Mizzi Antschel:	present	Mikhailowka to Gaissin. They ceased to live some time later.
Mrs Trebitsch:	present	I died of heart failure on the 20th of Aug., 1942, at the death-camp at Mikhailowka.
Prof Heimer:	present	I was shot dead on the 20th of August, 1942, in the camp of Mikhailowka.
Mr Kiermayer:	present	I was shot dead on the 20th of August, 1942, in the camp of Mikhailowka (owned by Dohrmann).
Mr Axelrod:	present	I was shot dead about August, 1942, in the camp of Nemirow (owned by Fix and Stöhr respectively).
Mr Schaffer:	present	I died of illness in the winter, 1942, in the camp of Kiblicz (owned jointly by Kaiser and Ufer).
Mrs Schaffer:	present	I was shot dead, March, 1943, in the camp of Kiblicz.
Young Ukrainian: Jewish mother from Teplik or Uman, with babe, newly born in the camp:	present	I was shot dead on the 29th of August, 1942, in the camp of Mikhailowka, together with my babe, and fourteen more slaves.
Solomon Wohlmann:	present	I was shot dead on the 29th of August, 1942, in the camp of Mikhailowka.
Mrs Haskil Zucker (his daughter) and her two little girls:	present	We were shot dead on the 10th of December, 1943, in the camp of Tarassiwka (owned by Dohrmann).
Mordko Seidner:	present	I was shot dead on the 29th of August, 1942, in the camp of Mikhailowka.

Dr Hermann Seidner, his son:	present	I was shot dead on the 10th of December, 1943, in the camp of Tarassiwka.
Ukrainian Jewish slave from Uman:	present	I was shot dead on the 11th of September, 1942, in the camp of Mikhailowka, on the night after my arrival from Uman.
Ukrainian Jewish girl-slave:	present	I had tried at an escape, was recaptured, and shot dead in the presence of the fellow-slaves who were toiling at the gravel-pit at Mikhailowka.
Ukrainian Jewish woman-slave:	present	I was shot dead together with twenty-four more women-slaves on the 14th of September, 1942, in the camp of Mikhailowka
Mr Goldenberg:	present	I was shot dead on the 10th of November, 1942, while being transferred from the stables to the school-building in the centre of the village Mikhailowka. .
Mr Dorbarmiker:	present	I was shot dead about the summer of 1942 in the camp of Berezowka (owned by Stöhr KG, München)
Mrs Fuchs, her sister:	present present	We were shot dead together on the 21st of Sept., 1942, in the maize-field opposite the toiling-site on the Strasse within the camp of Mikhailowka
Sali, Mrs Fuch's daughter:	present	I was shot dead on the 10th of December, 1943, in the camp of Tarassiwka.
Mrs Kron:	present	I was shot dead on the 28th of Sept., 1942, in the maize-field of Mikhailowka.
her daughter:	present	I was shot dead on the 10th of December, 1943, in the camp of Tarassiwka.
Mrs Bromberger: her daughter	present	I was shot dead together with Mrs Kron on the 28th of Sept., 1942, in the maize-field.
Mrs Weisselberg: her son-in-law Wihl Weisselberg: her grandson, Poldi: her granddaughter, Lia Weisselberg:	present present present present	We were shot dead on the 10th of December, 1943, in the camp of Tarassiwka.
Mia Goldschläger:	present	I died on the 4th of October, 1942 from illness in the camp of Mikhailowka.
Her sister, a teacher:	present	I was shot dead on the 10th of December, 1943, in the camp of Tarassiwka.
Mrs Lublin: of Mikhailowka. Mr Lublin: daughter over 22: daughter, in her teens: daughter, in her teens:	present present present present present	I was shot dead on the 5th of October, 1942, in the maize-field We were shot dead on the 10th of December, 1943, in the camp of Tarassiwka.
Mrs Koifman: her daughter-in-law: her son-in-law: her grandchild:	present present present present	I was shot dead on the 5th of October, 1942, in the maize-field, together with Mrs Lublin. We were shot dead after our transfer from Mikhailowka to the camp of Naraewka (owned by the firm Karl Kaiser, Hanau).

Mr Jurgrau:	present	We were shot dead after our transfer from Mikhailowka to the
Mrs Jurgrau:	present	camp of Naraewka (owned by the firm Karl Kaiser, Hanau)
their daughter:	present	

Dr Arnold Goldenberg: present I made a suicidal attempt on the 6th of October, 1942, but since by the 7th of October, 1942, I had not breathed my last – I had been in the care of our two fellow-slave doctors – I was shot dead on the 7th of October near the latrines in the camp of Mikhailowka.

Misha: present I was shot dead on the Strasse on the very toiling plot in Mikhailowka, on the 20th of October, 1942, by the Lithuanian guard Aliosha Wisotzkas.

Lothar Vogelhut, 17, his present I was shot dead on the Strasse, Mikhailowka, on the 2nd of
mother, Mrs Vogelhut, present November, 1942, by the Lithuanian guard Aliosha Wisotzkas.
Adele (?): I was shot dead on the 10th of December, 1943, in the camp of Tarassiwka.

Liuba, Ukrainian Jewess: present I was shot dead together with 106 Ukrainian Jews and Jewesses on the 12th of November, 1942, in the camp of Mikhailowka.

Mr Korn: present I was shot dead on the Strasse, Mikhailowka, by the Lithuanian Wisotzkas.

Mrs Korn née Besen: present I died of inanition on the 30th of November, 1942, in the camp of Mikhailowka.

Their son, Mussia, 18: present I died of internal t.b. on the 3rd of March, 1943, in the camp of Mikhailowka.

Wika Wolloch, relative: present I died of illness late December, 1942, in the camp of Mikhailowka.

Aisic: present I was shot dead on the 12th of December, 1942, in the camp of Mikhailowka, by OT-man Karl Ullerich.

Widow Dr Mehler: present I died of inanition and eaten up of lice about the end of November, 1942, in Mikhailowka.

Mrs Locker: present I died of inanition on the 17th of November, 1942, in Mikhailowka.

her son, Dr Alter Locker: present I was shot dead on the 10th of December, 1943, in Tarassiwka.

Mrs Stammler: present I died of illness on the 8th of November, 1942, in Mikhailowka.
Mr Stammler: present I was shot dead on the 10th of December, 1943, in Tarassiwka.

Isaak Gruber: present
Mrs Gruber: present We were shot dead some time after our transfer on the 14th of
little daughter: present December, 1942, from Mikhailowka.
little daughter: present

Mr Jablonower: present We were shot dead some months after our transfer on the 14th
Mrs Jablonower: present of December, 1942, from Mikhailowka.

Mrs Kudisch: present I died of typhus late November, 1942, in Mikhailowka.
Mr Kudisch: present We were shot dead some months after our transfer on the 14th
little daughter: present of December, 1942, from Mikhailowka.
little daughter: present

Prof Henner:	present	We were shot dead after our transfer on the 14th of December,
Mrs Henner:	present	1942, from Mikhailowka.
Mrs Rosa Kreindler- Weiss:	present	I was shot dead (after my transfer on the 14th of December, 1942, to the camp of Ivangorod) on the 8th of June, 1943, together with 12 more slaves when we were taken to Krasnapolka for our execution (camp owner: Eras KG, Nuremberg).
Jeweller Fischmann:	present	We were shot dead some time after our transfer on the 14th of
Mrs Fischmann:	present	December, 1942, from Mikhailowka.[2]
their baby:	present	
Grandmother:	present	
Mr Suchavaler:	present	We were shot dead some months after our transfer on the 14th
Mrs Suchavaler:	present	of December, 1942, from Mikhailowka.
their baby:	present	
Mr Lebel:	present	We were shot dead some months after our transfer on the 14th
Mrs Lebel:	present	of December, 1942, from Mikhailowka.[1]
their infant:	present	
their newly-born babe:	present	
Selma Meerbaum, 18:	present	I died of typhus on the 16th of December, 1942, in the camp of
Mrs Eisinger, her mother:	present	Mikhailowka.
Mr Eisinger, her step- father:	present	We were shot dead on the 10th of December, 1943, in the camp of Tarassiwka.
Prof Dr Moses Gottlieb:	present	I died of inanition on the 17th of December, 1942, in the camp of Mikhailowka.
Tudorache Take Gheorghe:	present	I was shot dead together with some more Romanian gypsies Christmas 1942, in the camp of Kiblicz (owners: Karl Kaiser, Hanau; Ufer, Koblenz).
Offenberger, 20:	present	I had already managed to slip under the barbed wire fence of the camp of Bugakow (owner: Stöhr, München) and was now in the open field when the Ukrainian interpreter Chjmjca aimed at me. The bullet went home. That happened on the 4th of February, 1943.
Rosenbach:	present	I was shot dead about August/September, 1942, by a Ukrainian militia-man, upon order of the commandant, sergeant major Michel Krommer, in the camp Braclaw (owners: Horst & Jüssen, Basaltwerke Neschen GmbH, Sinzig).
Mr Rüber:	present	We were shot dead by the commandant, sergeant major Michel
Mrs Rüber:	present	Krommer at the quarry Braclaw, owned by the firm Horst & Jüssen. It was about the 21st of September, 1942.
Mr Roth:	present	I was shot dead.
Mrs Roth:	present	I died of typhus at the camp of Mikhailowka.
Teacher Schuller:	present	I ceased to live.

1. 120 slaves were on that day transferred to the camp in Ivangorod

Mrs Scolar:[2]	present	My little boy was among those selected, so I voluntarily joined
her 9 year old boy:	present	the group and was shot dead together with him in the camp of
		Teplik (jointly owned by Eras KG, Nuremberg, Ufer, Koblenz and
		Karl Kaiser, Hanau) on the 21st of September, 1942.
Infant-boy Marcowitz:	present	We were shot dead somewhere outside the camp of Teplik in the
Infant-girl Marcowitz:	present	spring, 1943, by Polizeiwachtmeister, Karl Klenk.
Infant-girl Grünberg:	present	
Dental-surgeon	present	I was shot dead on the night of the 6th of February, 1943, in the
Gottesmann:	present	camp of Braclaw (owners: Horst & Jüssen).
Mrs Gottesmann:	present	
Mr Gänser:	present	We had managed one night to abscond from the camp of
Mrs Gänser:	present	Braclaw in the Spring, 1943, but were soon recaptured. Upon
Miss Rosenbach:	present	order of Paul Reiniger of the firm Basaltwerke, Neschen, joint
Miss Rosenbach, sisters:	present	owner of the camp, we were shot dead.
Mr Goldschmidt:		
Mr Schwarz, hairdresser:	present	We were shot dead in February, 1943, in the camp of Nemirow
Mrs Schwarz:	present	(Stöhr, KG, München); I, because I was going with child. That
		upon order of the commandant, Polizeimeister Alfred Jähnig.
Mr Buxbaum:	present	We were shot dead about March, 1943, in the camp of
Mrs Buxbaum:	present	Nemirow.
Aisic Schlossberg;	present	I was shot dead about March, 1943, in the camp of Nemirow.
Spokesman for the Jewish	present	I was shot dead in February, 1943, in the camp of Krasnapolka
slaves:		(owner: Eras KG, Nuremberg) upon the order of the comman-
		dant, OT-meister Johannes Schulte of Landesstrassenbauamt
		Meschede.
Dr Schajowicz:	present	I died of typhus about early March, 1943; I was the spokesman
		for the Jewish slaves in the camp of Teplik.
Sucher Israel:	present	I died of typhus in the spring, 1943, in the camp of Teplik.
his son, Manek, 14:	present	I was shot dead in the autumn, 1943, together with all the slaves
		behind a garden on the outskirts of Krasnapolka (In July the
		slaves had been transferred from Teplik).
Mr Grapper (Dorohoi):	present	I was shot dead in August, 1943, in the camp of Krasnapolka. It
		was a German police-officer who killed me on the toiling-plot
		with a pistol.
Mrs Metsch:	present	I was shot dead in the summer, 1943, in the camp of
		Krasnapolka.
Dr Metsch:	present	I was shot dead in the autumn, 1943, together with all the slaves
		behind a garden on the outskirts of Krasnapolka.
Lutz Adler:	present	I was shot dead in the autumn, 1943, together with all the slaves
		of Krasnapolka.
Mr Mader:	present	We were shot dead ...
his daughter:	present	

2. Mr Scolar Aram managed in the summer, 1943, to run away from the camp.

Mr Schifter:	present	
Mrs Schifter-Făgădău:	present	We were shot dead ...
daughter:	present	
daughter:	present	
Isaak Landmann:	present	We were shot dead in the autumn, 1943 together with all the
Anutza Landmann:	present	slaves of Krasnapolka.
Schapira, cousin:	present	
Mr Scheiner:	present	I was shot dead in the summer, 1943, in the camp of Krasnapolka.
Mr Abraham Kiesler:	present	We were shot dead on the 26th of April, 1943, in the camp of
Mrs Malka Kiesler:	present	Mikhailowka.
Mr Kellmer:	present	I was shot dead on the 26th of April, 1943, in the camp of Mikhailowka.
Mrs Kellmer:	present	I was shot dead on the 10th of December, 1943, in the camp of Tarassiwka.
Mrs Dvora Semmel:	present	I was shot dead on the 26th of April, 1943, in the camp of Mikhailowka.
her daughter, Cylla:	present	I was shot dead on the 26th of April, 1943, in the camp of Mikhailowka.
her niece:	present	I was shot dead on the 10th of December, 1943, in the camp of Tarassiwka.
Mr Schor:	present	We were shot dead on the 26th of April, 1943, in the camp of
Mrs Schor:	present	Mikhailowka.
daughter:	present	We were shot dead on the 10th of December, 1943, in the camp
daughter:	present	of Tarassiwka.
Izku Herschmann:	present	I was shot dead on the 26th of April, 1943, in the camp of Mikhailowka.
Mrs Herschmann:	present	I was shot dead on the 10th of December, 1943, in the camp of Tarassiwka.
Hersch Schärf:	present	We were shot dead on the 26th of April, 1943, in the camp of
Mrs Schärf:	present	Mikhailowka.
Ludo Adler:	present	I was shot dead on the 26th of April, 1943, in the camp of Mikhailowka.
his wife, Lilli:	present	
father-in-law, Dr Markus	present	We were shot dead on the 10th of December, 1943, in the camp
Rudich, mother-in-law,		of Tarassiwka.
Fani Rudich, brother-in-	present	
law, Gerry Rudich:	present	
Mr David Ungar:	present	I was shot dead on the 26th of April, 1943, in the camp of Mikhailowka.
Mrs Anna Ungar:	present	I joined my husband voluntarily.
Architekt Hammerling:	present	We were shot dead after our transfer on the 17th of Sept., 1942,
Mrs Hammerling:	present	from Mikhailowka to Gaisin.
Geldman, 9 year old boy:	present	I was shot dead on the 5th of February, 1943, in the camp of Braclaw (Horst & Jüssen).

Engineer Mandel:	present	I joined voluntarily the group of the selected in the camp of
his child:	present	Braclaw (Dohrmann, Remscheid) to be shot dead together with my child.[3] It happened on the 22nd of September 1942.
Popplinger:	present	I was shot dead on the 22nd of Sept., 1942, in the camp of Braclaw (Dohrmann, Remscheid).
Eng. Dermann, one-armed:	present	I was shot dead on the 5th of Feb., 1943, in the camp of Braclaw (Dohrmann).
his mother, Mrs Dermann:	present	I joined my son voluntarily, to be shot dead together.
Fruchter:	present	I was shot dead after my transfer from Braclaw to Gaisin.
Erbsenthal (Erbsendahl?):	present	They fetched me in August, 1943, from Tarassiwka to Gaisin,
Mrs Erbsenthal:	present	where I was shot dead. I was shot dead on the 10th of December, 1943, in the camp of Tarassiwka (owned by Dohrmann).
Mr Bertold Brüll:	present	We were shot dead.
Mrs Daks Brüll:	present	
Jessica Brüll, 2 year old:	present	I died some time after transfer on the 14th of Dec., 1942, from Mikhailowka to Ivangorod.
Mr Mejikhes:	present	We were shot dead after our transfer from Mikhailowka to
Mrs Mejikhes:	present	Naraewka on the 16th of Sept., 1942.[4]
their daughter:	present	
Mr Meiselmann:	present	
Mrs Meiselmann:	present	We were shot dead some months after our transfer from
Mr Meiselmann jr:	present	Mikhailowka to Ivangorod.
Miss Meiselmann:	present	
Miss Toni Schneeberg:	present	I was shot dead on the 10th of December, 1943, in the camp of Tarassiwka.
Miss Mizzi Harth:	present	I was shot dead on the 10th of December, 1943, in the camp of Tarassiwka.
Max Guttmann:	present	I was shot dead on the 10th of December, 1943, in the camp of Tarassiwka.
Seidner:	present	I was shot dead on the 10th of December, 1943, in the camp of Tarassiwka.
Dampf, hairdresser:	present	I was shot dead on the 10th of December, 1943, in the camp of Tarassiwka.
Brüll:	present	I was shot dead on the 10th of December, 1943, in the camp of Tarassiwka.
Avram Naiman (Uman):	present	I was shot dead on the 10th of December, 1943, in the camp of Tarassiwka.
Mr Koch:	present	We were shot dead on the 10th of December, 1943, in the camp
Mrs Koch:	present	of Tarassiwka.
Dr Kiermayer:	present	We were shot dead on the 10th of December, 1943, in the camp
Mrs Susi Kiermayer:	present	of Tarassiwka.

3. According to OT Fritz Mühl, many mothers joined voluntarily their children, to be shot together.
4. 150 slaves were on that day transferred to Naraewka.

Lawyer Cashdan:	present	We were shot dead on the 10th of December, 1943, in the camp
Mrs Cashdan:	present	of Tarassiwka.
Mr Weininger:	present	
Mrs Weininger:	present	We were shot dead some time after our transfer to Ivangorod on
Poldi Weininger:	present	the 14th of Dec., 1942.
Hannerl Weininger:	present	
Mr Rabinovici:	present	We were shot dead on the 10th of December, 1943, in the camp
Mrs Surica Rabinovici:	present	of Tarassiwka.
Mrs Steiner:	present	We were shot dead on the 10th of December, 1943, in the camp
Nori Steiner, 13 year old boy:	present	of Tarassiwka.
Marcel Gâtlan (Hârlău):	present	I was shot dead on the 10th of December, 1943, in the camp of Tarassiwka.
Mr Jakob Landmann:	present	
Mrs Bertha Landmann:	present	We were shot dead on the 10th of December, 1943, in the camp
their son, Turi, 19:	present	of Tarassiwka.
brother-in-law, David Semmel:	present	
sister-in-law, Rosa Semmel-Tabak:	present	
Mr Barasch:	present	
Mrs Barasch:	present	We were shot dead on the 10th of December, 1943, in the camp
son:	present	of Tarassiwka.
daughter:	present	
Mr Simon Goldstein:	present	We were shot dead on the 10th of December, 1943, in the camp
Mrs Goldstein:	present	of Tarassiwka.
Hardy, 15 years:	present	
Mr Sigmund Ebner:	present	
Mrs Ebner:	present	We were shot dead on the 10th of December, 1943, in the camp
son, Harry:	present	of Tarassiwka.
son:	present	
Bernhard (Zoniu) David:	present	We were shot dead on the 10th of December, 1943, in the camp
Mrs Kusia David:	present	of Tarassiwka.
Miss Clara Schärf:	present	I was shot dead on the 10th of December, 1943, in the camp of Tarassiwka.
Mr Stammler:	present	I was shot dead on the 10th of December, 1943, in the camp of Tarassiwka.
Mrs Stammler:	present	I died of typhus towards the middle of November, 1942, in the camp of Mikhailowka.
Mr Thau:	present	We were shot dead on the 10th of December, 1943, in the camp
Mrs Thau:	present	of Tarassiwka.
Mrs Segal:	present	We were shot dead on the 10th of December, 1943, in the camp
Miss Paula Segal:	present	of Tarassiwka.

Mr Otto Freyer:	present	
Mrs Freyer:	present	We were shot dead on the 10th of December, 1943, in the camp
Trude Freyer:	present	of Tarassiwka
Lothar Freyer:	present	
Mrs Metsch:	present	We were shot dead on the 10th of December, 1943, in the camp
her daughter, Yuta:	present	of Tarassiwka.
Mr Simon Ausländer:	present	We were shot dead on the 10th of December, 1943, in the camp
Mrs Ausländer:	present	of Tarassiwka.
daughter:	present	
Mr Körner:	present	We were shot dead on the 10th of December, 1943, in the camp
Mrs Körner:	present	of Tarassiwka.
daughter:	present	
Mrs Kreisel:	present	
girl, Selma, 11:	present	We were shot dead ...
girl:	present	
Mr Ozrud:	present	We were shot dead on the 10th of December, 1943, in the camp
Mrs Ana Ozrud:	present	of Tarassiwka.
Mrs Enzenberger:	present	We were shot dead on the 10th of December, 1943, in the camp
Mucki, 2 year old boy:	present	of Tarassiwka.
Eng. Heinz Rosengarten:	present	We were shot dead on the 10th of December, 1943, in the camp
Mrs Annie Rosengarten:	present	of Tarassiwka.
Mr Nathan Segall:	present	I was shot dead on the 10th of December, 1943, in the camp of Tarassiwka.
Mrs Segall:	present	I was shot dead on the 10th of December, 1943, in the camp of Tarassiwka.
daughter, Ruth:	present	I was shot dead on the 10th of December, 1943, in the camp of Tarassiwka.
daughter, Livia:	present	I was shot dead on the 10th of December, 1943, in the camp of Tarassiwka.
Eddie Weiss, Livia's fiancé:	present	I was shot dead on the 10th of December, 1943, in the camp of Tarassiwka.
Mr Meschulem Weiss:	present	I was shot dead on the 10th of December, 1943, in the camp of Tarassiwka.
Mrs Weiss:	present	I was shot dead on the 10th of December, 1943, in the camp of Tarassiwka.

OT-man Hermann Schneider giving evidence: 'I vividly recall two SDs who after the action were quarrelling which of them had aimed better.'

9

Chronology of Daghani's Career and his Life with Anişoara

22 February 1909	Born as the son of Mina and Viktor Korn, a German-speaking Jewish couple living at 14 Kreuzgasse, Suczawa, Bukovina (then a province of the Habsburg Empire).
Early 1920s	Suczawa, now in Romania, renamed Suceava; attended secondary school.
Late 1920s	Travelled to Munich and Paris, where he may have attended art classes.
Early 1930s	Moved to Bucharest and adopted the name Dagani, based on 'dagan', the Hebrew word for 'corn'; worked in a publishing house and then an import–export firm.
1931/2	Military service in the Romanian army.
27 June 1940	Married in Bucharest to Anişoara Rabinovici, known as Anna, whom he called Nanino.
28 June 1940	Northern part of Bukovina ceded to the Soviet Union.
November 1940	Earthquake in Bucharest, during which the Daghanis' home was damaged; the couple moved to Cernauţi (formerly Czernovitz) in the Soviet-occupied region.
22 June 1941	Nazi Germany invaded the Soviet Union.
Early July 1941	German and Romanian occupation of Bukovina.
Early October 1941	Jews evicted from southern Bukovina; massacre of approximately 5,000 Jews in Bukovina; Jews were allowed to do menial tasks – Daghani became a street sweeper.
11 October 1941	The Daghanis were sent with other Jews to the lower town of Cernauţi.
27 January 1942	A German soldier was found injured in the street in Cernauţi;

	around 200 males including Daghani were taken to the police headquarters to be executed as a reprisal. The soldier had been knocked down by an inebriated Ukrainian.
7 June 1942	The Daghanis were in a group deported to the quarry (Cariera de Piatră) near Ladijin (Ladyžino), in Transnistria.
11 June 1942	Arrival in Ladijin.
18 August 1942 to early November 1942	The group was transported across the river Bug to Mikhailowka and housed in stables; worked as slave labourers for the August Dohrmann engineering company, part of the Organisation Todt (OT), constructing Durchgangsstrasse IV (DG IV), a strategic supply road linking occupied Poland with southern Ukraine.
Early November 1942	Rehoused in the village school at Mikhailowka.
20 June 1943	The Daghanis were moved to Gaisin to work on a mosaic at the Dohrmann company headquarters.
15 July 1943	The Daghanis escape began with the help of the cobbler Abrasha, a member of the local resistance. They went into hiding at night in a derelict house in Gaisin.
16 and 17 July 1943	They spent the night concealed in the garden of Abrasha's neighbour, followed by a night hiding in a potato field.
18 July 1943	Dressed in peasant clothes, they travelled by cart from Gaisin to the market at Sobelewka, where they lodged with tailors who were persuaded to help them on the next stage of their escape.
19 July 1943	They arrived in Bershad on other side of river Bug, where they hid in the ghetto.
7 August 1943	Partisans attacked the camp at Mikhailowka; five Jewish slave labourers escaped and the remaining inmates were taken to Tarassiwka.
10 December 1943	All the Jews at Tarassiwka were killed by a unit of the Sicherheitsdienst (SD), assisted by Lithuanian auxiliaries.
25 December 1943	The Romanian Red Cross arranged for the transfer of the Daghanis to Tiraspol.
31 December 1943	They left Bershad.
5 January 1944	Arrival in Tiraspol.
16 March 1944	They were given repatriation papers to return to Bucharest.

19 March 1944	Arrival in Bucharest.
Late August 1944	Liberation of Bucharest by the Red Army.
1 December 1944	An excerpt from Daghani's slave labour camp diary published in the magazine *Răspântea*.
28 February 1945 to 29 December 1958	The Daghanis lived at 26 Strada Naum Romniceanu, Bucharest.
1947	Arnold Daghani, *Groapa este în livada de vişini*, published by Socec & Co, Bucharest.
1948	The Daghanis began applying for exit visas to leave Romania.
1958	Daghani had a one-man exhibition at the Patriarch's Palace, Bucharest.
25 December 1958	They received exit visas, due to expire on 31 December 1958.
29 December 1958	They left Bucharest travelling to Athens and then on to Jerusalem.
5 January 1959	Arrival in Israel.
April 1959	Daghani had a one-man exhibition in the Foyer Culturel, French Embassy, Tel Aviv.
1960	Arnold Daghani, *Lasst Mich Leben!*, published by Weg und Ziel Verlag, Tel Aviv.
27 September 1960	The Daghanis left Israel for London.
October to November 1960	They spent two months in Milan.
5 December 1960	They travelled to Jona, Switzerland, to stay at 'Grünfels', the home of Lotte Stiefel, a friend whom they met in Israel.
1961	Arnold Daghani, *The Grave is in the Cherry Orchard*, was published in London in a special issue of *Adam: International Review*, 29, 291–3, edited by Miron Grindea.
1 to 8 January 1961	Daghani signed a contract with the Centro Mondiale Commerciale, Rome, to exhibit his work.
8 January 1961	The Daghanis travelled from Rome to Jona.
13 January 1961	They travelled from Jona to London.
Spring 1961	Daghani had a one-man exhibition at the Woodstock Gallery, London.

9 April 1961	They travelled from London to Jona via Paris. They were refused a UK visa because they had no fixed address.
17 April to 30 September 1961	They stayed at 'Grünfels', Jona, with Lotte Stiefel.
April to May 1961	Daghani was included in a group exhibition at the Ashgate Gallery, Farnham, Surrey.
Summer 1961	Daghani was included in the group exhibition *Artists of Fame and Promise* at the Leicester Galleries, London.
3 October 1961	The Daghanis went to the Count Michael Károlyi Memorial Foundation, Vence, for six months.
4 October 1961 to March 1962	They lived in a prefabricated pavilion on the estate of the Countess Catherine Károlyi, part of the Count Michael Károlyi Memorial Foundation, Vence.
March 1962 to 1970	They lived at 'Mira Courmettes', in a cul-de-sac leading off the Boulevard Maréchal, Vence.
February to March 1963	Daghani was included in a group exhibition at the National Society, London.
March 1963	Daghani was included in a group exhibition at the Royal Institute of Painters in Watercolours, London.
April 1963	Daghani had a one-man exhibition of Stations of the Cross at the Church of St Katharine Cree, Leadenhall Street, London.
30 May 1963	The dedication of windows by Daghani in St Hugh's Church, Vence.
October to December 1963	The Daghanis visited London to see Anişoara's mother, but she died shortly before they arrived.
May 1964	The Daghanis visited Vienna with the Austrian Consul General from London; correspondence about the possibility of obtaining Austrian citizenship.
October 1965	Daghani gave his testimony to the Public Prosecutor in Lübeck for the judicial inquiry into the crimes committed in the slave labour camps of Ukraine.
April to May 1968	Daghani had a one-man exhibition, *Homage to Music*, at the University of Surrey, Farnham.
September to October 1970	Daghani had a one-man exhibition at which he showed *Swinging Art in the Twentieth Century and Some of its Excrescences* and the *Love* series, at the Institute of Contemporary Arts, London.

31 December 1970	The Daghanis moved from Vence into a first-floor flat at 18 Oberwiesstrasse, Jona.
17 November 1977	The Daghanis moved from Jona to a first-floor flat at 1 Palmeira Square, Hove, near Brighton, where they were neighbours of Miron Grindea and his wife Carola, the sister of Anişoara.
May 1984	Daghani had a one-man exhibition, *Arnold Daghani, A Relentless Spirit in Art 1944–1984*, at The Gallery, Brighton Polytechnic, as part of the Brighton Festival. A television programme on Arnold Daghani was made by TV South.
August 1984	Anişoara died.
6 April 1985	Daghani died in a Hove nursing home.

POSTHUMOUS EXHIBITIONS

1987	One-man exhibition, William Hardie Ltd at the Andrew Grant Gallery and at Edinburgh College of Art, Edinburgh.
1987 to 1988	One-man exhibition, William Hardie Ltd at the Washington Gallery, Glasgow.
1988	One-man exhibition, Morin-Miller Galleries, New York.
1990	One-man exhibition, Breyberry Contemporary Romantics and Master Paintings, Kingham, Oxford.
1991	One-man exhibition, The National Museum of Art, Bucharest.
1992	Arnold Daghani Festival of one-man exhibitions at the Barbican Centre, London; Library Gallery, University of Surrey, Farnham; The Ben Uri Gallery, London; and John Bonham/Murray Feely Fine Arts, London, organized by Grove Fine Arts, London.
1993	One-man exhibition, Museum of Art, Constanţa, Romania.
1998 to 1999	One-man exhibition, *Arnold Daghani: An Idiosyncratic Artist*, Wolseley Fine Arts, London.
November 1999 to April 2000	One-man exhibition, *Visual Witness: Arnold Daghani Exhibitions at the University of Sussex*, University Library and Gardner Arts Centre, University of Sussex, Falmer.
February to March 2000	One-man exhibition, *Arnold Daghani: An idiosyncratic artist*, Lewis Elton Gallery, University of Surrey, Farnham.

Summer 2000	One-man exhibition, *Playback: Commemorative Works by Arnold Daghani*, part of the official cultural programme at the international conference *Remembering For The Future 2000*, Keble College, Oxford.
2001	Group exhibition, *Legacies of Silence*, Imperial War Museum, London.
2003	Group exhibition, *Masoret: The History of Brighton and Hove's Jewish Community*, New Brighton History Centre, Brighton.
2004 to 2007	One-man exhibition, *Verfolgt-Gezeichnet: Arnold Daghani*, Stiftung für Eisenplastik, Sammlung Dr Hans Koenig, Zollikon, Switzerland and venues in Germany.
2005	Group exhibition, part of *Refugee Week 2005*, Hove Town Hall, Hove, Brighton.

WORKS IN PUBLIC COLLECTIONS

University of Sussex
University of Surrey
University of Warwick
Guildhall Art Gallery, London
Ben Uri Gallery, London
King's College, University of London
Yad Vashem, Jerusalem
National Museum of Art, Bucharest
Romanian Academy, Bucharest
Bucur Church, Bucharest
Museum of Art, Constanţa, Romania
Albertina, Vienna
YIVO, New York
Private collections worldwide

IMAGES IN THE PUBLIC DOMAIN

Book Covers

Appelfeld, A., The Healer (London: Quartet Books, 1992), cover shows *Jewish Scholar* (1961), Grove Fine Arts Ltd, London.

Niewyk, D.L., (ed.), The Holocaust (Problems in European Civilization series), third edition (Boston, MA and New York: Houghton Mifflin, 2003), cover shows *Transnistria*, YIVO, New York.

Tester, K., *The Social Thought of Zygmunt Bauman* (London: Palgrave Macmillan, 2004), cover shows *Nanino at the Window*, Arnold Daghani Collection, University of Sussex.

CD Cover

The Life and Death Orchestra, *Songs for the Betrayed World* (1999), cover shows *To Nanino: Happy New Year*, Arnold Daghani Collection, University of Sussex.

Bibliography

ARCHIVAL SOURCES

Arnold Daghani Collection, University of Sussex (ADC).
Letters from Arnold Daghani to Daniela Miga, Museum of Art, Constanţa, Romania.
Center for Advanced Holocaust Studies, United States Holocaust Memorial Museum (USHMM), Washington, DC.
Centrul pentru Studierea Istoriei Evreilor din Romania (Centre for the Study of the History of the Romanian Jews) (CSIER), Bucharest.

UNPUBLISHED BOOKS, FOLIOS AND TYPESCRIPTS BY ARNOLD DAGHANI IN THE
ARNOLD DAGHANI COLLECTION, UNIVERSITY OF SUSSEX

A Pictorial Autobiography, Vols. I–III (1940–60; 1960–63; 1963–76), books, C53–55.
1942 1943 And Thereafter (Sporadic records till 1977) (1942–77), folio, G2.
What a Nice World (1943–77), book, G1.
Memoirs: Switzerland (c. 1946–79), folio, C21.
Homo Ludens or The Most Personal Catalogue of Books etc. (1949–82), book, C26.00.
A Large, a Big Question Mark (1968), book, C39.
Matters of Ethics: Memoirs (1979–83), book, C36.
Let Me Live (1980s), typescript (AM), H5.

COPIES OF TESTIMONIES IN THE ARNOLD DAGHANI COLLECTION,
UNIVERSITY OF SUSSEX

Daghani, A., 'Zeugenschaftliche Vernehmung', Staatsanwaltschaft Lübeck bei dem Landesgericht, 2 P Js 1629/64, 9 June 1965: vorgeladen Arnold

Daghani (twenty-four-page transcript) (ZV).

Segall, N., 'Gedächtnisprotokoll eines Augenzeugen', 21 October 1943; an English translation of this report, titled 'Record from Memory of an Eyewitness', with Daghani's remarks, is contained in *Let Me Live* (six-page transcript).

PUBLICATIONS OF DAGHANI'S DIARY

Groapa este în livada de vişini (Bucharest: Socec & Co, 1947).

Lasst Mich Leben! German translation by Siegfried Rosenzweig (Tel Aviv: Weg und Ziel Verlag, 1960).

The Grave is in the Cherry Orchard, in Miron Grindea (ed.), *Adam: International Review* (London) 29, 291–3 (1961).

Lasst Mich Leben! Stationen im Leben des Künstlers Arnold Daghani, German translation by Felix Rieper of the extended version of Daghani's diary and memoirs, Felix Rieper and Mollie Brandl-Bowen (eds) (Springe: zuKlampen Verlag, 2002).

Arnold Daghani: Groapa este în livada de vişini, Lya Benjamin (ed.) (Bucharest: Editura Hasefer, 2004).

POSTHUMOUS SCHOLARSHIP ON ARNOLD DAGHANI

Bohm-Duchen, M., *Arnold Daghani* (London: Diptych, 1987).

Braun, H. and D. Schultz (eds), *Verfolgt-Gezeichnet: Der Maler Arnold Daghani* (Springe: zuKlampen Verlag, 2006).

Ernst, H., 'Das Kreuz mit dem Kreuz: Arnold Daghani und Marc Chagall', *Lamed* (Zeitschrift Stiftung Zürcher Lehrhaus) (August 2007), pp.7–15.

Schultz, D., 'Displacement and Identity: Arnold Daghani in Socialist Realist Romania', *Centropa*, 3, 2 (May 2003), pp.116-31 (an earlier version was published on www.artmargins.com, June 2002).

Schultz, D., 'Religion and Identity in the Work of Arnold Daghani', in Francis Ames-Lewis, Peter Martyn and Piotr Paszkiewicz (eds), *Art-Ritual-Religion* (Warsaw: Instytut Sztuki PAN, 2004), pp.109–19.

Schultz, D., 'Forced Migration and Involuntary Memory: The Work of Arnold Daghani', in Wendy Everett and Peter Wagstaff (eds), *Cultures of Exile: Images of Displacement* (Oxford: Berghahn, 2004), pp.67–86.

Schultz, D., 'The Possibilities of Pictorial Narrative: Word-Image-History in the Work of Arnold Daghani', in Hannu Salmi (ed.), *History in Words and Images* (Turku: University of Turku, 2005), pp.149–56; available as an eBook at http://www.hum.utu.fi/projects/historia/konferenssit/HistoryInWordsAndImages.htm.

Schultz, D., 'Pictorial Narrative, History and Memory in the Work of Arnold Daghani', in Grace Lees-Maffei (ed.), *Show/Tell: Relationships between Text, Narrative and Image: Working Papers on Design*, vol. 2 (University of Hertfordshire), available as an e-journal at www.herts.ac.uk/artdes1/research/papers/wpdesign/index.html (2007).

Schultz, D., 'Methodological Issues: Researching Socialist Realist Romania', in Vojtech Lahoda (ed.), *Local Strategies, International Ambitions: Modern Art and Central Europe 1918–1968* (Prague: Artefactum, 2007), pp.223–8.

Schultz, D., 'Crossing Borders: Migration, Memory and the Artist's Book' in Maruška Svašek (ed.), *Moving Subjects, Moving Objects: Migrant Art, Artefacts and Emotional Agency* (Oxford: Berghahn, 2009).

Schultz, D., and E. Timms, *Pictorial Narrative in the Nazi Period: Felix Nussbaum, Charlotte Salomon and Arnold Daghani*, special issue of *Word & Image*, 24, 3 (July-September 2008).

Timms, E., *Memories of Mikhailowka: Labour Camp Testimonies in the Arnold Daghani Archive* (Brighton: University of Sussex Centre for German-Jewish Studies, Research Paper No.4, June 2000).

Van der Heijden, C., 'Daghani, Daghani', short story in *Daghani, Daghani* (Amsterdam: Contact, 1989).

SECONDARY SOURCES

Amishai-Maisels, Z., 'Art Confronts the Holocaust', in M. Bohm-Duchen, (ed.), *After Auschwitz: Responses to the Holocaust in Contemporary Art* (Sunderland and London, Northern Centre for Contemporary Art in association with Lund Humphries, 1995), pp.49–77.

Ancel, J., *Contribuţii la Istoria României: Problema Evreiasca 1933–1944* (Bucharest: Editura Hasefer, 2003).

Benjamin, L., *Prigoăna si Rezistenţă în Istoriă Evreilor din România 1940–1944* (Bucharest: Editura Hasefer, 2001).

Bercovici-Korber, M., *Deportiert: Jüdische Überlebensschicksale aus Rumänien 1941–1944: Ein Tagebuch* (Konstanz: Hartung-Gorre Verlag, 1993).

Blanchot, M., The Writing of the Disaster, translated by Ann Smock (Lincoln, NE and London: University of Nebraska Press, 1995).

Blatter, J. and S. Milton, Art of the Holocaust (London: Orbis, 1982).

Bloxham, D., '"Extermination through Work": Jewish Slave Labour under the Third Reich', Holocaust Educational Trust Research Papers, 1, 1 (1999–2000).

Böhne, U., Fassungen bei Ernst Jünger (Meisenheim: Hain, 1972).

Carmelly, F. (Steigman) (ed.), Shattered! 50 Years of Silence: History and Voices of the Tragedy in Romania and Transnistria (Scarborough, ON: Abbeyfield, 1997).

Celan, P., 'Speech on the Occasion of Receiving the Literature Prize of the Free Hanseatic City of Bremen', in P. Celan, P., Collected Prose, translated by Rosmarie Waldrop (Manchester: Carcanet Press, 1986), pp.33–5.

Chalfen, I., Paul Celan: A Biography of his Youth, translated by M. Bleyleben (New York: Persea, 1991).

Costanza, M. S., The Living Witness: Art in the Concentration Camps and Ghettos (New York and London: Macmillan, 1982).

Enzyklopädic des Holocaust: Die Verfolgung und Ermordung der europäischen Juden (Munich and Zurich: Piper, 2002).

Felman, S., 'Education and Crisis, Or the Vicissitudes of Teaching', in S. Felman, and D. Laub, Testimony: Crises of Witnessing in Literature, Psychoanalysis, and History (New York and London: Routledge, 1992), pp.1–56.

Glasberg Gold, R., Ruth's Journey: A Survivor's Memoir (Gainesville, FL: University Press of Florida, 1993).

Golbert, R.L., 'Holocaust Sites in Ukraine: Pechora and the Politics of Memorialisation', Holocaust and Genocide Studies, 8, 2 (2004), pp.205–33.

Goldhagen, D.J., Hitler's Willing Executioners: Ordinary Germans and the Holocaust (London: Little, Brown, 1996).

Gutman, I. (ed.), Encyclopedia of the Holocaust (New York: Macmillan, 1990).

Hausleitner, M., B. Mihok and J. Wetzel, Rumänien und der Holocaust: Zu den Massenverbrechen in Transnistrien, 1941–1944 (Berlin: Metropol, 2001).

Hillesum, E., An Interrupted Life: The Diaries of Etty Hillesum (New York: Owl, 1996).

Ioanid, R., The Holocaust in Romania: The Destruction of Jews and Gypsies under the Antonescu Regime, 1940–1944 (Chicago, IL: Ivan R. Dee, 2000).

Kaienburg, H., Vernichtung durch Arbeit: Die Wirtschaftsbestrebungen der SS und ihre Auswirkungen auf die Existenzbedingungen der KZ-Gefangenen (Bonn: J.H. Dietz Verlag, 1990).

Kaienburg, H., *Die Wirtschaft der SS* (Berlin: Metropol, 2003).

Kampf, A., *Chagall to Kitaj: Jewish Experience in 20th Century Art* (London: Lund Humphries, 1990).

Langer, L.L., *Holocaust Testimonies: The Ruins of Memory* (New Haven, CT and London: Yale University Press, 1991).

Meyer, F., *Marc Chagall* (New York: Harry N. Abrams, 1964).

Muniu, E., *Pogromurile din Basarabia şi atte Câteva Intâmplâri* (1947).

Overy, R.J., *War and Economy in the Third Reich* (Oxford: Clarendon Press, 1994).

Rückerl, A., *NS-Verbrechen vor Gericht: Versuch einer Vergangenheitsbewältigung* (Heidelberg: Müller, 1982).

Tonkin, E., *Narrating Our Past: The Social Construction of Oral History* (Cambridge: Cambridge University Press, 1992).

Travers M., *German Novels of the First World War and their Ideological Implications, 1918–1933* (Stuttgart: Heinz, 1982).

Vidal-Naquet, P., *Assassins of Memory: Essays on the Denial of Holocaust* (New York: Columbia University Press, 1992).

Vlasopolos, A., *No Return Address: A Memoir of Displacement* (New York: Columbia University Press, 2000).

Weissglas, I., 'Ghetto und Deportation', in H. Wiesner (ed.), *In der Sprache der Mörder: Eine Literatur aus Czernowitz, Bukowina* (Berlin: Literaturhaus, 1993), pp.141–52.

White, H., *Figural Realism: Studies in the Mimesis Effect* (Baltimore, MD and London: Johns Hopkins University Press, 1999).

Index

First names are given for Mikhailowka inmates, engineers and guards; otherwise only the initial and surname are given. Names of publications beginning with the letters 'A' or 'The' will be listed under the first significant word. Page references to endnotes will be followed by the letter 'n' and the number of the endnote.